Reading
EXPLORER 4

Paul MacIntyre

HEINLE
CENGAGE Learning

Australia • Brazil • Japan • Korea • Mexico • Singapore • Spain • United Kingdom • United States

HEINLE
CENGAGE Learning

Reading Explorer 4
Paul MacIntyre

VP and Director of Operations: Vincent Grosso
Publisher: Andrew Robinson
Executive Editor: Sean Bermingham
Senior Development Editor: Derek Mackrell
Assistant Editor: Sarah Tan
Technology Development Manager: Debie Mirtle
Technology Project Manager: Shi-May Wei
Director of Global Marketing: Ian Martin
Director of US Marketing: Jim McDonough
Content Project Manager: Tan Jin Hock
Senior Print Buyer: Mary Beth Hennebury
National Geographic Coordinator: Leila Hishmeh
Contributing Writers: Julie Deferville, Angela Dove
Cover/Text Designer: Page 2, LLC
Compositor: Page 2, LLC
Cover Images: (Top) Tino Soriano/National Geographic
Image Collection, (bottom) Jason Edwards/National
Geographic Image Collection

Credits appear on pages 223–224, which constitutes
a continuation of the copyright page.

Acknowledgments
The Author and Publishers would like to thank the following
teaching professionals for their valuable feedback during
the development of this series.

Jamie Ahn, English Coach, Seoul; **Heidi Bundschoks**,
ITESM, Sinaloa México; **José Olavo de Amorim**, Colégio
Bandeirantes, São Paulo; **Marina Gonzalez**, Instituto
Universitario de Lenguas Modernas Pte., Buenos Aires;
Tsung-Yuan Hsiao, National Taiwan Ocean University,
Keelung; **Michael Johnson**, Muroran Institute of Technology;
Thays Ladosky, Colégio Damas, Recife; **Ahmed Mohamed
Motala**, University of Sharjah; **David Persey**, British Council,
Bangkok; **David Schneer**, ACS International, Singapore;
Atsuko Takase, Kinki University, Osaka; **Deborah E. Wilson**,
American University of Sharjah

Additional thanks to Yulia P. Boyle, Jim McClelland, and Jim
Burch at National Geographic Society; and to Nancy Douglas
for her helpful comments and suggestions.

This series is dedicated to the memory of Joe Dougherty,
who was a constant inspiration throughout its development.

Student Book ISBN-13: 978-1-4240-2936-5
Student Book ISBN-10: 1-4240-2936-8
Student Book + Student CD-ROM ISBN-13: 978-1-4240-2939-6
Student Book + Student CD-ROM ISBN-10: 1-4240-2939-2
Student Book (US edition) ISBN-13: 978-1-4240-4373-6
Student Book (US edition) ISBN-10: 1-4240-4373-5

Heinle
20 Channel Center Street
Boston, Massachusetts 02210
USA

Cengage Learning is a leading provider of customized learning solutions
with office locations around the globe, including Singapore, the United
Kingdom, Australia, Mexico, Brazil, and Japan. Locate our local office at:
international.cengage.com/region

Cengage Learning products are represented in Canada by Nelson
Education, Ltd.

Visit Heinle online at **elt.heinle.com**
Visit our corporate website at **www.cengage.com**

Printed in Canada
1 2 3 4 5 6 7 – 13 12 11 10 09

▯ Contents

Get ready to Explore Your World!

People in Loma Linda, **California** have one of the world's longest life expectancies. Why do they live so long? **p. 195**

In the spring of 2001, a mysterious outbreak infected 160 people in **Canada**. What caused it? **p. 39**

A scientist in **Switzerland** has shown a surprising relationship between love and smell. What did he find? **p. 25**

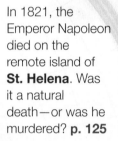

In 1821, the Emperor Napoleon died on the remote island of **St. Helena**. Was it a natural death—or was he murdered? **p. 125**

NORTH AMERICA

In June, 2004, an astronomer in **Arizona** noticed something terrifying in the night sky. What was it? **p. 167**

The wetlands of **Brazil's** Pantanal are home to the anaconda—the world's longest snake. How long is it? **p. 202**

SOUTH AMERICA

Easter Island is famous for its astonishing statues. Who built them—and why? **p. 102**

In **Argentina**, the tango is much more than just a dance. What makes it so special? **p. 117**

The world's largest bell, in **Moscow's** Red Square, has never rung. Why? **p. 152**

The **Mongol** leader Genghis Khan conquered much of the known world. But was he really a ruthless killer? **p. 139**

The writer Basho has been called the "Shakespeare of **Japan**." Why are his poems so popular? **p. 11**

EUROPE

ASIA

China's Jiuzhaigo Nature Reserve receives more than 7,000 tourists every day. Why does it attract so many people? **p. 52**

AFRICA

Naturalist Iain Douglas-Hamilton survived a terrifying incident in **Kenya's** Samburu National Reserve. What happened to him? **p. 95**

AUSTRALIA

In Accra, **Ghana**, a vast market is piled high with old and broken electronics. Where does all this "e-waste" come from? **p. 181**

A type of lizard in the desert of **Australia** drinks through its foot. How does it do it? **p. 61**

Scientists are collecting DNA in **Papua New Guinea**, and many other parts of the world. What does this evidence tell us about our distant past? **p. 75**

ANTARCTICA

Scope and Sequence

Welcome to Reading Explorer!

In this book, you'll travel the world, explore different cultures, and discover interesting topics. You'll also become a better reader!

Reading will be easier—and you'll understand more—if you ask yourself these questions:

What do I already know?
- Before you read, look at the photos, captions, chart and maps. Ask yourself: *What do I already know about this topic?*
- Think about the language you know—or may need to know— to understand the topic.

What do I want to learn?
- Look at the title and headings. Ask yourself: *What is this passage about? What will I learn?*
- As you read, check your predictions.

What have I learned?
- As you read, take notes. Use them to help you answer questions about the passage.
- Write down words you learn in a vocabulary notebook.

How can I learn more?
- Practice your reading skills and vocabulary in the Review Units.
- Explore the topics by watching the videos in class, or at home using the CD-ROM.

Now you're ready to explore your world!

title   photo   caption   heading

map

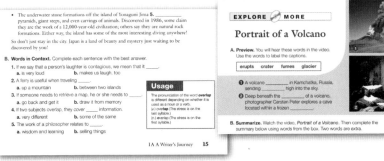

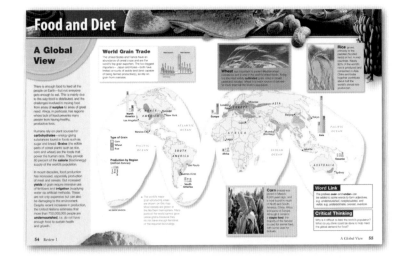

Words and Pictures

A moss covered ▶ stone with writing stands at Natadera Temple, Japan.

WARM UP

Discuss these questions with a partner.

1. Are there any famous travel writers from your country?

2. Do you know any photographers? What kinds of photographs do they take?

3. There is an expression, "A picture is worth a thousand words."

What do you think it means? Do you think it is true?

1A

The snow we saw together—
does it fall
this year as well?

Sadly, I part from you;
Like a clam[1] torn from its shell,
I go, and autumn too.

[1] A **clam** is a kind of shellfish that can be eaten.

A Writer's Journey

Before You Read

A. Discussion. Matsuo Basho (1644–1694) was a writer of *haiku*, Japanese three-line poems like the ones above. Haiku are often about the natural world. Read the poems, and answer the questions below.

1. What examples of nature are found in the poems?
2. What feelings is Basho trying to express?
3. Which poem do you prefer? Why?

B. Scan. Scan the reading and photo captions to answer the questions.

1. What is the name of Basho's great work in Japanese? In English?
2. Find three cities in Japan that the author of the passage visited.
3. Which river's fast-flowing water did Basho write a poem about?

ON THE POET'S TRAIL

▲ Basho's journal, *Narrow Road to a Far Province*, describes a path on Natagiri Pass that is still used by travelers today.

1 In May 1689, accompanied by his friend and follower Sora and carrying only a backpack, writing materials, and clothes, Japanese poet Matsuo Basho walked for five months
5 through the villages and mountains of Japan. This journey resulted in his great work, *Oku no Hosomichi* or *Narrow Road to a Far Province*. "It was as if the very soul of Japan had itself written it," said the early 20th-century Buddhist
10 poet Miyazawa Kenji. Today, thousands of people visit the place of Basho's birth, see the shrine[1] where he is buried, and travel parts of the trail he walked. Over 300 years later, writer Howard Norman and *National Geographic*
15 photographer Michael Yamashita decided to follow Basho's route. Here are extracts from Norman's diary of the journey.

Basho's masterpiece begins, "Each day is a journey, and the journey itself home." His words
20 are on my mind as I prepare to walk in the footsteps of this great poet, along his narrow road—the 2,000-kilometer (1,200-mile) path he followed through Japan over 300 years ago. I, too, have brought writing materials and will
25 keep a journal of my impressions along the way.

SEPTEMBER 2, TOKYO

I have arrived in Tokyo to begin my travels north. We are received by Mr. Ichihara of the Oku no Hosomichi network in his library and
30 office near the Sumidagawa River where Basho, Sora, and a few friends in a boat commenced their journey from Edo on May 16, 1689. Dressed in traditional Japanese clothes, Mr. Ichihara bows. He has an open, friendly
35 manner and a contagious intensity of spirit. "Look!" Mr. Ichihara rubs the stomach of Basho's statue. "He was a little chubby[2] when he set out. You'll see, in the statues of him at the end of the Oku no Hosomichi he looks
40 thin and tired, and yet full of knowledge and joy—and sadness, which all makes sense."

We enjoy a nice Japanese dinner. Early in the evening I hire a boat, which slowly navigates the Sumidagawa River almost to Tokyo Bay—Basho's
45 path. We pass under the river's many famous bridges, some dating back to Basho's time, and we turn around at the fish market. It is dark now. How could Basho, writing in 1689, have imagined the ten million lights of Tokyo—or
50 finding it difficult to see the stars because of them?

[1] A **shrine** is a religious place or structure that is associated with a particular person or object.
[2] A **chubby** person is somewhat fat.

◄ A statue of Basho stands outside a temple in Hiraizumi, Japan.

▼ A fisherman, carrying a long bamboo rod, stands in the Mogami River, Japan. Basho wrote a poem about the fast-flowing water of this river.

SEPTEMBER 14, MATSUSHIMA CITY

Many people arrive at Matsushima on ferries. The ferries sail past Niwo Island, whose shape
55 resembles a submarine, then past Kane Island with its four water tunnels, and others. Moments off our own ferry, looking around at the shops, hotels, and restaurants of Matsushima, my guide declares that the town is unpleasant to look at.
60 "Too much concrete," he says.

To escape present-day reality (and daydream of the past), I sit down on a bench and read how Basho described Matsushima:

"Now, though it's been only too often
65 observed, Matsushima presents a magnificent vista³ . . . All sorts of islands gather here, steep ones pointing to sky, others creeping⁴ upon waves. Or some are piled double on each other, or even
70 triple, and some divided at one end and overlapping at the other. Some bear others on their backs; some seem to embrace them, as if caressing⁵ their offspring⁶ . . . The feeling: one of intense beauty . . ."

75 ## SEPTEMBER 21, NIIGATA PREFECTURE

We cross the Umikawa and Himekawa Rivers where they run into the sea. Basho called this region "the most perilous⁷ place in the north."
80 Today there's a road, of course, high up along the steep cliffs with concrete supports and wire netting to keep the rocks from crashing down. But the names of the passes retain their old warnings, such as *koma gaeshi*, which means
85 "send back your horses." What happened here? Basically, about 800 years ago a woman tried to flee from a powerful official with her small child along the cliffs. Crashing waves threw them into the sea. Someone observed this
90 and reported that at one terrible moment the currents tore the woman from her child, and suddenly they were pulled in opposite directions, then drowned. It is the saddest place I've ever been.

³ A **vista** is a view from a particular place, especially a beautiful view from a high place.
⁴ To **creep** somewhere means to move there quietly and slowly.
⁵ If you **caress** someone or something, you stroke them gently and affectionately.
⁶ You can refer to a person's children or to an animal's young as their **offspring**.
⁷ Something that is **perilous** is very dangerous.

SEPTEMBER 24, OTSU CITY

95

Today along the Nagara River I watch how three fishermen in wooden boats have tightened string "necklaces" around six cormorants' necks. Cormorants are birds that

100 can be trained to dive and catch fish, which the fishermen retrieve by reaching into the cormorants' throats. This demonstration of an age-old fishing technique is both for tourists and to feed their families. I watch this for an

105 hour or so, until finally the cormorants are fed the fish they themselves caught!

We are anxious to get to Genjyu-an, the peaceful shrine near Lake Biwa where Basho's remains lie. A man steps from the modest gift shop to

110 show us the grave itself. Incense is burning. In the small pond there are two turtles. I dip the long-handled wooden dipper in a bucket and pour water over the gravestone.[8] The basho tree (a kind of banana tree from which the poet

115 took his name) is flowering. There is the song of insects and, as if welcoming the evening, the cry of a bird. The train station is close by; there are noises of car traffic, students on bicycles, and crowded streets.

▲ Pine, rock, and sea form a beautiful view along the Sea of Japan.

120 I see the man closing up shop. He notices that I am still there. "It's good to say a prayer. It's up to you which one." He bows to me, and then bows to the gravestone. "I'll wait to lock the gate."

125 In the centuries since his death, Basho has become many things to many people—wise man, outsider artist, wanderer, and, above all, a great poet. His *Narrow Road* contains humor (even about himself), details of his

130 trip, religious wisdom, artistic descriptions, and even complaints. At the same time, his book provides a kind of timeless spiritual map for the traveler. Linguist Helen Tanizaki once described Basho this way: "He's like a quirky[9]

135 philosopher tour-guide who pretty much leaves readers alone to experience traveling in those remote places for themselves."

---

[8] A **gravestone** is a stone that marks a grave, the place where a dead person is buried.

[9] Something or someone that is **quirky** is odd or unpredictable in appearance, character, or behavior.

Reading Comprehension

Critical Thinking

What do you think Miyazawa Kenji meant when he said about the *Narrow Road*, "It was as if the very soul of Japan had itself written it."?

A. Multiple Choice. Choose the best answer for each question.

Gist

1. What is this reading mainly about?
   a. criticism of Basho's work
   b. the best places to visit in Japan
   c. impressions of Basho's trail
   d. why Basho wrote *Narrow Road*

Detail

2. How does Mr. Ichihara describe Basho at the start of his journey?
   a. full of sadness
   b. chubby
   c. having an intensity of spirit
   d. full of knowledge

Paraphrase

3. Which of the following is closest in meaning to "Now, though it's been only too often observed, Matsushima presents a magnificent vista" on lines 64–66?
   a. The view from Matsushima is wonderful, even though many people have seen it.
   b. Matsushima's view needs to be seen often before it is truly appreciated.
   c. Matsushima's view is less magnificent because it has become so familiar.
   d. Although it presents a magnificent view, Matsushima is actually a disappointment.

Detail

4. Which statement is NOT true about fishing on the Nagara river?
   a. The cormorants had string tied around their necks.
   b. The fishermen control more than one bird each.
   c. The birds dropped their fish at the fishermen's feet.
   d. The fishing was partly a demonstration for tourists.

Inference

5. Which region would the writer probably describe as the most tragic?
   a. Sumidagawa
   b. Niwo island
   c. Umikawa and Himekawa
   d. Otsu

B. Completion. Complete the labels with information about the places the author visited. Use no more than four words from the reading.

① Tokyo We hired a boat and passed under the Sumidagawa River's _____.

② Matsushima City Our travel guide didn't like the town because there was

_____.

③ Niigata Prefecture We visited the place on the coast where two rivers _____.

④ Otsu City Finally, close to Lake Biwa, we reached the _____ where Basho's grave is located.

Vocabulary Practice

A. Completion. Complete the information using the correct form of words from the box. One word is extra.

commence	embrace	flee	navigate	overlap	resemble

Many tourists arriving in Japan naturally
1. _____ their sightseeing in large cities such as Tokyo, Osaka, and Kyoto, not far from the international airports where they arrive. But, if you stay in the city, you're only seeing one side of Japan. Join the more adventurous tourists who
2. _____ the crowded city streets and escape into a beautiful landscape of forests and islands that stretches the length of Japan. Here are three suggestions to get you started!

▲ Okunoin Cemetery, Koyasan, Japan

- At the island of Miyajima, take a kayaking trip where you can **3.** _____ much of the island's 27-kilometer coastline and discover its sea caves, shellfish farms, and beaches.

- Koyasan, a beautiful World Heritage Site, is famous for its many temples. Here monks **4.** _____ a religion known as Shingon Buddhism, and happily share the experience with visitors.

- The underwater stone formations off the island of Yonaguni Jima **5.** _____ pyramids, giant steps, and even carvings of animals. Discovered in 1986, some claim they are the work of a 12,000-year-old civilization; others say they are natural rock formations. Either way, the island has some of the most interesting diving anywhere!

So don't just stay in the city. Japan is a land of beauty and mystery just waiting to be discovered by you!

B. Words in Context. Complete each sentence with the best answer.

1. If we say that a person's laughter is contagious, we mean that it _____.
  a. is very loud   **b.** makes us laugh, too

2. A ferry is useful when traveling _____.
  a. up a mountain   **b.** between two islands

3. If someone needs to retrieve a map, he or she needs to _____.
  a. go back and get it   **b.** draw it from memory

4. If two subjects overlap, they cover _____ information.
  a. very different   **b.** some of the same

5. The work of a philosopher relates to _____.
  a. wisdom and learning   **b.** selling things

Usage

The pronunciation of the word **overlap** is different depending on whether it is used as a noun or a verb.
(*v.*) over**lap** (The stress is on the last syllable.)
(*n.*) **o**verlap (The stress is on the first syllable.)

Yamashita took this photograph of fishermen on the west coast of India for a series of articles on the 13th century explorer Marco Polo.

Michael Yamashita has combined his passions of photography and travel for over 25 years as a photographer for *National Geographic Magazine*. In 1999, an assignment for a series of articles on Marco Polo took him from Venice, through Iraq and Afghanistan, to the islands of Southeast Asia. His other assignments have included recreating the voyages of Chinese explorer Zheng He, photographing the border of North and South Korea, traveling the length of the Great Wall, and following the route of Japanese writer Matsuo Basho.

To be a professional photographer, Yamashita says, it's vital to be "in the right place to get the right subject at the right time." But, sometimes, good fortune can play an important role; as Yamashita says; "Professional photographers are paid to be lucky!"

Before You Read

A. Discussion. Read the information above about *National Geographic* photographer Michael Yamashita. What do you think makes a good photograph? What do you think is needed to be a good photographer?

B. Scan. Do you think these statements about Michael Yamashita are true (**T**) or false (**F**)? Check (✔) your answers. Then read the passage to see if you were correct.

	T	F
1. He studied photography in college.	☐	☐
2. He used to be an English teacher.	☐	☐
3. He started taking photographs when he was a child.	☐	☐

An Interview with
Michael Yamashita

▲ Yamashita stood up to his waist in a temple pond to get this photo of a frog just about to jump.

Q: Is it true that before becoming a photographer, you were an English teacher?

Yeah, I spent four years in Japan in the early '70s, and two of those years I was teaching. There was a huge demand in Japan for English. The Japanese studied English at school, but didn't speak much English, so as a native speaker I could help out. It was a great job.

I was in Japan at the time to get in touch with my roots, trying to see how Japanese I might be. Growing up in the States with a Japanese name and face, I really never felt 100 percent American because I didn't look like the American majority. We were the only Asian family in the town where I lived. So, after studying history in the States, I decided to go to Japan and have the experience of living there.

Q: Did you know any Japanese before you went there?

No. I learned the hard way, which was total immersion,[1] working in a company where nobody spoke English. In the beginning it was tough. The only things I knew were the names of food, since I grew up with Japanese food.

My parents were both fluent in Japanese, but they only used Japanese at home as sort of the secret language. For example, when Christmas was coming, they would sing in Japanese about what presents they were going to get. There was also the pressure of fitting in. As a young boy in the United States, I tried to be like everyone else. So, until I traveled to Japan, knowing Japanese was something that never really interested me. If anything, I avoided learning it.

Q: And it was in Japan that you bought your first camera. Is that right?

I did. Like every amateur, I bought a camera to essentially record what I was seeing and doing, to send pictures back to family and friends. I spent some time learning about it, and I just got really obsessed by the whole process.

The more I got into photography, the more I loved it. Every few months I left Japan to renew my visa, and so I went to a different country each time, taking pictures just to show friends and family. As my pictures got better, people told me I should show them to other photographers. Eventually, I met an agent and decided I wanted to be a professional.

[1] If you learn a language by **total immersion**, you learn by living in a culture where the language is spoken.

Q: As a professional photographer, what would you say makes a good photograph?

In the case of *National Geographic* magazine, I like to call them "page stoppers." They are pictures with such great visual impact that the viewer has to stop turning the pages. You're arrested[2] by the framing,[3] the light, the color, or the subject, and you stare at it. Then you're likely to read the captions and be drawn into reading the whole story. For me, that is an ideal picture.

Q: For photographing a story like *Basho's Trail*, how much planning is involved and how much is improvisation?[4]

I prepare as much as I can. I read about six different translations of Basho's book, *Narrow Road to the Deep North*. I thought about what happened on each section of the route: where he talks about the banana leaf, and where on the Mogami River he wrote a poem about swift[5] water.

So, certain things I was looking for, but others were not so place-specific. Basho mentions the moon many times, so I knew I had to do a moon picture, which sounds easy. But the moon is only full once a month, and the sky may be cloudy. Or, if the moon is rising too early, or too late, I wouldn't be able to see it. But I try my best to be in the right place to get the right subject at the right time.

▼ Moonrise over Matsushima's pine-covered islands

▲ A maple leaf on rocks in a waterfall on the Mogami River, Japan

Q: Were there other important moments you remember while doing that article?

Well, there's that frog photo. It was in summer the first week I was there. I was shooting some banana leaves under the roof of a Japanese temple. It was pouring rain, and it was beautiful. As I was walking back to the car, I looked down into this little pond and saw a frog sitting on a leaf. So, my job was to get a good picture of it.

I started out shooting from the land, but the shot wasn't quite right. Then I got into the water. I was up to my waist in this smelly temple pond, early in the morning, concentrating on a frog and thinking "Thank God the caretakers[6] of the temple haven't arrived yet!" I managed to anticipate the moment just before it was ready to jump, and that's when I took the photo. You'll see that the frog is just about to turn to its right, and in the next picture, it was flying.

[2] If you **arrest** a process, you stop it from continuing.
[3] The **framing** of a photograph refers to where the photographer sets the borders of the photograph.
[4] If you **improvise**, you make or do something using whatever you have or without having planned it in advance.
[5] Something that is **swift** moves very quickly.
[6] A **caretaker** is a person who takes care of a house or property when the owner is not there.

▲ Yamashita is particularly fond of this photo of a group of Tajik schoolchildren: "I got a very natural photograph of them preparing for school in incredible light."

100 **Q: Are there other photos from your career that you're particularly fond of?**

One time I was in a little village in Tajikistan, waiting to shoot something at sunrise for an article on Marco Polo. I was wandering about 105 with nobody around when I saw a kid walking down the road. Then more kids joined up. I followed them, and they ended up in this schoolyard. By then the sun was rising behind me. It was extremely bright, and focused on 110 those kids.

If you look at that picture, the shadow is right behind them. That means that, if they look toward me, they can't see me because I'm in the glare of the sun. So, I got a very 115 natural picture of them preparing for school in incredible light.

Q: Finally, what do you think it takes to become a great photographer?

Well, there is not that much economic 120 motivation, considering the difficulty of selling pictures and getting in the door. What it takes is basically passion; you have to be really obsessed by your craft.[7] Especially today, with the competition 125 being what it is, to be a success you really have to eat and drink photography. It's passion that drives you forward.

[7] You can use **craft** to refer to any activity that involves doing something skillfully.

Reading Comprehension

A. Multiple Choice. Choose the best answer for each question.

Main Idea
1. Why did Yamashita become a professional photographer?
a. There is a lot of money in photography.
b. He didn't enjoy being an English teacher.
c. He became passionate about photography.
d. He had always hoped to work for *National Geographic Magazine*.

Paraphrase
2. In lines 9–10, the phrase "to get in touch with my roots" is nearest in meaning to _____.
a. to show others what I have become
b. to meet other members of my family
c. to learn the history of my country
d. to learn about where my family came from

Critical Thinking

Which of Michael Yamashita's photos in this unit do you like best? What qualities of the photo do you like?

Detail
3. According to Yamashita, what is a "page stopper"?
a. an excellent photograph in a magazine
b. a photograph taken in the sun's glare
c. a photograph with a great caption
d. a really interesting story that contains photographs

Detail
4. How did Yamashita prepare himself to take pictures for the article *Basho's Trail*?
a. He took lots of photos in Japan.
b. He bought a new camera.
c. He read several versions of a book by Basho.
d. He tried not to prepare too much.

Inference
5. Which of the following would Yamashita probably agree with?
a. A good photographer doesn't need luck.
b. Getting a first job as a professional photographer is easier than it was before.
c. Passion is the most important factor for becoming a good photographer.
d. There are many financial reasons for becoming a professional photographer.

B. Classification. Match each description (**a–f**) with the correct photograph.

The photo was taken . . .

a. as the photographer was leaving.
b. in very bright light.
c. at just the right moment.
d. in the early morning.
e. with the sun behind him.
f. on temple grounds.

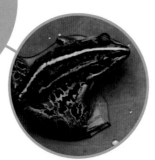

Vocabulary Practice

A. Completion. Complete the information with the words in the box. Two words are extra.

ideal	route	glare	obsessed	passion
motivate	fluent	amateur	anticipated	concentrate

Although you may not be a professional photographer yet, here are two photography courses to help untrained, **1.** _____ photographers learn to take professional-quality photographs. All you need to begin is your **2.** _____ for photography.

Nature Photography

Nature photographers go off the well-traveled **3.** _____ to take unforgettable photographs of nature. In this course, you will **4.** _____ on learning the mysteries of photographing nature outdoors. The instructors will show you inspired photos that are sure to **5.** _____ you to take your own great photographs. You will learn the same methods expert nature photographers use. Learn how to photograph nature in any light, from the **6.** _____ of the midday sun to nighttime photography.

Travel Photography

The **7.** _____ travel photographer is a master of photographing a wide variety of subjects, including people, nature, festivals and celebrations, as well as cities and their architecture. In this course, you will improve your travel photography by learning all of the elements above. Methods for using flash will also be discussed. Soon you will be taking better travel photographs than you could ever have **8.** _____ .

B. Definitions. Use the words in the box in **A** to complete the definitions.

1. A(n) _____ is someone who does something as a hobby and not as a job.

2. If you are _____ about something, you keep thinking about it and cannot think about anything else.

3. If you have a(n) _____ for something, you have a very strong interest in it and like it very much.

4. The _____ person or thing for a particular task or purpose is the best possible person or thing for it.

5. _____ is very bright light that is difficult to look at.

6. If you _____ someone to do something, you make them feel determined to do it.

7. A(n) _____ is a way from one place to another.

8. If your speech, reading, or writing is _____, you speak, read, or write easily, smoothly, and clearly with no mistakes.

9. If you _____ an event, you realize in advance that it may happen and you are prepared for it.

Word Partnership

Use **route** with:
(*n.*) **escape** route, **parade** route;
(*adj.*) **main** route, **scenic** route, **alternative** route, **different** route, **direct** route, **shortest** route

EXPLORE MORE

Portrait of a Volcano

A. Preview. You will hear these words in the video. Use the words to label the captions.

| erupts | crater | fumes | glacier |

1 A volcano _____ in Kamchatka, Russia, sending _____ high into the sky.

2 Deep beneath the _____ of a volcano, photographer Carsten Peter explores a cave located within a frozen _____.

B. Summarize. Watch the video, *Portrait of a Volcano*. Then complete the summary below using words from the box. Two words are extra.

Kamchatka, Russia

| obsession | flee | navigate | amateur | concentration |
| anticipate | commence | fluent | ideal | passion | route |

Kamchatka, in eastern Russia, has over one hundred and twenty volcanoes. Volcanoes are photographer Carsten Peter's **1.** _____. He and his team are on an expedition to photograph some, including the highest active volcano in Asia—Klutchevskaya.

Carsten and his team **2.** _____ their investigations at a recently erupted volcano. The team **3.** _____ through snow, mud, and toxic fumes to an acid lake in a crater. They use a rubber raft in their photographs to show the size of the crater. But, the acid in the water will quickly destroy the raft. Carsten is able to take just a few photos before they are forced to **4.** _____ the lake.

Next, they follow a(n) **5.** _____ that takes them south to Mutnovskaya volcano. A magnificent glacier lies beneath the smoking crater, making it the **6.** _____ subject for an adventure photographer. Although he has taken many excellent photographs, Carsten will not stop, because he is **7.** _____ with taking that one perfect picture.

Carsten and his colleague enter an ice cave cut into the glacier by hot water. Although they **8.** _____ that the cave could soon come crashing down, they ignore the danger. They move in, deeper and deeper, until they are blocked by an acid waterfall. It threatens to destroy Carsten's equipment. Carsten needs all his **9.** _____ to keep his equipment working but, in the end, he gets the picture he needs.

C. Think About It.

1. Why do you think Carsten Peter is so passionate about volcanoes? Do you know anyone who has a strong passion for a hobby or occupation?

2. If you were a professional photographer or travel writer, what would you most like to photograph, or write about?

To learn more about travel writers and photographers, visit elt.heinle.com/explorer

22 Unit 1 Words and Pictures

UNIT 2
Love and Attraction

Discuss these questions with a partner.

1. In what ways do you think science might explain feelings of love?

2. What is it that makes one person attractive to another?

3. What are some things that animals do, or have, to attract a mate?

▲ A pair of king penguins share a private moment on South Georgia Island.

23

Aspects of Love

Before You Read

A. Discussion. Check (✔) whether you agree or disagree with the following statements about love. Then explain your answers to a partner.

	Agree	Disagree
1. The idea of romantic love is a modern one.	❏	❏
2. The feeling of love is caused by chemicals in the brain.	❏	❏
3. Attitudes about love are the same in all cultures.	❏	❏
4. Arranged marriages are likely to last longer than ones started in romance.	❏	❏
5. The feeling of romantic love usually only lasts a short time.	❏	❏

B. Scan. You are going to read about some specialists' beliefs about love. Quickly scan the reading. Then match the people on the left with their professions on the right.

1. Thomas Lewis   _____ a. Swiss university professor

2. Helen Fisher   _____ b. Italian university professor

3. Donatella Marazziti   _____ c. psychiatrist

4. Claus Wedekind   _____ d. anthropologist

Love: A Chemical Reaction?

▲ An overjoyed bride and groom at their wedding in Varese, Italy.

1   Some anthropologists[1] once thought that romance was a Western idea, developed in the Middle Ages.[2] Non-Western societies, they thought, were too occupied with social and
5   family relationships for romance. Today, scientists believe that romance has existed in human brains in all societies since prehistoric[3] times. In one study, for example, men and women from Europe, Japan, and the Philippines were asked to
10   fill out a survey to measure their experiences of passionate love. All three groups said that they felt passion with the same extreme intensity.

But though romantic love may be universal, its cultural expression is not. To the Fulbe people
15   of northern Cameroon, men who spend too much time with their wives are insulted[4] and looked down on. Those who fall deeply in love are thought to have fallen under a dangerous spell. For the Fulbe, to be controlled by love is
20   seen as shameful.

In India, marriages have traditionally been arranged, usually by the bride and groom's parents, but today love marriages appear to be on the rise, often in defiance of parents' wishes.
25   The victory of romantic love is celebrated in Bollywood films. However, most Indians still believe arranged marriages are more likely to succeed than love marriages. In one survey of Indian college students, 76 percent said
30   they would marry someone with all the right qualities even if they weren't in love with the person. Marriage is considered too important a step to leave to chance.

---

[1] **Anthropology** is the scientific study of people, society, and culture.
[2] **The Middle Ages** was the period in European history between 476 A.D. and about 1500 A.D.
[3] **Prehistoric** people and things existed at a time before information was written down.
[4] If someone **insults** you, they say or do something that is rude or offensive.

▲ A young Indian couple embrace in their home.

Finding the Right Person

35 Some psychiatrists,[5] such as Thomas Lewis from the University of California, hypothesize that romantic love is rooted in experiences of physical closeness in childhood—for example, how we felt in our mother's arms. These feelings of
40 comfort and affection are written on our brain, and as adults our constant inclination is to find them again. According to this theory, we love whom we love not so much because of the future we hope to build, but rather because of
45 the past we hope to live again. The person who "feels right" has a certain look, smell, sound, or touch that activates very deep memories.

Evolutionary psychologists explain, however, that survival skills are inherent in our choice
50 of a mate. According to this hypothesis, we are attracted to people who look healthy—for example, a woman with a 70 percent waist-to-hip ratio is attractive because she can likely bear children successfully. A man with rugged
55 features probably has a strong immune system[6] and therefore is more likely to give his partner healthy children.

On the other hand, perhaps our choice of a mate is a simple matter of following our noses.
60 Claus Wedekind of the University of Lausanne in Switzerland conducted an interesting experiment with sweaty[7] T-shirts. He asked 49 women to smell T-shirts previously worn by a variety of unidentified men. He then asked the
65 women to rate which T-shirts smelled the best and which the worst.

▲ A young couple in matching shirts in Shanghai, China. Their shirts read, "Our love will . . . go on forever."

He found that women preferred the smell of a T-shirt worn by a man who was the most genetically different from her. This genetic
70 difference means that it is likely that the man's immune system possesses something hers does not. By choosing him as the father of her children, she increases the chance that her children will be healthy.

Is It All Just Chemicals?
75 According to other researchers, love may be caused by chemicals in the body. Donatella Marazziti, a professor at the University of Pisa in Italy, has studied the biochemistry[8] of lovesickness.[9] Having been in love twice herself
80 and felt its overwhelming power, Marazziti became interested in exploring the similarities between love and obsessive-compulsive disorder (OCD).[10]

[5] **Psychiatry** is the branch of medicine concerned with the treatment of mental illness.
[6] The body's **immune system** protects it from diseases of all kinds.
[7] **Sweat** is the salty, colorless liquid that comes through your skin when you are hot, sick, or afraid.
[8] **Biochemistry** is the study of the chemical processes that occur in living things.
[9] A **lovesick** person experiences overwhelming feelings of love.
[10] If someone has **obsessive-compulsive disorder**, they cannot stop doing a particular thing, such as washing their hands.

▲ A group photo of Marion and Emily Grillot's family. The couple, from Ohio, U.S.A., have been married for 58 years. They have 20 children and 77 grandchildren.

85 Marazziti examined the blood of 24 people who had fallen deeply in love within the past six months, and measured their levels of serotonin. Serotonin is a powerful chemical in the brain and body that is connected with our
90 moods, emotions, and desires. She found that their levels of serotonin were 40 percent lower than normal people—the same results she found from people with OCD. Her conclusion was that love and mental illness may be
95 difficult to tell apart.

Another scientist, anthropologist Helen Fisher, from Rutgers University, U.S.A., has been looking at love with the aid of an MRI machine.[11] She recruited subjects who were
100 "madly in love," and once they were inside the MRI machine, she showed them two photographs, one neutral, the other of their loved one.

What Fisher saw fascinated her. When each
105 subject looked at his or her loved one, the parts of the brain linked to reward and pleasure "lit up." Love "lights up" these areas using a chemical called dopamine. Dopamine creates intense energy, exhilaration, focused attention,
110 and motivation to win rewards.

Dopamine levels do eventually drop, though, and studies around the world confirm that a decrease in passion is the norm.

Fisher has suggested that relationships frequently
115 break up after about four years because that's about how long it takes to raise a child through infancy.[12] Passion, that wild feeling, turns out to be practical after all. A couple not only needs to bring a child into this world; they also need
120 a bond that continues long enough to raise a helpless human infant.

Maintaining Love

Eventually, all couples find that their passion declines over time. For relationships that
125 get beyond the initial stage of passion to have a real chance of lasting, a chemical called oxytocin may be the key. Oxytocin is a hormone our body produces that promotes mutual feelings of connection and bonding.
130 It is produced when we hug our long-term husbands and wives or our children. In long-term relationships that work, oxytocin is believed to be abundant in both partners.

According to Helen Fisher, couples who want
135 their relationships to last should make an effort to keep a close physical relationship. Through frequent physical contact, they can trigger the production of more oxytocin—and in this way feel closer to each other.

---

[11] An **MRI machine** allows medical staff to get a picture of the soft parts inside a patient's body using a powerful magnetic field.
[12] **Infancy** is the period of your life when you are a baby or very young child.

Reading Comprehension

A. Multiple Choice. Choose the best answer for each question.

Gist **1.** Another title for this reading could be _____.
  a. *Science Can Conquer Passion*
  b. *The Right Way to Choose a Mate*
  c. *Explaining Why We Fall in Love*
  d. *The Case for Arranged Marriage*

Reference **2.** Which choice best expresses the meaning of *this theory* on line 42?
  a. Marriage is too important to leave to chance.
  b. Without the approval of family, romantic love rarely succeeds.
  c. Romantic love is based on pleasant memories that we try to find again.
  d. Memories of comfort and affection can satisfy our need for romantic love.

Detail **3.** According to evolutionary psychology, why would a woman choose a man with rugged features?
  a. to improve her immune system
  b. to have healthier children
  c. to protect her from animals and other threats
  d. because he is more likely to have a 70 percent waist-to-hip ratio

Inference **4.** Why did Marazziti probably choose to study similarities between love and OCD?
  a. She wanted to better understand her own experiences.
  b. She had naturally low serotonin levels.
  c. Others researchers felt it was an important area to study.
  d. She suffered from a mental illness.

Detail **5.** According to researchers, which of the following chemicals is most closely related to successful long-term relationships?
  a. dopamine   c. serotonin
  b. oxytocin   d. none of the above

B. Matching. Match the people with their ideas about love. One idea is extra.

  1. Thomas Lewis thinks that   _____
  2. The Fulbe think   _____
  3. Anthropologists thought   _____
  4. Most Indians think   _____
  5. Helen Fisher believes   _____

  a. romance was a Western invention.
  b. arranged marriages have the best chance of success.
  c. we are most attracted to people who look healthy.
  d. it is shameful to be controlled by love.
  e. love is linked to childhood experiences of closeness.
  f. relationships evolved to last long enough to raise a child through infancy.

Critical Thinking

The author writes that a particular chemical may be the key to lasting relationships. How do you feel about relationships relying on a chemical?

Vocabulary Practice

A. Matching. Read the information below and match each word in **red** with its definition.

The Origins of Valentine's Day

Although Valentine's Day may seem like a modern event, its roots go back over 2,000 years. This day of romance evolved from the Roman celebration called Lupercalia, which was held every year on February 15. When the emperor Constantine made Christianity the official religion of the Roman Empire, around A.D. 313, the holiday continued and was renamed for Saint Valentine.

According to the story, in about A.D. 270, Roman Emperor Claudius II, seeking to recruit more soldiers for his army, prohibited young men from marrying. Valentine, it is said, was a priest who performed marriages in secret despite the ban. For his defiance of the emperor, Valentine was killed—on February 14, the story goes.

One of the first Valentine's Day cards was sent in 1415 from France's Duke of Orléans to express his affection for his wife while he was held prisoner in England. Today, giving your sweetheart a Valentine's Day card has become the norm for lovers in many countries around the world.

a. a way of behaving that is considered normal in a particular society _____

b. behavior showing you are not willing to obey _____

c. feelings of love for someone _____

d. referring to the actions and feelings of people who are in love _____

e. to select or persuade someone to join an organization _____

B. Completion. Complete the sentences below with the correct form of the words from the box. One word is extra.

inherent	trigger	mutual	norm	abundant	inclination

1. Chocolate may be _____ romantic—scientists have found that it contains chemicals that cause you to feel like you're in love.

2. However, chocolate, which may cause feelings of love in some people, can _____ severe headaches for others.

3. By giving a Valentine's Day gift, a person in love sometimes discovers that the love is _____, and that their feelings are returned.

4. According to a recent bizarre scientific study, women with large chins have a greater _____ to cheat in relationships.

5. Science tells us that a(n) _____ of certain chemicals in the brain causes the racing heart, blushing, and sweaty hands of someone in love.

Usage

Use **the norm** to mean that something is usual and expected.

2B Animal Attraction

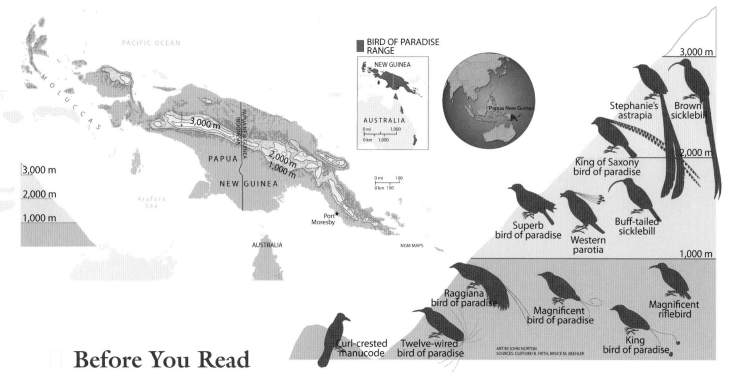

BIRD OF PARADISE RANGE

NEW GUINEA

AUSTRALIA

PACIFIC OCEAN

MOLUCCAS

PAPUA NEW GUINEA
INDONESIA

PAPUA

NEW GUINEA

Arafura Sea

Port Moresby

AUSTRALIA

NGM MAPS

3,000 m
2,000 m
1,000 m

Papua New Guinea

3,000 m
2,000 m
1,000 m

Stephanie's astrapia
Brown sicklebill
King of Saxony bird of paradise
Superb bird of paradise
Western parotia
Buff-tailed sicklebill
Raggiana bird of paradise
Magnificent bird of paradise
Magnificent riflebird
Curl-crested manucode
Twelve-wired bird of paradise
King bird of paradise

ART BY JOHN NORTON
SOURCES: CLIFFORD B. FRITH, BRUCE M. BEEHLER

Before You Read

New Guinea and its surrounding islands are home to 34 species of birds of paradise. Mountainous New Guinea has habitats at various altitudes.[1] Most birds of paradise are habitat specialists that live within a single mountain range and altitude. This isolation reduces the flow of genes between populations, allowing the birds to evolve separately into their wonderful varieties.

[1] A location's **altitude** is its height above sea level.

A. Quiz. Read the information and look at the chart above.
Then circle **T** (true), **F** (false), or **NG** (not given).

1. In its lifetime, a bird of paradise usually travels widely.	T	F	NG
2. Stephanie's astrapia has very long tail feathers.	T	F	NG
3. The main reason birds of paradise stay isolated is to avoid conflict.	T	F	NG
4. Isolation has caused birds of paradise to differ greatly from each other.	T	F	NG
5. The superb bird of paradise lives at altitudes below 1,000 m.	T	F	NG

B. Predict. Look quickly at the title, headings, photos, and captions on pages 31–33.
Check (✔) the information you think you'll read about.

❐ commercial uses of birds of paradise
❐ why birds of paradise have such beautiful feathers
❐ what birds of paradise eat
❐ when birds of paradise were discovered by Europeans

Feathers of Love

1 Covered in soft, black feathers, the noble performer bows deeply to his audience. From the top of his head grow several long feathers that tap the ground as he begins his dance. This
5 dancing bird is Carola's parotia, just one of the fascinating and unique birds of paradise that live on the island of New Guinea. What is the reason for the dance show? This male bird is attempting to impress a row of females that are
10 watching him from a branch above.

Keeping the females' attention isn't easy, so he really gives it his all. He pauses for dramatic effect, then commences his dance again. His neck sinks and his head moves up and down,
15 head feathers bouncing. He jumps and shakes his feathers until his performance attracts the attention of one of the females—the one that will be his mate.

An Amazing Performance

20 In the dense and humid jungle of New Guinea is nature's most absurd theater, the very special mating game of the birds of paradise. To attract females, males' feathers resemble costumes worthy of the stage. The bright reds,
25 yellows, and blues of their feathers stand out sharply against the green of the forest. It seems that the more extreme the male's costume and

▲ A red bird of paradise practicing his display

colors, the better his chance of attracting a mate.

30 Not only do most male birds of paradise have extremely beautiful feathers, they know how to use them. Each species has its own type of display behavior. Some dance remarkably complex dances on the ground, in areas that
35 they have cleared and prepared like their own version of a dance floor.[1] Others perform their display high in the trees.

The male red bird of paradise shows off his delightful red and yellow feathers in a
40 display sometimes called a "butterfly dance," spreading and moving his wings intensely like some giant butterfly. The male Carola's parotia has at least six different dance moves, including one in which he spreads out his feathers like a
45 dress in a move called the "ballerina[2] dance." While some birds of paradise perform alone, others, like Goldie's birds of paradise, often perform together, creating an eye-catching performance that female birds find impossible
50 to resist. Hanging from nearby branches, male Goldie's birds prominently display the clouds of soft red feathers that rise from their backs as they flap[3] their wings with great energy. Excited females soon arrive to choose the one
55 that pleased them the most.

[1] In a restaurant or night club, the **dance floor** is the area where people can dance.
[2] A **ballerina** is a woman who dances ballet, a type of artistic dance.
[3] If a bird or insect **flaps** its wings, the wings move quickly up and down.

The Evolution of Color

These brilliantly colored birds of paradise have evolved over millions of years from ancient birds whose feathers were dark and boring in comparison. Of today's 38 brightly colored birds of paradise species, 34 of them live only on New Guinea and the surrounding islands. These birds of paradise invite us to solve a mystery of nature. It seems to be a contradiction[4] that such extreme feathers and colors could have been favored by the process of evolution. After all, these same brightly colored feathers that attract mates also make them much more noticeable to predators[5] and slow the birds down, making fleeing from those predators more difficult. The answer lies in the safe environment in which the birds live, and a process of evolution known as "sexual selection."

"Life here is pretty comfortable for birds of paradise. The island's unique environment has allowed them to go to extremes unheard of elsewhere," says biologist Ed Scholes of New York's Museum of Natural History. Under harsher conditions, he says, "evolution simply wouldn't have come up with these birds." Fruit and insects are abundant all year in the forests of New Guinea, and predators are few. The result is a perfect environment for birds.

Sexual selection has thus been the driving force in the evolution of birds of paradise. Freed of other pressures, birds of paradise began to specialize in attracting mates. Over millions of years, they have slowly undergone changes in their color, feathers, and other talents. Characteristics that made one bird more attractive than another were passed on and enhanced over time. "The usual rules of survival aren't as important here as the rules of successful mating," Scholes adds.

The diversity of New Guinea's birds also springs from its varied environments: from humid coastal plains to high-elevation cloud forests, from swamps[6] to mountains rising as high as 5,000 meters (16,000 feet). The landscape has many physical barriers that isolate animal populations, allowing them to develop into separate and distinct species.

Bird Performers, Human Dancers

The people of New Guinea have been watching the displays of the birds of paradise for centuries. "Locals will tell you they went into the forest and copied their rituals from the birds," says anthropologist Gillian Gillison of the University of Toronto, who lived among New Guinea tribes for more than a decade. At local dance performances, now more tourist entertainment than true ritual, the painted dancers still evoke the birds with their movements and beautiful costumes. "By wearing the feathers," Gillison says, ". . . you capture the animal's life force. It makes you a warrior."[7]

[4] If an aspect of a situation is a **contradiction**, it is completely different from other aspects and makes the situation confusing, or difficult to understand.
[5] A **predator** is an animal that kills and eats other animals.
[6] A **swamp** is an area of very wet land with wild plants growing in it.
[7] A **warrior** is a fighter or soldier, especially in former times, who was very brave and experienced in fighting.

◀ A pair of displaying Goldie's birds of paradise

▲ A Papua New Guinean tribesman wearing in his nose feathers from a King of Saxony bird of paradise.

In the past, demand for the birds' beautiful feathers resulted in a huge amount of hunting. At the peak of the trade, in the early 1900s, 80,000 skins a year were exported from New Guinea for European ladies' hats. However, surprisingly few birds die for these costumes nowadays. Ceremonial feathers are passed down from generation to generation. Local people are still permitted to hunt birds of paradise for traditional uses. However, hunters usually target older male birds, leaving younger males to continue breeding.[8]

There are more serious threats to the birds' welfare. An illegal market in feathers still exists. Large farms use up thousands of acres of forest where birds of paradise once lived, as does large-scale industrial logging.[9] Oil prospecting and mining[10] also present dangers to New Guinea's wildest forests. Meanwhile, human populations continue to grow. Land is owned by different local families whose leaders disagree about which areas should be protected.

However, there may be some good news for the birds. David Mitchell, a conservationist, is using local villagers to record where the birds display and what they eat. He hopes not only to gather data, but also to encourage protection of the birds' habitat. The strategy seems to be working. "I had come to cut down some trees and plant yam vines,"[11] says Ambrose Joseph, one of Mitchell's farmers. "Then I saw the birds land there, so I left the trees alone." For millions of years these impressive birds have danced to find their mates. They'll keep dancing for as long as the forest offers them a stage.

[8] When animals **breed**, they have babies.
[9] **Logging** is the business of cutting down trees for use as wood.
[10] **Mining** is the business of digging deep into the earth to obtain valuable materials.
[11] A **yam** is a root vegetable, like a potato, that grows in tropical areas. A **vine** is a plant that grows up or over things.

Reading Comprehension

A. Multiple Choice. Choose the best answer for each question.

Main Idea

1. Why do birds of paradise dance and display their feathers?
   a. to frighten away predators
   b. to attract a mate
   c. to exercise and clean their bodies
   d. to show possession of an area

Vocabulary

2. In line 12, the phrase *gives it his all* is closest in meaning to _____.
   a. tries as hard as possible
   b. gives everything away
   c. stops paying attention
   d. starts to lose hope

Detail

3. Which type of bird dances in a group?
   a. male Carola's parotia
   b. female Carola's parotia
   c. male Goldie's bird of paradise
   d. female Goldie's bird of paradise

Detail

4. Which factor is NOT mentioned as a reason for the birds' unusual characteristics?
   a. widespread availability of fruits and insects
   b. variety of environments
   c. lack of predators
   d. the island's geographical location

Detail

5. Why do local people continue to hunt birds of paradise?
   a. to eat them
   b. to sell them to tourists
   c. to make costumes
   d. to keep their numbers down

Critical Thinking

Besides the feathers of birds of paradise, what other animal characteristics might sexual selection be responsible for?

B. True or False. Read the sentences below and circle **T** (true), **F** (false), or **NG** (not given).

1. Male birds of paradise display for females both in trees and on the ground.　　　　　　　　　**T　F　NG**

2. The red bird of paradise is known for its "ballerina dance."　　**T　F　NG**

3. Traditional dancers of New Guinea today dance mainly to entertain tourists.　　　　　　　　　**T　F　NG**

4. New Guinean hunters of birds of paradise kill mainly younger male birds.　　　　　　　　　**T　F　NG**

5. Most of the remaining birds of paradise live in the mountains.　**T　F　NG**

Vocabulary Practice

A. Completion. Complete the information using the correct form of words from the box. Two words are extra.

dense	absurd	prominent
species	undergo	evoke
harsh	ritual	noble
bounce		

▲ A researcher crosses a river in Papua New Guinea.

Jennifer Holland is a writer who went to Papua New Guinea to do research for an article on birds of paradise. She later shared some of her most memorable experiences.

Her favorite **1.** _____ of bird of paradise is Carola's parotia, whose dance **2.** _____ includes motions such as bowing, flapping, **3.** _____, and moving its neck side to side to move the **4.** _____ wire-like feathers on its head, in hopes of winning one of the watching females. "Its mating dance is so **5.** _____ that I could hardly keep from laughing."

For a couple of nights, Holland stayed in a tiny village with a large local family. It is the custom of the local people to build a fire pit in the center of the room, and smoke forms a **6.** _____ cloud inside the house. Because she was not accustomed to it, the smoke was very **7.** _____ on her eyes and her lungs. "My eyes watered constantly, I coughed like a new smoker, and I had to step outside regularly to get fresh air—much to the delight of the local kids who sat on the steps waiting for us to emerge."

On one of the country's smaller islands, Holland met a little boy who was terrified because he had never seen someone who looked like her before. The adults and older kids laughed and tried to comfort him, but he continued to cry, as if seeing her **8.** _____ the image of a monster come to eat his family.

B. Definitions. Match words from the box in **A** with the correct definition. Two words are extra.

1. easily visible, obvious _____

2. to have something necessary or unpleasant happen to you _____

3. to cause a particular memory, idea, emotion, or response to occur _____

4. unpleasantly or harmfully hard, bright, or rough _____

5. swing or move up and down _____

6. a series of actions that people regularly carry out in a particular situation _____

7. ridiculous or not making sense _____

8. belonging to a high social class and having a title _____

Thesaurus   **absurd** Also look up: (*adj.*) crazy, foolish

The Love Bird

A. Preview. Read the passage below and match each word in blue with its definition.

Where romance is concerned, no animal takes the process of **courtship** as seriously as a male bird of paradise. They are known to perform **elaborate** and time-consuming dances on the forest floor or up in the **canopy**, while the females watch from their **perch**.

1. the highest, spreading branches of a forest _____

2. behavior meant to lead to mating _____

3. a resting place for a bird _____

4. complex _____

B. Summarize. Watch the video, *The Love Bird*. Then complete the summary using the correct form of words from the box. Two words are extra.

▲ A female Wilson's Bird of Paradise watches and judges a male from above.

prominent	affection	dense	norm	recruit	species
inherent	elaborate	harsh	inclination	evoke	mutual

C. Think About It.

Australian riflebirds are found in the **1.** _____ rainforests of northeastern Australia. These interesting and colorful **2.** _____ of birds are part of the birds of paradise family. Riflebirds may have got their name from the close resemblance of their color to the uniform of early British army riflemen. Males have brighter colors than females, which they use in their courtship displays.

One male hops from side to side with wings outstretched in a(n) **3.** _____ dance. He is hoping to win the female's **4.** _____. However, his dancing does not always **5.** _____ the desired reaction. Although he tries his dance many times, the feeling is clearly not **6.** _____, and she simply leaves him. Her action might seem **7.** _____, but this is a reminder of how serious this game is. Only good dancers will be allowed to reproduce.

If a male makes the right impression, females will be more **8.** _____ to mate with him. For example, a successful male might push out his chest to make it more **9.** _____. Loudly clapping his wings is another method used to **10.** _____ females.

1. Why do you think only male riflebirds have beautiful feathers and perform attractive dances, and not females?

2. Do riflebirds and humans have anything in common in the way they look for partners?

To learn more about love and attraction, visit elt.heinle.com/explorer

UNIT 3
Food and Health

Discuss these questions with a partner.

1. Have you ever eaten something that made you sick?

2. What kinds of foods can be dangerous? Why?

3. In what ways can the world increase its supply of food?

▲ A genetically engineered lettuce is washed with water to remove bacteria.

37

Food Safety

▲ A health educator in Kansas, U.S.A., uses glow powder to demonstrate how bacteria can cover skin if people don't wash their hands properly.

Before You Read

Usually we can't see, smell, or taste the bacteria that make us sick.
Whether people are getting sicker from food today than they were 50 years ago is a matter of debate. What *is* different are the bacteria. Advances in processing and sanitation in the developed world have diminished some foodborne threats, but new hazards come with changes in lifestyle and food production.

E. coli 0157:H7
First identified as a cause of disease in 1982, *E. coli* produces a powerful toxin that can lead to kidney failure. Infections generally result from eating undercooked ground beef.

Salmonella
Almost any food can carry *Salmonella* bacteria, but chicken and eggs are especially high-risk carriers. Infections have leveled off, yet an emerging variety shows high rates of drug resistance.

Listeria
Able to survive refrigeration, *Listeria* is found in many foods, including soft cheeses and processed meats like hot dogs. Pregnant women, babies, and people with weakened immune systems are most at risk.

A. Matching. Read the information above and match each word in blue with its definition. Then match the words below with their definitions.

1. foodborne   ___ **a.** poisonous substance created by an organism
2. toxin   ___ **b.** very small organisms that can cause disease
3. bacteria   ___ **c.** parts and processes of the body that fight illness
4. immune system   ___ **d.** carried into our bodies in the things we eat

B. Skim. Skim the first two paragraphs of the reading passage. What incident caused the U.S. government to take foodborne illness more seriously?

How Safe Is Our Food?

1 A week before Christmas, 1992, Lauren Beth Rudolph ate a cheeseburger from a fast food restaurant in California. On Christmas Eve, suffering from severe stomach pain, Lauren
5 was admitted to the hospital. There she endured three heart attacks before eventually dying on December 28. She was six years old.

The burger Lauren ate was contaminated with the virulent[1] bacteria *E. coli* 0157:H7.
10 Her death was the first in an outbreak[2] that caused 732 illnesses in five states and killed four children. The *E. coli* bacteria are so virulent that it takes no more than a few of them to cause deadly infection. "We used to
15 think of foodborne[3] illness as little more than a stomachache," says Joseph Levitt of the U.S. government's Food and Drug Administration. "After the [Rudolph case] we realized this was no issue of stomachaches, but a serious and
20 compelling[4] public health problem."

Bacteria to Blame

There is more risk involved in our everyday activity of eating than you might think. It is estimated that each year in the United States
25 76 million people suffer from foodborne diseases; 325,000 of them are hospitalized and 5,000 die. In the developing world, contaminated food and water kill almost two

▲ A sausage-and-pepper sandwich stall in New York, U.S.A. Customers at stalls like this rely on government food inspectors to make sure the food they eat is safe.

million children a year. In most cases, virulent
30 types of bacteria are to blame.

Bacteria are an integral part of a healthy life. There are 200 times as many bacteria in the colon[5] of a single human as there are human beings who have ever lived. Most of these
35 bacteria help with digestion, making vitamins, shaping the immune system, and keeping us healthy. Nearly all raw food, too, has bacteria in it. But, the bacteria
40 that produce foodborne illness are of a different, more virulent kind."

[1] A **virulent** disease or poison is extremely powerful and dangerous.
[2] If there is an **outbreak** of something unpleasant, such as violence or a disease, it suddenly starts to happen.
[3] **Foodborne** bacteria enter people's bodies in the foods they eat.
[4] A **compelling** reason is one that convinces you that something is true, or that something should be done.
[5] Your **colon** is part of your intestines — the tubes in your body through which food passes when it has left your stomach.

▲ Dishes contain colonies of Campylobacter, a disease-causing bacteria found on retail chickens tested at the University of Arkansas, U.S.A.

Many of the bacteria that produce
foodborne illnesses are present in the
intestines of the animals we raise for
food. When a food animal containing
dangerous bacteria is cut open during
processing, bacteria inside the animal can
contaminate meat. Fruits and vegetables
can pick up the dangerous bacteria if
washed or watered with contaminated
water. A single bacterium, given the
right conditions, divides rapidly enough
to produce colonies of billions over the
course of a day. This means that even
only lightly contaminated food can
become highly infectious. The bacteria
can also hide and multiply on sponges,
dish towels, cutting boards, sinks, knives,
and kitchen counters, where they're
easily transferred to food or hands.

Changes in the way in which farm
animals are raised are also affecting the
rate at which dangerous bacteria can
spread. In the name of efficiency and
economy, fish, cattle, and chickens are raised
in giant "factory" farms, which confine large
numbers of animals in tight quarters. Cattle,
for example, are so crowded together under
such conditions that even if only one animal
is contaminated with *E. coli* 0157:H7, it
will likely spread to others.

Tracking the Source

Disease investigators like Patricia Griffin, are
working to find the sources of these outbreaks
and prevent them in the future. Griffin, of the
U.S. CDC (Centers for Disease Control and
Prevention), has worked in the foodborne-
disease business for 15 years. Outbreaks like
the incident that killed Lauren Beth Rudolph
turned her attention to the public food safety
threat that exists in restaurants and in the food
production system. Food safety is no longer
just a question of handling food properly in
the domestic kitchen. "Now," Griffin says,
"we are more aware that the responsibility
does not rest solely with the cook. We know

▲ To fight Salmonella, graduate student Lisa Bielke sprays
"healthful bacteria" onto chicks in an experiment to determine
if those bacteria can out-compete harmful bacteria in the
chicks' intestines.

that contamination often occurs early in the
production process—at steps on the way from
farm or field or fishing ground to market."

Griffin's job is to look for trends in food-
related illness through analysis of outbreaks.
Her staff tries to identify both the food
source of an outbreak and the contaminating
bacteria. To link cases together, the scientists
use a powerful tool called PulseNet, a network
of public health laboratories connected by
computer that matches types of bacteria using
DNA.[6] PulseNet allows epidemiologists[7] to
associate an illness in Nebraska, say, with one
in Texas, tying together what might otherwise
appear as unrelated cases. Then it's the job
of the investigators to track down what went
wrong in the food's journey to the table. This
allows them to determine whether to recall[8]
a particular food or to change the process by
which it's produced.

---

[6] **DNA** is a material in living things that contains the code for their
structure and many of their functions.
[7] **Epidemiologists** are scientists who study outbreaks of disease.
[8] When sellers **recall** a product, they ask customers to return it to them.

▲ At a vegetable shipping facility near Cartago, Costa Rica, workers wear sanitary clothes, and all the vegetables are washed in clean water.

In January 2000, public health officials in Virginia noted an unusual group of patients sick with food poisoning from salmonella. Using PulseNet, the CDC identified 79 patients in 13 states who suffered infection from the same type of salmonella bacteria. Fifteen had been hospitalized; two had died. What was the common factor? All had eaten mangoes during the previous November and December. The investigation led to a single large mango farm in Brazil, where it was discovered that mangoes were being washed in contaminated water containing a type of salmonella bacteria. salmonella contamination is a widespread problem, and more recently other salmonella cases have been detected. In the spring of 2001, for example, almonds from a farm in California infected 160 Canadians with salmonella.

The mango and almond outbreaks had a larger lesson; we no longer eat only fruits and vegetables in season and that are grown locally, as we once did. Instead, we demand our strawberries, peaches, mangoes, and lettuce year-round. As a result, we are depending more and more on imports. Eating food grown elsewhere in the world means depending on the soil, water, and sanitary[9] conditions in those places, and on the way their workers farm, harvest, process, and transport the products.

Reducing the Risk

There are a number of success stories that provide hope and show us how international food production need not mean increased risk of contamination. Costa Rica has made sanitary production of fruits and vegetables a nationwide priority. Produce is packed carefully in sanitary conditions; frequent hand washing is compulsory, and proper toilets are provided for workers in the fields. Such changes have made Carmela Velazquez, a food scientist from the University of Costa Rica, optimistic about the future. "The farmers we've trained," she says, "will become models for all our growers."

In Sweden, too, progress has been made in reducing the occurrences of foodborne disease at an early stage. Swedish chicken farmers have virtually eliminated salmonella from their flocks[10] by diligently cleaning up their chicken houses and by using chicken feed that has undergone heating to rid it of the dangerous bacteria. Now the chickens that Swedes buy are salmonella-free. The success of these pioneers suggests that it is indeed feasible for companies and farms to produce safe and sanitary food, while still turning a profit.

▲ A Danish egg producer fights salmonella by running eggs under ultraviolet rays to kill surface bacteria.

[9] **Sanitary** means concerned with keeping things clean and healthy.
[10] A **flock** of birds, sheep, or goats is a group of them.

Reading Comprehension

A. Multiple Choice. Choose the best answer for each question.

Gist **1.** What is the reading mainly about?
   a. avoiding foodborne bacteria by eating at home, not in restaurants
   b. poor sanitary conditions in restaurants and farms around the world
   c. the importance of advanced technology in the fight against foodborne bacteria
   d. dangerous foodborne bacteria, its sources, detection, and control

Inference **2.** What is Levitt's opinion about the government's attitude before the Rudolph case?
   a. It already took foodborne illness very seriously.
   b. It was concerned about the number of stomachaches in California.
   c. It didn't see foodborne illness as a serious public health problem.
   d. It focused too much on food outbreaks in fast food restaurants.

Detail **3.** Why is even a single disease-causing bacterium dangerous?
   a. It can mix with other bacteria.
   b. It can become billions in a day.
   c. Just one can kill a six-year-old child.
   d. It can move more rapidly alone.

Detail **4.** What is PulseNet used for?
   a. to match types of bacteria using DNA
   b. to identify restaurants with poor sanitary conditions
   c. to connect patients with foodborne illness to doctors
   d. to catalog sanitary food production methods

Reference **5.** In line 162, *these pioneers* refers to _____.
   a. international food producers who can still turn a profit
   b. people who improve sanitary conditions in Costa Rica and Sweden
   c. scientists who create new bacteria-resistant foods
   d. journalists who write stories about outbreaks of foodborne illness

> **Critical Thinking**
>
> What do you think can be done to protect ourselves from foodborne illnesses?

B. Matching. Match each cause (**1–5**) with its effect (**a–e**).

Causes
   1. cutting open food animals in processing   _____
   2. improving sanitary conditions on farms   _____
   3. the use of "factory" farms   _____
   4. all-year demand for fresh vegetables   _____
   5. heating of feed   _____

Effects
   a. greater dependence on imports
   b. Salmonella-free chickens
   c. meat is contaminated by bacteria
   d. fewer cases of contaminated produce
   e. bacteria easily spread from animal to animal

Vocabulary Practice

▲ According to the Alabama Peanut Producers Association, Americans consume 1.5 kilograms of peanut butter per person every year.

A. Definitions. Read the information below and match each word in **red** with its definition.

A food contamination scare recently occurred in the United States involving one of the country's most beloved foods—the peanut. In late 2008 to early 2009, nine people died and almost 700 people nationwide were reported to have been affected by salmonella poisoning. However, the real number of victims was likely to be much higher. The U.S. Center for Disease Control estimates that for every reported case of salmonella, 38 cases go unreported.

The cause of the salmonella was found to be peanut products. Peanuts are used in a wide variety of products and are an integral part of health bars, cookies, ice cream varieties, and even dog biscuits. Although the Food and Drug Administration (FDA) does not have the authority to order a compulsory recall, stores across the country voluntarily removed peanuts and peanut products from store shelves.

Using DNA technology, the FDA traced the exact variety of salmonella back to a company called Peanut Company of America, which was likely not diligent enough in its testing and cleanliness. The company has since gone out of business.

a. necessary because a law or someone in authority says you must _____

b. being an essential part of something _____

c. happening or existing in all parts of a country _____

d. hard-working in a careful and thorough way _____

e. dirty or harmful because of dirt, chemicals, or radiation _____

B. Words in Context. Complete each sentence with the best answer.

1. If contamination is confined, it _____.
   a. occurs within a certain area   b. has spread to many areas

2. The body's digestive system primarily _____.
   a. fights disease   b. takes nutrients from food

3. If a project is feasible, it _____ be done.
   a. can   b. can't

4. An optimistic person believes that the future will be _____ than today.
   a. worse   b. better

5. A person might be called a pioneer in business because he or she _____.
   a. started a new type of company   b. wrote a history of a company

> ## Word **Link**
> The suffix **–wide** has the meaning of *extending throughout*, e.g., city**wide**, nation**wide**, world**wide**.

Genetic Engineering

Before You Read

From the Lab to Your Dinner Plate

Scientists like this researcher are busy altering the genes of the animals and plants we use for food. The genes of corn have been altered to create new varieties that are resistant to insects and to herbicides. A new, golden-colored rice, high in vitamin A, is also the product of genetic alteration. A new, genetically altered variety of salmon grows faster than natural salmon. While these "biotech" varieties seem to offer clear benefits, critics continue to point out the risks of genetic alteration of foods.

A. **Discussion.** Read the information above. What benefits and risks might be associated with the examples mentioned?

B. **Predict.** The following three questions are headings in the reading passage. What answers do you think will appear in the passage? Read the passage to check your ideas.

   1. Are biotech foods safe for humans?
   2. Can biotech foods harm the environment?
   3. Can biotech foods help feed the world?

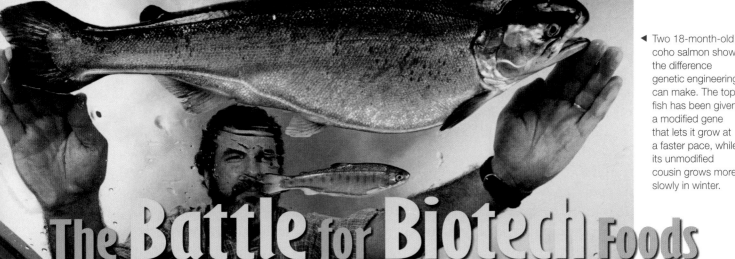

The Battle for Biotech Foods

Two 18-month-old coho salmon show the difference genetic engineering can make. The top fish has been given a modified gene that lets it grow at a faster pace, while its unmodified cousin grows more slowly in winter.

1　Genetic engineering of crops and animals through the manipulation of DNA is producing a revolution in food production. It is also starting a battle between those who
5　believe in its promise and critics who doubt and fear it. The potential to improve the quality and nutritional value of the vegetables and animals we eat seems unlimited. Such potential benefits notwithstanding, critics fear
10　that genetically engineered products, so-called biotech foods, are being rushed to market before their effects are fully understood.

Q: What are biotech foods?

Biotech foods are produced from animals
15　and plants that have been genetically altered. Genetic alteration is nothing new. Humans have been altering the genetic traits[1] of plants for thousands of years by keeping seeds from the best crops and planting them in following
20　years, and by breeding varieties to make them taste sweeter, grow bigger, or last longer. In this way we've transformed the wild tomato from a fruit the size of a small stone to the giant ones we have today. From a plant called
25　teosinte with an "ear" barely an inch long has come our foot-long[2] ears of sweet white and yellow corn.

On the other hand, the techniques of genetic engineering are new, and quite different
30　from conventional breeding. Conventional breeders always used plants or animals that were related, or genetically similar. In so doing, they transferred tens of thousands of genes. By contrast, today's genetic engineers can transfer
35　just a few genes at a time between species that are distantly related or not related at all. There are surprising examples: rat genes have been inserted into lettuce plants to make a plant that produces vitamin C, and moth genes have
40　been inserted into apple trees to add disease resistance. The purpose of conventional and modern techniques is the same—to insert a gene or genes from an organism that carries a desired trait into an organism that does not
45　have the trait. Several dozen biotech food crops are currently on the market, among them varieties of corn, soybeans, and cotton.
50　Most of these crops are engineered to help farmers deal with age-old[3] farming problems: weeds,[4] insects, and
55　disease.

---

[1] A **trait** is a particular characteristic, quality, or tendency that someone or something has and which can be inherited.
[2] One **inch** = 2.54 cm; One **foot** = 12 inches (30 cm).
[3] An **age-old** story, tradition, or problem has existed for many generations or centuries.
[4] A **weed** is a wild plant that grows in gardens or fields of crops and prevents the plants that you want from growing properly.

▲ The papaya ringspot virus threatened the entire Hawaiian papaya industry until 1998, when farmers were given seeds genetically modified to improve resistance.

Q: Are biotech foods safe for humans?

As far as we know. So far, problems have been few. In fact, according to Steve L. Taylor, of the Department of Food Science and Technology at the University of Nebraska, "None of the current biotech products have been implicated[5] in allergic reactions or any other healthcare problem in people." Some biotech foods might even be safer than conventional varieties. Corn damaged by insects often contains high levels of fumonisins, toxins[6] that are carried on the backs of insects and that grow in the wounds of the damaged corn. Lab tests have linked fumonisins with cancer in animals. Studies show that most corn modified for insect resistance has lower levels of fumonisins than conventional corn damaged by insects.

However, biotech foods have had problems in the past. One problem occurred in the mid-1990s when soybeans were modified using genes from a nut. The modified soybeans contained a protein[7] that causes reactions in humans who are allergic to nuts. While this protein was discovered before any damage was done, critics fear that other harmful proteins created through genetic modification may slip by undiscovered. The technique of moving genes across dramatically different species, such as rats and lettuce, also makes critics nervous. They fear something could go very wrong either in the function of the inserted gene or in the function of the host[8] DNA, with the possibility of unexpected health effects.

Q: Can biotech foods harm the environment?

Most scientists agree that the main safety issues of genetically engineered crops involve not people but the environment. Allison Snow is a plant ecologist at Ohio State University known for her research on "gene flow," the natural movement of plant genes from one population of plants to another. She worries that genetically engineered crops are being developed too quickly and released before they've been adequately tested.

On the other hand, advocates of genetically engineered crops argue that some genetically modified plants may actually be good for the land, by offering an environmentally friendly alternative to pesticide,[9] which tends to pollute water and harm animals. Far less pesticide needs to be applied to cotton plants that have been genetically modified to produce their own natural pesticide. While applied chemical pesticides kill nearly all the insects in a field, biotech crops with natural pesticide only harm insects that actually try to eat those crops, leaving the rest unharmed.

▼ At a test field in Colorado, U.S.A, a farmer demonstrates a genetically modified corn plant that outperforms its conventional cousin.

[5] If someone is **implicated** in a crime or bad situation, they are involved in it or responsible for it.

[6] A **toxin** is any poison produced by an animal, bacteria, or plant.

[7] **Protein** is a substance found in food like meat, eggs, or milk, that you need to be healthy.

[8] The **host** is the animal or plant into which the foreign DNA is inserted.

[9] **Pesticides** are chemicals that farmers put on their crops to kill harmful insects.

▲ Out of every ten rice plants that scientists at Cornell University, U.S.A., modify, only one or two will be suited for future development. Researchers must monitor dozens of specimen dishes to determine which plants will offer improvements over the original rice.

Q: Can biotech foods help feed the world?

115 "Eight hundred million people on this planet are malnourished,"[10] says Channapatna Prakash, a native of India and a scientist at the Center for Plant Biotechnology Research at Tuskegee University, "and the number
120 continues to grow." Prakash and many other scientists argue that genetic engineering can help address the urgent problems of food shortage and hunger by increasing crop quantities and nutritional value, offering crop
125 varieties that resist pests and disease, and providing ways to grow crops on land that would otherwise not support farming.

According to the World Health Organization, for example, between 100 million and 140
130 million children in the world suffer from vitamin A deficiency.[11] Some 500,000 go blind every year because of that deficiency, and half of those children die within a year of losing their sight. "Golden rice," a biotech variety
135 named for its yellow color, is thought by some to be a potential solution to the suffering and illness caused by vitamin A deficiency.

Skeptics, however, claim that golden rice is little more than a public relations exercise by
140 the biotechnology industry, which they say has exaggerated its benefits. "Golden rice alone won't greatly diminish vitamin A deficiency," says Professor Marion Nestle of New York

University. "Beta-carotene,[12] which is already
145 widely available in fruit and vegetables, isn't converted to vitamin A when people are malnourished. Golden rice does not contain much beta-carotene, and whether it will improve vitamin A levels remains to be seen."

150 Q: What next?

Whether biotech foods will deliver on their promise of eliminating world hunger and bettering the lives of all remains to be seen. Their potential is enormous, yet they carry
155 risks. If science proceeds with caution, testing new products thoroughly and using sound judgment, the world may avoid the dangers of genetic modification, while enjoying its benefits.

▲ For the Wathome family in eastern Kenya, biotechnology's risks are greatly outweighed by its rewards. Before getting genetically modified disease-free banana seedlings, they barely had enough to eat. Now they sell a surplus.

[10] Someone who is **malnourished** is weakened from not eating enough or the right kinds of food.
[11] **Deficiency** in something, especially something that your body needs, is not having enough of it.
[12] **Beta-carotene**, a natural substance found in red or orange fruit and vegetables, is used in the body to create vitamin A.

Reading Comprehension

A. Multiple Choice. Choose the best answer for each question.

Purpose

1. What is the author's purpose in writing the passage?
   a. to make biotech foods seem as attractive as possible
   b. to show both sides of the biotech foods issue
   c. to convince the reader that biotech foods are dangerous
   d. to explain why biotech foods will not be successful

Detail

2. Which of the following is NOT practiced by conventional breeders?
   a. using related organisms to breed
   b. altering the genetic traits of organisms
   c. creating organisms with desired traits
   d. transferring just a few genes at a time

Critical Thinking

What is your opinion of biotech foods? Which arguments presented in the text do you think are the strongest?

Inference

3. What is the danger of fumonisins?
   a. They might possibly cause cancer in humans.
   b. They could cause insect resistance to modified corn.
   c. They might cause insects to damage corn plants.
   d. They could decrease the numbers of insects.

Detail

4. According to WHO, about how many children die within a year of going blind from vitamin A deficiency?
   a. 140 million   b. 100 million   c. 500,000   d. 250,000

Main Idea

5. What is the main idea of the final paragraph?
   a. With care, the potential of biotech foods could possibly be realized.
   b. The risks of biotech foods seem to outweigh any possible benefits.
   c. The world has already seen great advances due to biotech foods.
   d. Biotech food development has been slowed by the many risks involved.

B. For and Against. Complete the chart using no more than three words from the reading in each blank.

Biotech Foods

Reasons for

1. There is nothing new about humans altering the _____ traits of plants. We've been doing it for thousands of years.

2. Not one current biotech food has been linked to _____ reactions or health problems in people.

3. Insect-resistant biotech plants offer an environmentally safe alternative to _____.

Reasons against

4. Even though we try to catch them all, harmful proteins created through genetic modifications may still _____.

5. Genetically engineered crops are sometimes released into the environment before they have been _____.

6. The benefits of golden rice are exaggerated. It is little more than a(n) _____.

Vocabulary Practice

A. Completion. Complete the information using the correct form of words from the box. Two words are extra.

allergy	battle	conventional
diminish	revolution	nutrition
pest	gene	skeptic
notwithstanding		

▲ A Cornell University researcher examines varieties of genetically modified rice.

According to a study, Chinese farmers growing rice whose **1.** _____ are modified to enhance insect resistance reduced their pesticide use by 80 percent. They also saw pesticide-related health problems drop sharply. In addition, the genetically modified (GM) rice seed boosted crop production by almost 10 percent. There has been resistance to using GM grains as food crops—but some think this news from China may signal an important and **2.** _____ change.

For the study, two types of rice were genetically altered to resist two common insect **3.** _____, which usually require heavy use of pesticides to control. The farmers were allowed to purchase the GM seed at the same price as **4.** _____ seed. During the study, the amount of pesticide used by farmers **5.** _____ because they saw less need for it. As a result, farmers' pesticide exposure dropped, and their health improved.

However, not everyone agrees that GM food is risk free; there are still many **6.** _____ who don't trust it. Some people are concerned that government regulation of GM rice will not be strict enough. There is also the fear that insects will become used to the modified plants and become stronger over time. As with all GM foods, people worry that there could be unexpected and life-threatening **7.** _____ reactions to them in humans. Such fears and concerns **8.** _____, proven examples of problems with GM foods have been quite rare.

B. Definitions. Use the correct form of words in the box in **A** to complete the definitions.

1. reduce in size, importance, or intensity _____

2. despite _____

3. a reaction whereby you become ill when you eat, smell, or touch something _____

4. a very great change in the way that something is done or made _____

5. usually used _____

6. insects or other small animals that damage crops or food supplies _____

7. a person who has doubts about things that other people believe _____

8. the process whereby the body takes things it needs from food _____

Word Partnership

Use **battle** with:
(adj.) **bloody** battle, **major** battle, **constant** battle, **legal** battle, **losing** battle, **uphill** battle; (v.) **prepare for** battle, **fight a** battle, **win/lose a** battle; (n.) battle **of wills**

The Smelliest Fruit

A. Preview. The durian fruit is considered one of the world's smelliest foods, yet is eaten by people all over Southeast Asia. Can you think of foods in other cultures which are both hated and loved for their unique taste and smell?

Here are some examples:

Chou tofu is tofu that has been soaked in a mixture of sour milk, vegetables, and meat juices. It means "smelly tofu" in Chinese.
Natto is traditional Japanese breakfast food made of sticky, slimy, rotted soy beans.
Stilton cheese is very moldy[1] cheese that is widely eaten in Europe.

[1] Something that is **moldy** is covered in fungus due to decay.

B. Summarize. Watch the video, *The Smelliest Fruit*. Then complete the summary below using words from the box. Two words are extra.

nationwide	nutrition	feasible	contaminated	battle
compulsory	diligently	diminishing	conventional	notwithstanding

In Malaysian Borneo, hotels are involved in a **1.** _____ with guests over a very smelly fruit called the durian. The smell of the durian is hard to describe, and has been compared to rotten fish or a rubbish dump. This is why it is **2.** _____ for guests to eat durians outside of the hotel. Hotel staff must **3.** _____ keep watch for this food, because guests often try to smuggle it into the hotel. Its offensive smell **4.** _____, the durian is loved by people **5.** _____ in Malaysia.

Other cultures have their own strong-smelling foods: for example, cheese in the West. Like some kinds of cheese, durian is very precious and expensive where it comes from, and people have even been killed for it.

When the fruit is in season in Kuching, a city in Malaysian Borneo, hotel managers must work harder to keep it out. A hotel that smells of durian will find the number of guests visiting it quickly **6.** _____. But since it's not **7.** _____ to check every single guest entering the hotel, a certain number of durians inevitably get through. There are several ways to clean a room that has been **8.** _____ by the durian smell. One is charcoal, which absorbs the odor slowly. Another way is to use a machine called an ionizer, which can remove the smell in three hours or less.

C. Think About It.

1. What do you think is the purpose of the durian's strong smell?

2. Are there any other foods or drinks you would like to see banned in public places?

To learn more about food and health, visit elt.heinle.com/explorer

A. Crossword. Use the definitions below to complete the missing words.

Across
1. ridiculous, does not make sense
2. existing in all parts of the country
6. a feeling of love or fondness
11. a way from one place to another
12. constantly thinking about something
14. an intense interest or feeling for something
15. part of a cell in a living thing that controls characteristics passed to its children
17. a series of actions regularly performed in a set manner
18. when you _____ something, it moves upward or away from the surface right after hitting it
19. a group of plants and animals with the same characteristics
20. a boat that transports people across a stretch of water

Down
1. you are _____ to something if you get a rash or fall ill after coming in contact with it
3. very impressive or distinguished in appearance
4. crowded, closely packed together
5. a process where food is broken down in the stomach
6. present in large quantities
7. to escape something
8. required
9. to direct a ship or plane on its course
10. one of the first people to develop or be involved in something
13. a person who has doubts about something others believe in
15. a light that is too bright and difficult to look at
16. to cause a particular idea, emotion, or response to occur

B. Notes Completion. Scan the information on pages 52–53 to complete the notes.

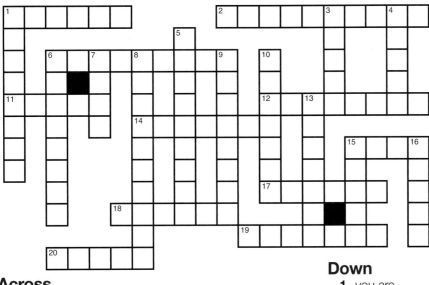

Field Notes

Site: Jiuzhaigou Nature Reserve

Location: _____, China

Information:
- Jiuzhaigou means _____ in Chinese.
- Lakes in Jiuzhaigou are especially clear because of high concentrations of _____. Their unusual colors can be attributed to the differing depths and _____.
- The _____ and _____ peoples have lived in this region for centuries.
- A Tibetan legend tells of the god Dago who gave a magical _____ to the goddess _____. She dropped the gift and the pieces formed Jiuzhaigou's lakes.
- The number of _____ is restricted in order to preserve Jiuzhaigou's natural beauty. Cars must also use "clean gas" to avoid polluting the atmosphere with _____.

Sites: **Jiuzhaigou Nature Reserve**

Location: **Sichuan Province, China**

Category: **Natural**

Status: **World Heritage Site since 1992**

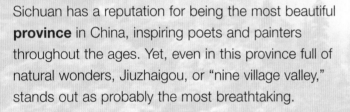

Jiuzhaigou

has provided dramatic scenery for movies such as Jet Li's *Hero*.

Sichuan has a reputation for being the most beautiful **province** in China, inspiring poets and painters throughout the ages. Yet, even in this province full of natural wonders, Jiuzhaigou, or "nine village valley," stands out as probably the most breathtaking.

Visitors to this valley named for its nine native Tibetan villages are greeted by a **mystical** landscape of snow-capped mountains, lakes, waterfalls, and forests. Jiuzhaigou's blue, green, and turquoise lakes are famed for their inherent beauty. The water is so clear that the bottom is often visible even at its deepest parts. This is due to a natural phenomenon where some lakes have a high concentration of calcium carbonate, a type of mineral which prevents bacteria and **algae** from growing. Varying depths and mineral **composition** in the lakes give them their otherworldly jewel-like colors.

This remote region was inhabited by Tibetan and Qiang peoples for centuries until loggers discovered it in the 1960s and began cutting down trees. The government, alarmed by the destruction, declared Jiuzhaigou a nature reserve in 1982. It was made a UNESCO World Heritage Site in 1992 and has since been one of China's most protected areas.

Glossary

algae: a type of plant that grows in water
composition: the way in which different parts are put together
emissions: gas released into the atmosphere
mystical: mysterious, spiritual, or beyond understanding
province: a large section of a country that has its own administration

A Gentle Giant

Once found throughout southern and eastern parts of China (see map), wild pandas are now confined to isolated patches of mountain forest in a few regions, including Jiuzhaigou.

Legends and Folklore

Dreamlike scenery and Tibetan spirituality have inspired countless legends surrounding the waters of Jiuzhaigou. In an ancient love story, the Tibetan god Dago gave a mirror polished by clouds and wind to the goddess Semo, who accidentally dropped it. The mirror pieces scattered, forming Jiuzhaigou's 118 lakes.

MONGOLIA

0 mi   600
0 km   600

BEIJING⊕

C H I N A

JIUZHAIGOU
NATURE
RESERVE

Remaining
habitat

INDIA

Historic range
of giant panda
(*Ailuropoda
melanoleuca*)

MYANMAR
(BURMA)

South
China

A Difficult Balance

Because of its outstanding natural beauty Jiuzhaigou has become a popular sightseeing destination. "Jiuzhaigou is spectacular by any definition of the word," says *National Geographic* photographer Michael Yamashita, who took the background photo. "It's hugely popular. It gets something like 20,000 visitors a day."

To deal with all those visitors, operators have had to build more hotels and restaurants while ferrying tourists in by the busload. It has become a battle to accommodate the steady flow of people without diminishing the natural beauty they have come to see. Officials are concentrating on limiting the impact of tourism by restricting the number of visitors. Cars must also travel on certain routes and use "clean energy" such as natural gas to reduce carbon dioxide **emissions**.

▲ Plant life grows on a dead tree trunk in Jiuzhaigou's Panda Lake.

Food and Diet

A Global View

There is enough food to feed all the people on Earth—but not everyone gets enough to eat. This is mainly due to the way food is distributed and the challenges involved in moving food from areas of **surplus** to areas of great need. Africa, in particular, has regions where lack of food prevents many people from having healthy, productive lives.

Humans rely on plant sources for **carbohydrates**—energy-giving substances found in foods such as sugar and bread. **Grains** (the edible parts of cereal plants such as rice, corn, and wheat) are the foods that power the human race. They provide 80 percent of the **calorie** (food energy) supply of the world's population.

In recent decades, food production has increased, especially production of meat and cereals. But increased **yields** of grain require intensive use of fertilizers and **irrigation** (supplying water via artificial methods). These are not only expensive but can also be damaging to the environment. Despite recent increases in production, the United Nations estimates that more than 750,000,000 people are **undernourished**, i.e., do not have enough food to sustain health and growth.

World Grain Trade

The United States and France have an abundance of cereal crops and are the world's top grain exporters. The two biggest importers—Japan and Korea—both have limited amounts of arable land (land capable of being farmed productively), so they rely on grain from overseas.

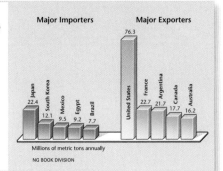

Major Importers

Major Exporters

Japan 22.4
South Korea
Mexico 12.1
Egypt 9.5
Brazil 9.2
7.7

United States 76.3
France 22.7
Argentina 21.7
Canada 17.7
Australia 16.2

Millions of metric tons annually

NG BOOK DIVISION

289
11 90
North America

NORTH AMERICA

Toronto
New York
Los Angeles

Mexico City

ATLANTIC OCEAN

PACIFIC OCEAN

SOUTH AMERICA

São Paulo

Buenos Aires

71 19 20
South America

Type of Grain

- Corn
- Wheat
- Rice

Production by Region (million tonnes)

Corn
Rice
Wheat

NG BOOK DIVISION

▲ The world's major grain-producing areas are shown on this map. Most cereals are grown in the northern hemisphere. Many parts of the world cannot grow cereal grains because they do not have enough farmland or the required technology.

Wheat was important in ancient Mediterranean civilizations and is one of the world's oldest foods. Today it is the most widely **cultivated** grain. Used in bread, pasta, and noodles, wheat is a major source of calories for more than half the world's population.

Rice grows primarily in the paddies (flooded fields) of hot, humid countries. Nearly 90 percent of the world's rice is produced and consumed in Asia. China and India together contribute about half the world's annual rice production.

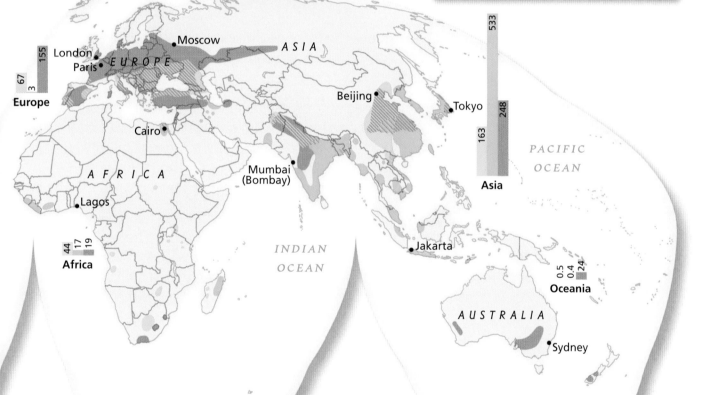

Moscow

London
Paris

ASIA

EUROPE

155
67
3

Europe

Beijing

Tokyo

Cairo

AFRICA

PACIFIC OCEAN

533
248
163

Asia

Mumbai
(Bombay)

Lagos

44
17
19

Africa

INDIAN OCEAN

Jakarta

0.5
0.4
24

Oceania

AUSTRALIA

Sydney

Corn (maize) was grown in Mexico 6,000 years ago and is now found in much of North and South America, China, Africa, and parts of Europe. Although it remains a **staple food**, the majority of the harvest is used for animal feed, with some used for biofuels.

Word Link

The prefixes **over-** and **under-** can be added to some words to form adjectives, e.g., *undernourished*, *overpopulated*, and verbs, e.g., *underestimate*, *overeat*, *overlook*.

Critical Thinking

Why is it difficult to feed the world's population? What do you think could be done to help meet the global demand for food?

A Global View   **55**

A. Definitions. Use the correct form of words in **bold** from pages 54 to 55 to complete the passage.

Humans around the world have for centuries **1.** _____ plants to supply their bodies' energy needs. **2.** _____ such as corn, wheat, and rice are especially good sources of the energy we need. That's one reason why they are **3.** _____ foods in the diets of most people. Some parts of the world have good land, fertilizer, and also plenty of water to **4.** _____ the fields. Those places have very high crop **5.** _____ and are able to grow more than they can use. The result is that they produce a **6.** _____ that can be kept for times of need or sold to other countries. On the other hand, as many as 750,000,000 people are **7.** _____ because they live in countries that have less food than they need.

B. Word Link. The prefixes **over–** and **under–** can be added to verbs to form new verbs. Read the information below and add *over-* or *under-* to create the correct new verb. Then answer the question. Use your dictionary to help you.

India is home to some 1,200 different species of birds. Although there are laws in place banning the capture and trade of these birds, as many as 300 species are regularly caught and traded. In a recent incident, more than 10,000 birds headed for foreign countries were found by the police at Mumbai International Airport. Birds **1.** _____**go** great stress during transport: for every bird that reaches its final destination, two die on the way.

Until 1991, India was one of the largest exporters of birds to the Middle East and other markets **2.** _____**seas**. In that year, India adopted a ban on all wild bird trade. Unfortunately, an **3.** _____**ground** trade in wild birds continues throughout the country. "The trade is not limited to domestic markets," said Abrar Ahmed of the Bombay Natural History Society. "There is continuous large-scale bird smuggling out of the country." Ahmed has **4.** _____**taken** a study of bird trading across India as part of his doctoral thesis.

Asad R. Rahmani, director of the Bombay Natural History Society, who **5.** _____**saw** Ahmed's study, noted that Ahmed had clever ways of working **6.** _____**cover** without raising the suspicions of trappers and traders of birds. The study brings to light aspects of the trade that have until now been **7.** _____**looked**.

For example, Ahmed has described the **8.** _____**lying** reasons why the bird trade is so common and so difficult to stop. One reason is a religious bird-release business. In several Indian religions, releasing a caged bird back into the wild is an important ritual, and people are willing to pay for the birds they will release.

C. Usage. Some words in English are nouns when the accent is on the first syllable, but verbs if the accent is on the second syllable. For example, **pro**ject is a noun, while pro**ject** is a verb. Look at the sentences below and check (✓) whether the accent of the word in **bold** is on the first or second syllable.

	Which Syllable	
	First	**Second**
1. Despite assurances of safety, many people still fear that they could **contract** diseases from genetically modified foods.	❐	❐
2. A common objection to genetically modified foods is that they are marketed before sufficient **research** can be done.	❐	❐
3. In order to win a food poisoning case in court, you need to prove that the **conduct** of the restaurant was the cause.	❐	❐
4. A number of leading food companies have decided to **reject** ingredients from cloned animals in their products.	❐	❐
5. A recent **survey** showed that many people think genetically modified foods will provide benefits in the future.	❐	❐
6. A private company recently opened a new laboratory **complex** devoted to the development of genetically modified plants.	❐	❐
7. The speaker didn't **contrast** public opinion of genetically modified foods in Europe with that in the United States.	❐	❐
8. It is possible to **extract** DNA from fruit using just materials that are easily available.	❐	❐
9. Plans to label genetically modified foods has led to **conflict** between the food industry and the government.	❐	❐

D. Word Link. We can add **–ance** or **–ence** to certain verbs to form nouns. Complete each chart with the missing verb or noun form of the word. Use your dictionary to help you. Then use the correct forms of the words to complete the sentences.

Verb	Noun
1. abound	
2. assist	assistance
3.	coherence
4. conserve	
5. correspond	
6.	emergence

Verb	Noun
7. infer	
8.	maintenance
9.	occurence
10.	pertinence
11. refer	
12. revere	

1. Basho's name will always be linked with the _____ of a new style of poetry: the 17-syllable poems known as haiku.
2. Basho's poem *Noon Doze* was inspired by an everyday _____ that might happen today or centuries ago: a short nap against a cool wall.
3. Though you will find many neon signs and skyscrapers in modern Tokyo, there is also a(n) _____ of shrines, parks, and gardens.

4. Basho's great journey was made mainly on foot but with occasional _____ by horse.

5. Haiku poems frequently include a _____ to a season.

6. Sometimes haiku poems include key nature words that we can use to _____ the season without directly stating it.

E. Word Partnership. Several phrasal verbs are of the form **get** followed by one or more particles (for example, *get* your idea *across*, *get around* to doing something). Complete the passage using the particles in the box.

back	around to	over	across	along	at	away	by

1. Sometimes actions (a gift or an invitation) can get your message _____ better than just words.

2. After a break up, make sure you give yourself time to get _____ the relationship before starting a new one.

3. In today's busy world, a couple might never get _____ discussing their future unless they plan a time to talk about it.

4. Marriage is no guarantee of a permanently happy relationship. Even married couples need to work at getting _____ with each other.

5. If you feel the romance has left your marriage, try getting _____ with your partner for a weekend at the sea, in the mountains, or wherever!

6. If there's a problem you don't understand in your relationship, honest communication, though sometimes difficult, is usually the best way to get _____ the truth.

7. Surprisingly, some relationship experts believe that, after breaking up, you can improve your chances of getting your partner _____ by *not* communicating for a month.

8. If money is tight and you are struggling just to get _____, work together to cut expenses. Don't ask relatives or friends for money if at all possible.

F. Choosing the Right Definition. Study the numbered definitions for *route*. Then write the number of the definition (**1–5**) that relates to each sentence below.

route /rut, raʊt/ (**routes, routing, routed**) **1** N-COUNT A **route** is a way from one place to another. ❑ ... the shortest route to the school. **2** N-COUNT In the United States, **Route** is used in front of a number in the names of main roads between major cities. ❑ *Route 780 heads west out of the city.* **3** N-COUNT You can refer to a way of achieving something as a **route**. ❑ That problem can be solved by two different routes. **4** V-T If vehicles, goods, or passengers **are routed** in a particular direction, they are made to travel in that direction. **5** PHRASE **En route** to a place means on the way to that place. ❑ They had an accident en route to Paris.

_____ **a.** **Route** 95 connects the cities of Boston, New York, and Washington, D.C.

_____ **b.** The poet Matsuo Basho died of an illness in 1694 while en **route** to Osaka.

_____ **c.** At points along Basho's **route** are stone monuments displaying his poems.

_____ **d.** Some travel agencies tend to **route** tourists to the same popular destinations.

_____ **e.** Some study photography in college, but others become photographers by other **routes**.

Design and Engineering

Discuss these questions with a partner.

1. What are some examples of recent fashion innovations?
2. How have the materials used to make clothes changed over the years?
3. Apart from clothes, what else can be made from fabric?

▲ Biomimetic paint, inspired by the lotus leaf, on wood blocks repels water and resists stains.

Design by Nature

▲ This man-made flying insect was inspired by the real-life blowfly (below). Wings powered by tiny motors beat up to 275 times per second. "A true fly's wings are remarkable . . .," says engineer Ron Fearing. "Our challenge is to get . . . a device [that's] ¹⁄₂₀ the weight of a paper clip."

Before You Read

Biomimetic engineers have a **concrete purpose** in mind: to create designs that **have the potential** to change our everyday lives. These engineers **draw inspiration** from designs found in nature, many of which are **unimaginably complex**. They then **apply** the design principles in order to improve existing technologies, or create entirely new ones. Recent applications of biomimetic research include new technologies used in engineering, medicine, and many other **fields**.

A. Matching. Read the information and match each word or phrase in **blue** with its definition.

1. _____ (to) get ideas
2. _____ (to) use (an idea, etc.)
3. _____ areas of research
4. _____ extremely difficult to understand
5. _____ possess the capability
6. _____ definite goal, or aim

B. Skim. Skim the first paragraph of the reading passage to answer these questions.

1. What is the name of the animal that interests biologist Andrew Parker?
2. What special ability does the animal have?
3. What does Parker want to do with the knowledge he has obtained?

Biomimetics

One cloudless midsummer day, Andrew Parker, an evolutionary biologist, knelt in the baking red sand of an Australian desert and gently placed the right back leg of a thorny devil into a dish of water. The thorny devil, a small lizard that has learned to survive in the baking heat of the Australian desert, has a secret that fascinated Parker. "Look, look!" he exclaimed, "Its back is completely drenched!"[1] Sure enough, in less than a minute, water from the dish had traveled up the lizard's leg, across its skin, and into its mouth. It was, in essence, drinking through its foot. The thorny devil can also do this when standing on damp sand—a vital competitive advantage in the desert. Parker had come here to solve the riddle of precisely how it does this, not from purely biological[2] interest, but with a concrete purpose in mind: to make a device to help people collect water in the desert.

From Natural Wonder to Useful Tool

Parker is a leading scientist in the field of biomimetics–applying designs from nature to solve problems in engineering, materials science, medicine, and other fields. His studies of the body coverings of butterflies and beetles have led to brighter screens for cell phones. He sometimes draws inspiration from nature's past: while visiting a museum in Warsaw, Poland, he noticed a 45-million-year-old fly trapped in amber[3] and observed how the shape of its eye's surface reduced light reflection. This shape is now being used in solar panels.[4]

▲ Drinking through its foot, the thorny devil lizard of the dry Australian desert demonstrates its ability to move water to its mouth using channels between its scales.

As the next phase in his plan to create a water-collection device inspired by the lizard, Parker sent his observations and experimental results to Michael Rubner and Robert Cohen, two colleagues at the Massachusetts Institute of Technology. On the one hand, Parker is full of inspiration and enthusiasm about the many possibilities of biomimetics. On the other, Rubner and Cohen are much more practical and focus on the ideas that actually have a chance of being applied successfully. This combination of biological insight and engineering pragmatism[5] is vital to success in biomimetics, and has led to several promising technologies.

Though Rubner and Cohen are certainly impressed by biological structures, they consider nature merely a starting point for innovation. Cohen says, "The natural structure provides a clue to what is useful . . . But maybe you can do it better." Ultimately, they consider a biomimetics project a success only if it has the potential to make a useful tool for people. "Looking at pretty structures in nature is not sufficient," says Cohen. "What I want to know is, can we actually transform these structures into [something] with true utility[6] in the real world?"

[1] If something is **drenched**, it is completely wet.
[2] **Biological** processes occur in the bodies of living things.
[3] **Amber** is a hard yellowish-brown substance used for making jewelry.
[4] A **solar panel** is a device used to collect electrical energy from the sun.
[5] **Pragmatism** means dealing with problems in a practical way.
[6] The **utility** of something is its usefulness.

The hook-and-loop design of Velcro (electron microscope image, left) that grips instantly, but lets go when pulled, was initially based on a type of seed called a cocklebur (right).

Unlocking Nature's Secrets

The work of Parker, Rubner, and Cohen is only one part of a growing global biomimetics
65 movement. Scientists around the world are studying and trying to copy a wide variety of nature's design secrets, with the goal of using them to create something useful. In the United States, researchers are looking at the shape
70 of humpback whale fins in order to improve windmills that generate electric energy. The shape of the body of a certain fish has inspired designers at Mercedes-Benz to develop a more efficient car design. By analyzing how termites[7]
75 keep their large nests at the right temperature and humidity, architects[8] in Zimbabwe hope to build more comfortable buildings. And in Japan, medical researchers have developed a painless needle that is similar in shape to the
80 proboscis[9] of a mosquito.

The Bio-Inspired Robot

Potentially, one of the most useful applications of biomimetics is the robot. Robots can perform tasks that might be too boring or
85 dangerous for humans, but such robots are extremely difficult to build. Professor Ronald Fearing of the University of California is creating a tiny robot fly that can be used in surveillance[10] or rescue operations. Fearing's
90 fly is a much simplified copy of the real thing. "Some things are just too mysterious and complicated to be able to replicate,"[11] he says. It will still be years before his robot fly can perform anything like an actual fly, but Fearing
95 is confident that over time he will close the gap between nature and human engineering.

At Stanford University in California, Mark Cutkosky is working on a robot gecko. As long ago as the fifth century B.C., the Greek
100 philosopher Aristotle was amazed at how this small lizard "can run up and down a tree in any way, even with the head downward." Cutkosky studied the extremely small structures on the gecko's feet that allow it to run up and down
105 vertical walls as easily as humans run down the street. He applied what he learned to create Stickybot, a robot that can walk up and down smooth vertical surfaces made, for example, of glass or plastic. The U.S. military, which funds
110 the project, hopes that one day Stickybot will be able to climb up a building and stay there for days, monitoring the area below. Cutkosky hypothesizes a range of non-military uses as well. "I'm trying to get robots to go places
115 where they've never gone before," he says. For now, Stickybot only climbs very clean and smooth surfaces quite slowly—quite unlike a real gecko, which can run up just about any surface very quickly.

[7] **Termites** are small insects.
[8] An **architect** is a person who designs buildings.
[9] A **proboscis** is a long mouth part, usually of an insect.
[10] **Surveillance** is the careful watching of someone, especially by an organization such as the police or the army.
[11] If you **replicate** something, you make a copy of it.

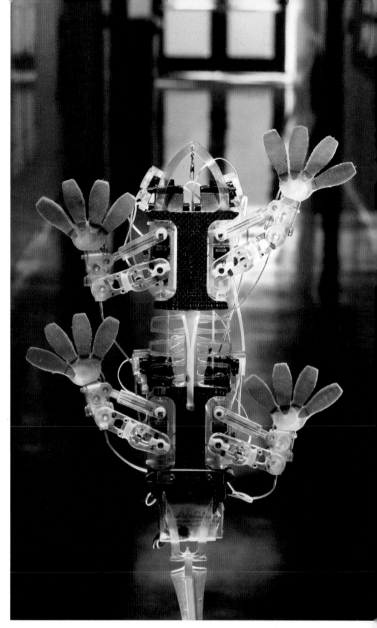

The Stickybot (right) climbs a glass wall, using toes based on those of the gecko (left).

¹²⁰ However, despite the promise of the field, and the brilliant people who work in it, biomimetics has led to surprisingly few business successes. Perhaps only one product has become truly famous—Velcro, which was ¹²⁵ invented in 1948 by Swiss chemist George de Mestral, who copied the way seeds called cockleburs stuck to his dog's fur. Some blame industry, whose short-term expectations about how soon a project should be completed and ¹³⁰ become profitable conflict with the time-consuming nature of biomimetics research. But the main reason biomimetics hasn't yet been a business success is that nature is inherently and unimaginably complex. For the present, ¹³⁵ engineers cannot hope to reproduce it.

Nonetheless, the gap with nature is gradually closing. Researchers are using more powerful microscopes, high-speed computers, and other new technologies to learn more from ¹⁴⁰ nature. A growing number of biomimetic materials are being produced. And although the field of biomimetics has yet to become a very successful commercial industry, it has already developed into a powerful new tool for ¹⁴⁵ understanding nature's secrets.

Reading Comprehension

A. Multiple Choice. Choose the best answer for each question.

Gist **1.** Another title for this reading could be _____.
- a. *The Life of the Thorny Devil*
- b. *Why Biomimetics Can't Succeed*
- c. *Technology Inspired by Nature*
- d. *Andrew Parker's Scientific Career*

Detail **2.** Why did Andrew Parker go to the Australian desert?
- a. to capture and bring back a thorny devil
- b. to understand how the thorny devil collects water
- c. to provide water to thirsty thorny devils
- d. to discover water in the Australian desert

Detail **3.** What has the study of termite nests inspired?
- a. more comfortable buildings
- b. improved windmills
- c. a more efficient car design
- d. a painless needle

Reference **4.** In line 91, what does *things* refer to?
- a. tasks
- b. robot flies
- c. copies
- d. parts of nature

Main Idea **5.** What is the main idea of paragraph 8 (starting line 120)?
- a. Velcro is the greatest business success biomimetics has ever had.
- b. Biomimetics would be more successful if industry were less demanding.
- c. Nature's complexity is why biomimetics has had few business successes.
- d. Today's engineers are unable to copy nature as well as de Mestral could.

Critical Thinking

Which feature of an animal or plant not mentioned in the reading do you think would be useful to replicate? Can you think of a practical use for it?

B. True or False. Read the sentences below and circle **T** (true) or **F** (false).

1. Parker hopes to create a water-collection device inspired by the thorny devil.   **T**   **F**

2. Rubner and Cohen are satisfied with understanding how nature works.   **T**   **F**

3. Studying humpback whale fins may be useful for improving windmills.   **T**   **F**

4. The body of a fish inspired a painless needle design.   **T**   **F**

5. Stickybot is perhaps the most famous biomimetic creation so far.   **T**   **F**

Vocabulary Practice

A. Completion. Complete the information with the correct form of words from the box. Two words are extra.

colleague	device	gap	vital
gradual	insight	nonetheless	
reproduce	riddle	vertical	

▲ The design of the Mercedes Bionic concept car is based on the shape of the tropical boxfish.

The tropical boxfish, roughly the shape of a box, looks like it would have trouble moving through the water. **1.** _____, the boxfish is in fact an excellent swimmer that cuts through the water extremely smoothly. It is such a good swimmer that engineers at Mercedes Technology Center in Sindelfingen, Germany, had a remarkable **2.** _____: to use the boxfish to design the shape of a car that can cut through air as efficiently as the boxfish moves through water.

A model of the boxfish was created for them by Ronald Fricke and his **3.** _____ at the Rosenstein Museum in the city of Stuttgart. The model was placed inside a wind tunnel, a(n) **4.** _____ that is used to study how air moves around solid objects. The boxfish shape reportedly performed over 65 percent better than today's compact cars. It should be possible to **5.** _____ that efficient shape for use in the body of a car to reduce its air resistance. Less air resistance would mean less fuel required to run it—something which is **6.** _____ to all drivers in times of expensive fuel.

Engineers set to work to try to solve the **7.** _____ of how this unlikely shape could be so efficient. Their efforts were successful, and the car they created is the Mercedes Bionic concept car. On the highway, it is able to travel as far as 35 kilometers on just one liter of fuel. The car is currently just for testing and not for sale. However, the company says it expects that, in the future, various features of the Bionic concept car will **8.** _____ be introduced into cars that it produces for sale to the public.

B. Definitions. Match words from the box in **A** with the correct definition.

1. an object that has been invented for a particular purpose _____

2. necessary or very important _____

3. an accurate and deep understanding of something _____

4. occuring in small stages over a long period of time, rather than suddenly _____

5. standing or pointing straight up _____

6. a space between two things or a hole in the middle of something solid _____

7. something that is very difficult to understand _____

8. people you work with, especially in a professional job _____

Word Partnership Use **vital** with: (adj.) **absolutely** vital; (n.) vital **importance**, vital **information**, vital **link**, vital **organs**, vital **part**, vital **role**

4B
The Future of Fashion

Before You Read

In this computer-generated image, goats hang by a thread to make a very real point. Goats bred by Nexia Biotechnologies in Montreal contain a spider gene that causes them to make a spider-silk protein in their milk. This protein is being used in a new **fiber** that's five times as strong as steel.

Spider silk joins a long list of fibers, both natural and **synthetic**, that have been used to create **textiles** that are then used to make, for example, clothing. Some recently created textiles are **high-tech** industrial secrets. Others are well-known and, like wool, have been used in textiles for thousands of years.

A. Completion. Complete the sentences below using the words in **blue**.

1. _____ are types of woven cloth.

2. _____ activities or equipment involve an advanced level of technology.

3. A _____ is a thin thread of a natural or artificial substance, especially one that is used to make cloth or rope.

4. _____ products are made from chemicals or artificial substances rather than from natural ones.

B. Predict. Look quickly at the photos, captions, and headings in the reading. Check (✔) the topics you think you'll read about.

- ❒ high-tech protective clothing
- ❒ extremely strong fabrics
- ❒ intelligent clothes
- ❒ famous fashion models

Dream-weavers

▶ This computer modified image demonstrates how a technologically advanced uniform being developed by the U.S. Army would enable soldiers to hide effectively.

1 Alex Soza is a young and extremely creative Danish fashion designer. He says his ideas come to him in dreams. "I daydream. That's how I get ideas." One of his inventions, a
5 jacket that stays suspended in the air like a balloon after it is taken off, arose from such a daydream. He explained, "I was on the subway, and this picture of a floating jacket popped into my mind." Alex Soza is one of
10 many dreamers and pioneers who are turning textile[1] fantasies into realities. Thanks to them, the world of high-tech textiles is an exciting place to be these days.

High-Tech Textiles

15 Not so long ago, all fibers[2] used to make textiles came from natural sources: wool from the hair of sheep, cotton from the cotton plant, silk from silk worms. The first true synthetic fiber didn't appear until 1935, when
20 scientists at the DuPont Company invented nylon. Nylon is just one of various industrially produced substances called polymers. Polymers can be pulled into a thread, which makes them well suited for use in textile manufacturing.

25 Synthetic textiles have come a long way since nylon. Kevlar, a textile which is stronger than steel, is used in bullet-proof vests and ropes used by astronauts in space. Other high-tech fibers can resist very high temperatures—
30 perfect for firefighters and race-car drivers. While not all companies are forthcoming about their products for fear of having their ideas stolen, Huges Vinchon, an executive at Dubar-Warneton, a manufacturer of high-tech textiles
35 in France, is happy to display some of the amazing synthetic fibers his company creates. There is an oil-eating textile that absorbs five times its weight in oil, and is perfect for cleaning up oil spills. Another absorbs
40 vibrations.[3] ("Can you imagine a motorboat you can't hear?" he says.) There is also an ordinary-looking cloth bag that is "completely water soluble,"[4] according to Vinchon. "It's strong enough to carry heavy objects. But if I
45 dip it in boiling water, it disappears."

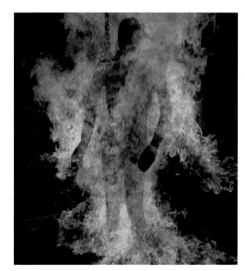

◀ A model human made of copper tests protective clothing for firefighters in temperatures of over 1,350°C (2,500°F).

[1] **Textiles** are types of woven cloth.
[2] A **fiber** is a thin thread of a natural or artificial substance, especially one that is used to make cloth or rope.
[3] If something **vibrates**, it shakes with repeated small, quick movements.
[4] If something is water **soluble**, it will dissolve in water.

Some high-tech textiles draw their inspiration from nature. Spider silk is a natural fiber that is five times as strong as steel. Unfortunately, spiders cannot be farmed, as they will eat each other. A Canadian biotechnology firm, Nexia, has come up with a possible alternative to spider farming: they have inserted the spider-silk protein gene into goats, thereby causing them to produce spider-silk protein in their milk. Nexia's head Jeff Turner is already dreaming of applications for the new fiber, named BioSteel. "Why use rockets to lift objects into orbit?[5] . . . Why not have a [big] satellite and dangle a rope down to earth and pull them up? . . . [There's] not a rope that will hold its weight at that length—but spider silk with its high strength-to-weight ratio could."

Wearable Electronics

Textiles have always been used in clothing, and modern, high-tech textiles may redefine what clothes are all about. "In the past, clothing protected us from the elements," says Ian Scott, head of technology for women's wear at British department store Marks & Spencer. "Then clothing became about fashion. The future is about clothing that can do something for you. It's no longer passive. It's active." One example of this active clothing that he hopes to sell in the next few years is an "intelligent bra," a sports bra that can sense stress and adjust its dimensions to give perfect support.

Other wearable electronics are being pioneered at a design laboratory in London run by the European manufacturer Philips Electronics. They are in the planning stages for various high-tech products, including an intelligent apron. This electronic apron acts as a kind of remote control device. It has a built-in microphone that allows the wearer to operate kitchen appliances using voice commands. Another planned product is the Queen of Clubs outfit. According to a Philips spokesperson, "Here's an outfit for the girl who's really into clubbing. Sensors[6] hidden in her clothes allow her to affect the lights and beat of the music. . . . So that she can make contact with other people across the dance floor, she has . . . pants with lights that flash when someone is trying to get in touch."

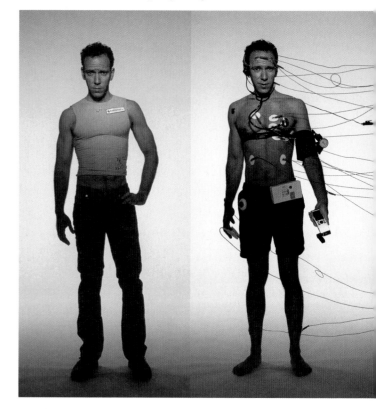

▲ Jeff Wolf, CEO of Sensatex, a technology company, demonstrates the smart shirt. Sensors in the shirt can replace all the equipment and wires shown on the right.

While there are many interesting clothing innovations to look forward to, the only item so far sold in stores was marketed a few years ago as the first wearable electronics jacket. The jacket, called the ICD+, sold for about a thousand dollars. It had an MP3 player and cell phone. Headphones were built into the hood, and it had a microphone in the collar. Clive van Heerden, director of Intelligent Fibres, pointed out that it was an early first step and a conservative one. "We want to make the jacket that makes the coffee and picks up the kids and keeps track of the shopping list, but it's not going to happen overnight."

[5] An **orbit** is the curved path in space that an object follows as it moves around a planet, moon, or star.

[6] A **sensor** is an instrument that reacts to certain physical conditions, such as heat or light.

▲ The CL75 is a flying
crane as tall as a 20-story building.
Made of fabric as thin as a shirt, it can lift as much as 75 tons.

Future Warriors

110 One of the most important areas of clothing innovation is for military purposes. High-tech textiles are everywhere at the U.S. Army research center in Natick, Massachusetts. As part of their Future Warrior program,
115 researchers are developing uniforms that will make a soldier difficult or impossible to see. Fibers in the uniform would take on the same color, brightness, and patterns of the surroundings of the wearer. A soldier dressed
120 in such a uniform would become nearly invisible to the enemy.

The researchers at Natick are also working on portable buildings that are made of what are essentially large, high-strength textile balloons.
125 Called air beams, these building materials would allow a team to build a structure large enough to hold airplanes in a fraction of the time a conventional metal structure would take. The largest air beams, about 0.75 meters
130 (2.5 feet) in diameter and 24 meters (78 feet) long, are so rigid that you can hang a heavy truck from one. Yet they can be packed into a truck. Whereas a conventional metal hangar[7] takes ten people five days to set up, one made
135 of air beams can be set up by six people in just two days.

Today's textile innovators are creating astonishing things. From Alex Soza's artistic jacket that defies gravity to smart aprons to
140 invisible military uniforms, high-tech textiles will soon be appearing in more and more parts of our lives. Who can foresee what these textile pioneers will dream up next? "It's about imagination!" says Alex Soza, with a bright
145 look in his eye. "It's a beautiful dream! It's turning science fiction into scientific fact!"

[7] A **hangar** is a large building in which aircraft are kept.

Reading Comprehension

A. Multiple Choice. Choose the best answer for each question.

Purpose **1.** What is the main purpose of the passage?
   a. to provide a historical overview of innovative fashion styles
   b. to introduce the reader to developments in high-tech textiles
   c. to convince the reader to buy the latest fashions
   d. to explain how modern fashions are often inspired by nature

Inference **2.** Why does Huges Vinchon mention a motorboat you can't hear?
   a. to evoke admiration for a fabric which can absorb vibrations
   b. to explain one of the properties of an oil-absorbing fabric
   c. to give an example of how quietly his textile factory runs
   d. to show that he is not afraid of having his ideas stolen

Inference **3.** Which person do you think would be most likely to design a coat made of paper with six arms that three people can wear together?
   a. Alex Soza
   b. Huges Vinchon
   c. Jeff Turner
   d. Ian Scott

Detail **4.** Which of these items has actually been sold in stores?
   a. the Queen of Clubs outfit
   b. the intelligent bra
   c. the intelligent apron
   d. the ICD+ jacket

Reference **5.** The word *they* on line 132 refers to _____.
   a. heavy trucks   c. metal hangars
   b. air beams   d. airplanes

Critical Thinking

Do you think the products mentioned in the reading will sell well if they become available in stores?

B. Matching. Match each futuristic fashion (**1–5**) with the correct description (**a–e**).

   1. Alex Soza's jacket   _____
   2. The intelligent bra   _____
   3. The Queen of Clubs outfit   _____
   4. The intelligent apron   _____
   5. The ICD+ jacket   _____

   a. can adjust its dimensions.
   b. had an MP3 player and a cell phone.
   c. allows you to operate kitchen appliances.
   d. lights up in response to music.
   e. was imagined in a daydream.

Vocabulary Practice

▲ A cyclist rides by *The Gates*, in New York's Central Park.

A. Completion. Complete the information using the correct form of words from the box. One word is extra.

fantasy	foresee	forthcoming
rigid	suspend	thereby

Christo and his wife Jeanne-Claude are two of the best-known living artists. However, the art they are famous for could never fit inside a museum. They are "environmental artists" who change the look of a place on a very large scale, often with colorful fabric, **1.** _____ allowing people to look at that place in a new way.

Once the couple has settled on an artistic idea, it takes an incredible amount of planning, work, and money in order to turn their **2.** _____ into reality. Some examples of their large-scale works are:

Wrapped Coast (1969). About 90,000 square meters (a million square feet) of fabric were used to wrap the coast of Little Bay in Sydney, Australia.

Surrounded Islands (1983). Eleven islands in Miami were surrounded by 600,000 square meters (6.5 million square feet) of floating pink fabric.

The Gates (2005). In New York City's Central Park, 7,503 metal gates with yellow fabric **3.** _____ from them were set up along the park's pathways.

Christo and Jeanne-Claude's **4.** _____ project is called *Over the River*. It involves hanging fabric over a distance of nearly 10 kilometers above the Arkansas River in Colorado in the United States. Although Christo and Jeanne-Claude are both in their seventies, they don't **5.** _____ that *Over the River* will be their last work of art. They are already planning future projects.

B. Words in Context. Complete each sentence with the best answer.

1. An example of a rigid material is _____.
   a. cotton   b. wood

2. If you bought some clothes at a fraction of their original price, you _____.
   a. saved money   b. spent too much

3. Gravity is particularly important when you are designing _____.
   a. a rocket   b. clothing

4. Military clothing is worn by _____.
   a. business people   b. soldiers

5. A portable device is easily _____.
   a. carried   b. used

Word Link

The prefix **fore–** has the meaning of *before*, e.g., **fore**see, **fore**cast, **fore**stall, **fore**ground.

Kinetic Sculpture

A. Preview. Read the information below and match each word in **blue** with its definition.

A kinetic sculpture is **literally** a piece of art on wheels. **Contestants** in the Kinetic Sculpture Race can focus on making their vehicles more kinetic (which means they are able to move on their own) or making them more eye-catching. Of course, they have to remember this is no simple race down the street, but a full **obstacle course** over a great distance!

1. actually; without any exaggeration   _____
2. a path along which objects are placed making it difficult to travel   _____
3. people who take part in a competition   _____

▲ Kinetic sculptures come in all shapes, sizes, and colors.

B. Summarize. Watch the video, *Kinetic Sculpture*. Then complete the summary below using words from the box. Two words are extra.

nonetheless	colleague	portable	rigid	foresee
fantasy	vital	device	vertical	thereby

The Kinetic Sculpture Race, held each year in Baltimore, is an unusual race between human-powered machines on an obstacle course. A kinetic sculpture is a work of art, but unlike ones in the museum, which cannot move, these are completely **1.** _____, as they must be driven over a long route through water, sand, mud, and ice.

These machines seem to come from a make-believe world of pure **2.** _____. At the same time, the machines must actually function, so good engineering is also **3.** _____ to success.

The race originated in the late 1960s when Hobart Brown raced his neighbors down Main Street on his son's bicycle, which he wildly decorated, **4.** _____ starting an event that would eventually become very popular.

Kinetic sculptures in the race range from small, simple **5.** _____ driven by one person to large, complex vehicles requiring many drivers. In this year's race, 21 teams participated. There are sometimes mechanical problems that are difficult to **6.** _____ at the start, but the race goes on **7.** _____. Contestants simply do their best to repair their machines along the way.

The most important part of the race seems not to win, but simply to have fun working together with people you know such as friends or **8.** _____ from work—or even with complete strangers!

C. Think About It.

1. Imagine that you are going to enter the race. What shape will your kinetic sculpture be?

2. Founder of the race, Hobart Brown, says in the video, "The true art work or the true art form is the participation of everyone from the kid up to the adult and the kid looks up to the adult and says I want to get older too." What do you think he means?

To learn more about design and engineering, visit elt.heinle.com/explorer

Human Journey

Discuss these questions with a partner.

1. How long ago did the first humans arrive in your country? Where did they come from?

2. What kinds of evidence help us learn about early humans?

3. What are the most remote inhabited places in the world? How did people first reach there?

▲ A reconstruction of a Neanderthal female.

5A The DNA Trail

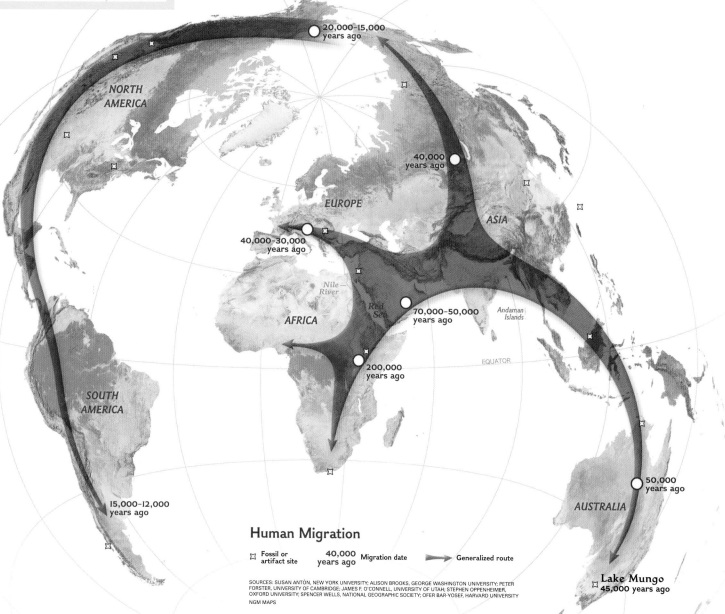

Human Migration

⛿ Fossil or artifact site   **40,000 years ago** Migration date   ➤ Generalized route

SOURCES: SUSAN ANTÓN, NEW YORK UNIVERSITY; ALISON BROOKS, GEORGE WASHINGTON UNIVERSITY; PETER FORSTER, UNIVERSITY OF CAMBRIDGE; JAMES F. O'CONNELL, UNIVERSITY OF UTAH; STEPHEN OPPENHEIMER, OXFORD UNIVERSITY; SPENCER WELLS, NATIONAL GEOGRAPHIC SOCIETY; OFER BAR-YOSEF, HARVARD UNIVERSITY
NGM MAPS

Before You Read

A. Completion. The map above shows the likely migration routes of our human ancestors as they populated the world. Study the map and complete the sentences below.

1. The first modern humans began spreading out from the continent of _____.

2. The continent most recently populated by modern humans is _____.

3. Modern humans crossed over to North America from the continent of _____.

4. Europe was populated by modern humans _____ years ago.

B. Skim. Skim the article on the following pages. What kinds of evidence are scientists looking for to help them understand the migrations of our human ancestors?

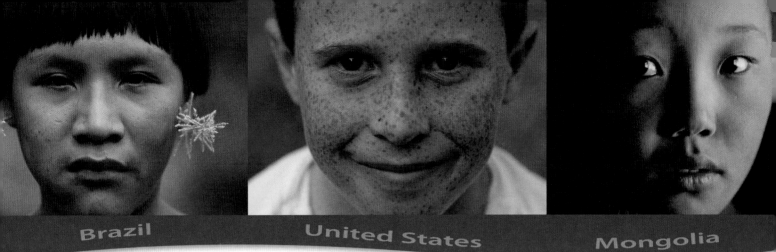

Brazil   United States   Mongolia

The Greatest Journey

Modern genetic evidence indicates humans left Africa as long as 70,000 years ago. Fanning out across the continents, they gave rise to new faces and races

1 Everybody loves a good story, and when it's finished, this may be the greatest one ever told. It begins in Africa with a group of people, perhaps just a few hundred, surviving
5 by hunting animals and gathering fruits, vegetables, and nuts. It ends about 200,000 years later with their six and a half billion descendants spread across the Earth, living in peace or at war, their faces lit by campfires[1]
10 and computer screens.

In between is an exciting tale of survival, movement, isolation, and conquest, most of it occurring before recorded history. Who were those first modern people in Africa?
15 What routes did they take when they left their home continent 50,000 years ago to expand into Europe and Asia? When and how did humans reach the Americas? For decades the only proof was found in a small number of
20 scattered bones and artifacts[2] our ancestors left behind on their journeys. In the past 20 years, however, increasingly refined DNA technologies have allowed scientists to find a record of ancient human migrations in
25 the DNA of living people.

Tracing Ancestry in DNA

"Every drop of human blood contains a history book written in the language of our genes," says population geneticist[3] Spencer
30 Wells. The human genetic code, or genome, is 99.9 percent identical throughout the world. But while the bulk of our DNA is the same, what's left is responsible for our individual differences—in eye color or disease risk, for
35 example. On very rare occasions, a small change, called a mutation, can occur, which is then passed down to all of that person's descendants. Generations later, finding that same mutation in two people's DNA
40 indicates that they share the same ancestor. By comparing mutations in many different populations, scientists can trace their ancestral connections.

These ancient mutations are easiest to find
45 in two places: in DNA that is passed from mother to child (called mitochondrial DNA, or mtDNA for short), and in DNA that travels from father to son (known as the Y chromosome, the part of DNA that determines
50 a child will be a boy). By comparing the mtDNA and Y chromosomes of people from various populations, geneticists can get a rough idea of where and when those groups separated in the great migrations around the planet.

[1] A **campfire** is a fire that is made outdoors, usually for warmth or cooking.
[2] An **artifact** is a human-made ornament, tool, or other object, especially one that is historically or culturally interesting.
[3] A **geneticist** is a scientist who studies DNA and genes.

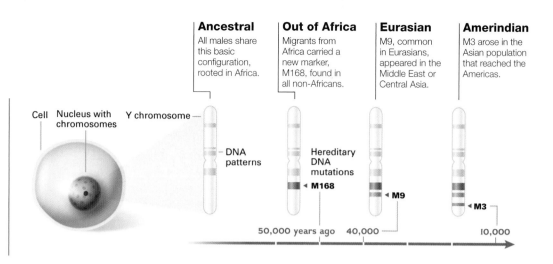

Genetic mutations act as markers, tracing a journey through time. The earliest known mutation to spread outside Africa is M168, which arose some 50,000 years ago. This graphic shows the Y chromosome of a Native American man with various mutations, including M168, proving his African ancestry.

Ancestral
All males share this basic configuration, rooted in Africa.

Out of Africa
Migrants from Africa carried a new marker, M168, found in all non-Africans.

Eurasian
M9, common in Eurasians, appeared in the Middle East or Central Asia.

Amerindian
M3 arose in the Asian population that reached the Americas.

Cell Nucleus with chromosomes Y chromosome

DNA patterns

Hereditary DNA mutations

◄ M168   ◄ M9   ◄ M3

50,000 years ago   40,000   10,000

Out of Africa

In the mid-1980s, a study compared mtDNA from women around the world and found that women of African descent showed twice as many genetic mutations as other women. Because mutations seem to occur at a steady rate over time, scientists were able to conclude that modern humans must have lived in Africa twice as long as anywhere else. They now calculate that all living humans are related to a single woman who lived roughly 150,000 years ago in Africa, a "mitochondrial Eve." If geneticists are right, all of humanity is linked to Eve through an unbroken chain of mothers. Eve was soon joined by "Y chromosome Adam," the genetic father of us all, also from Africa. DNA studies have confirmed that all the people on Earth, with all their shapes and colors, can trace their ancestry to ancient Africans.

What seems virtually certain is that at a remarkably recent date—probably between 50,000 and 70,000 years ago—one small group of people, the ancestors of modern humans, left Africa for western Asia, either by migrating around the northern end of the Red Sea or across its narrow southern opening.

Once in Asia, genetic evidence suggests, the population split. One group stalled[4] temporarily in the Middle East, while the other commenced a journey that would last tens of thousands of years. Moving a little further with each new generation, they followed the coast around the Arabian Peninsula, India, and Southeast Asia, all the way to Australia. "The movement was probably imperceptible,"[5] says Spencer Wells. "It was less of a journey and probably more like walking a little farther down the beach to get away from the crowd."

Although archeological[6] evidence of this 13,000-kilometer (8,000-mile) migration from Africa to Australia has almost completely vanished, genetic traces of the group that made the trip do exist. They have been found in the DNA of indigenous[7] peoples in the Andaman Islands near Myanmar, in Malaysia, and in Papua New Guinea, and in the DNA of nearly all Australian aborigines. Modern discoveries of 45,000-year-old bodies in Australia, buried at a site called Lake Mungo, provide some physical evidence for the theories as well.

People in the rest of Asia and Europe share different but equally ancient mtDNA and Y-chromosome mutations. These mutations show that they are descendants of the group that stayed in the Middle East for tens of thousands of years before moving on. Perhaps about 40,000 years ago, modern humans advanced into Europe.

[4] If a process **stalls**, or if someone or something stalls it, the process stops but may continue at a later time.

[5] Something that is **imperceptible** is so small it is not noticed or cannot be seen.

[6] **Archeology** is the study of the past through examination of the remains of things such as buildings, tools, and other objects.

[7] **Indigenous** people or things belong to the country in which they are found, rather than coming there or being brought there from another country.

▲ Spencer Wells, head of the National Geographic Society's Genographic Project. It will analyze DNA from hundreds of thousands of people to map how prehistoric humans populated the planet.

Peopling the Americas

115 About the same time as modern humans pushed into Europe, some of the same group that had paused in the Middle East spread east into Central Asia, where they eventually reached as far as Siberia, the Korean peninsula,
120 and Japan. Here begins one of the last chapters in the human story—the peopling of the Americas. Most scientists agree that today's Native Americans descend from ancient Asians who crossed from Siberia to Alaska in
125 the last ice age, when low sea levels would have exposed a land bridge between the continents. They probably traveled along the coast—perhaps a few hundred people moving from one piece of land to the next, between
130 a freezing ocean and a wall of ice. "A coastal route would have been the easiest way in," says Wells. "But it still would have been a hell of a

trip." Once across, they followed the immense herds[8] of animals into the mainland and spread
135 to the tip of South America in as little as a thousand years.

Genetic researchers can only tell us the basic outlines of a story of human migration that is richer and more complex than any ever
140 written. Most of the details of the movements of our ancestors and their countless[9] individual lives in different times and places can only be imagined. But thanks to genetic researchers, themselves descendants of mtDNA Eve and
145 Y-chromosome Adam, we have begun to unlock important secrets about the origins and movements of our ancient ancestors.

---

[8] A **herd** is a large group of animals of one kind that live together.
[9] **Countless** means very many.

Reading Comprehension

A. Multiple Choice. Choose the best answer for each question.

Gist

1. Another title for this reading could be _____.
   a. *Finding Y Chromosome Adam*
   b. *Who Were the First Humans?*
   c. *What DNA Teaches Us About Our History*
   d. *The Discovery of DNA in Africa*

Paraphrase

2. Which of the following is closest in meaning to *Every drop of human blood contains a history book written in the language of our genes* on lines 27–29?
   a. An individual's DNA contains mutations that indicate the person's ancestral history.
   b. The organization of information in a history book is similar to the organization of DNA within a gene.
   c. Every drop of blood contains enough DNA information to fill a history book.
   d. Although people speak different languages, all human blood contains the same language.

Detail

3. What happened to the first group of humans that moved from Africa into Asia?
   a. Most of the migrants turned back into Africa.
   b. They divided into two groups.
   c. Most of the migrants moved directly into Europe.
   d. They paused in the Middle East for tens of thousands of years.

Sequence

4. Which area was first to be populated by human migrants?
   a. Europe   c. western Asia
   b. Australia   d. South America

Detail

5. What of the following is NOT cited as evidence for the great migration to Australia?
   a. archeological evidence discovered in Asia
   b. DNA of people in Southeast Asia
   c. DNA of native people in Australia
   d. discovery of human remains in Australia

Critical Thinking

What evidence does the author use to show that humans began in Africa? Is it possible that this theory is wrong? Why or why not?

B. Fact or Theory. Which of these statements are facts (**F**) and which are theories (**T**)?

1. Mutations are easiest to find in mtDNA and in the Y chromosome.   **F   T**

2. All people are linked to "mitochondrial Eve" through an unbroken chain of mothers.   **F   T**

3. Almost no archeological evidence of the human journey from Africa to Australia has been found.   **F   T**

4. Bodies discovered at Lake Mungo are about 45,000 years old.   **F   T**

5. Humans traveled along the coast of a land bridge between Siberia and Alaska.   **F   T**

Vocabulary Practice

▲ Before modern humans entered Europe and Asia, the Neanderthals had lived there for 200,000 years.

A. Completion. Complete the information using the correct form of words from the box. One word is extra.

bury	conquer	descendant
bulk	mainland	immense
refine	scatter	vanish proof

Before modern *Homo sapiens* migrated out of Africa perhaps 60,000 years ago, scientists tell us that another group, Neanderthals, had occupied Europe and Asia for maybe 200,000 years. Although there were probably no more than 15,000 of them at their population's peak, groups of Neanderthals were **1.** _____ over a(n) **2.** _____ area throughout Europe, into the Middle East, and even as far east as Mongolia.

In 1856, the first Neanderthal bones were found **3.** _____ in Germany's Neander Valley by workers digging for stones. These thick bones indicated that Neanderthals were shorter than modern humans, but physically stronger. Their tools were rough and simple, and not as **4.** _____ as those of later *Homo sapiens*. Additionally, their food was not as varied; the **5.** _____ of their diet was the meat of large and medium-sized animals.

At some point after modern humans entered Europe and Asia, the Neanderthals **6.** _____ from Earth. The reason for their disappearance remains a mystery. There are, however, a number of theories. As modern *Homo sapiens* **7.** _____ their lands, they may have killed the Neanderthals off. Other possible causes include diseases introduced by the newcomers, or climate change.

Another theory was that the Neanderthals had children with *Homo sapiens*, and gradually became part of their group. However, 1997 DNA analysis by geneticist Svante Pääbo and his colleagues at the University of Munich determined that Neanderthal DNA is not included in the DNA of modern humans. This is rather convincing **8.** _____ that the majority of Neanderthals probably died out, and people alive today are not their **9.** _____.

B. Definitions. Match words from the box in **A** with the correct definition.

1. the largest part of a country or continent, contrasted to the islands around it _____

2. a fact, an argument, or a piece of evidence showing that something is true or exists _____

3. related people in later generations _____

4. spread over an area in a messy or irregular way _____

5. suddenly disappear, often in a way that cannot be explained _____

6. extremely large or great _____

7. take complete control of another group's land by force _____

8. improve something by making small changes to it _____

Word Partnership

Use **proof** with: (adj.) **convincing** proof, **final** proof, **living** proof, proof **positive**; (v.) **have** proof, **need** proof, **offer** proof, **provide** proof, **require** proof, **show** proof.

5B Fantastic Voyage

The illustration above pictures some of history's most amazing ocean navigators, the early Polynesians. **Anthropologists** believe that the Polynesians are descendants of an earlier group of Pacific Ocean explorers called the Lapita. Together, in **canoes** perhaps similar to the one shown above, they **expanded** their world to include nearly every island in the Pacific Ocean, landed in New Zealand, South America, and may even have gone to North America.

Where did these brave adventurers come from? What drove them again and again to sail their canoes over the **horizon** in search of new lands? How did they accomplish such amazing **feats** of navigation, finding and colonizing hundreds of distant islands scattered across an ocean that covers nearly a third of the earth?

Before You Read

A. Matching. Read the information above and match each word in **blue** with its definitions.

1. became larger _____

2. scientists who study people or culture _____

3. impressive achievements _____

4. wooden boats of a traditional style _____

5. the line where the sky seems to meet the land or sea _____

B. Scan. Scan the picture captions in the reading to find the answers to these questions.

1. Where was a Lapita pot uncovered?
   a. on Bora Bora   b. at a carnival   c. on Éfaté Island

2. On which island was the temple of Taputaputea?
   a. Raiatea   b. Easter Island   c. Hawaii

3. How long ago did the Lapita people travel east from New Guinea?
   a. 1,000 years ago   b. 3,000 years ago   c. 5,000 years ago

Beyond the Blue Horizon

1 It is mid-afternoon on a beach on the island of Bora Bora in French Polynesia, and it feels like a carnival.[1] The air smells of barbecue, and thousands of cheering spectators crowd
5 the shore to see the end of the Hawaiki Nui Va'a, a challenging 130-kilometer (80-mile) Polynesian canoe[2] race that virtually stops the nation. "This is our heritage," says Manutea Owen, a former canoe champion and a revered
10 hero on his home island of Huahine. "Our people came from over the sea by canoe. Sometimes when I'm out there competing, I try to imagine what they must have endured and the adventures they had crossing those
15 huge distances."

Pioneers of the Pacific

Manutea Owen's ancestors colonized nearly every island in the South Pacific Ocean in what was perhaps the most remarkable feat[3]
20 of human navigation before humans went to the moon. Only recently have scientists begun to understand where these amazing voyagers came from, and how, with simple canoes and no navigation equipment, they could manage
25 to find and colonize hundreds of distant islands scattered across an ocean that covers nearly a third of the globe. This expansion[4] into the Pacific was accomplished by two extraordinary civilizations: the Lapita and the Polynesians.

30 From about 1300 to 800 B.C., the Lapita people colonized islands that stretch over millions of square kilometers, including the

▲ The Hokule'a, a modern Hawaiian voyaging canoe built on ancient designs, arrives in Hawaii after a 6,100-kilometer (3,800-mile) voyage.

Solomon Islands, the Santa Cruz Islands, Vanuatu, Fiji, New Caledonia, and Samoa.
35 Then, for unknown reasons, they stopped. There was an interval of around 1,000 years before the civilization of the Polynesians, descendants of the Lapita, launched a new period of exploration. Then, they outdid the
40 Lapita with unbelievable feats of navigation, expanding the boundaries of their oceanic world until it was many times the size of that explored by their ancestors. Their colonies included the Cook Islands, French Polynesia,
45 Easter Island, and Hawaii, eventually reaching South America around 1000 A.D.

▲ This Lapita pot was recently uncovered in a 3,000-year-old burial site on Éfaté Island, Vanuatu.

[1] A **carnival** is a public festival with music, processions, and dancing.
[2] A **canoe** is a small wooden boat that you move through the water using a stick with a wide end called a paddle.
[3] If you refer to something as a **feat**, you admire it because it is an impressive and difficult achievement.
[4] If something **expands**, it becomes larger.

◄ The island of Raiatea in French Polynesia was a departure point for ancient voyagers who discovered Hawaii and New Zealand. After filling their canoes with supplies, sailors left from the temple of Taputaputea, the spiritual center of their world.

How Did They Do It?

There is one stubborn question for which archeology has yet to provide any answers: how did the Lapita and early Polynesian pioneers accomplish, many times over, a feat that is analogous to a moon landing? Very little evidence remains to help scientists understand their remarkable sailing skills. Unfortunately, no one has found an intact Lapita or early Polynesian canoe that might reveal how they were sailed. Nor do the oral histories[5] and traditions of later Polynesians offer any insights as to how they were able to navigate areas of open ocean hundreds or even thousands of kilometers wide without becoming lost. "All we can say for certain is that the Lapita had canoes that were capable of ocean voyages, and they had the ability to sail them," says Geoff Irwin, a professor of archeology at the University of Auckland. Nonetheless, with little evidence, scientists have been able to develop some theories about the secrets of these explorers' success.

Sailors have always relied upon the so-called "trade winds," winds that blow steadily and in predictable directions over the ocean's surface. Geoff Irwin notes that the Lapita's expansion into the Pacific was eastward, against steady trade winds. Sailing against the wind, he argues, may have been the key to their success. "They could sail out for days into the unknown . . . , secure in the knowledge that if they didn't find anything, they could turn about and catch a swift ride home on the trade winds." For returning explorers, successful or not, the geography of their own archipelagoes[6] provided a safety net, ensuring that sailors wouldn't sail past and be lost again in the open ocean. Vanuatu, for example, is a chain of islands 800 kilometers (500 miles) long with many islands within sight of each other. Once sailors hit that string of islands, they could find their way home.

Irwin hypothesizes that once out in the open ocean, the explorers would detect a variety of clues to follow to land: seabirds and turtles that need islands on which to build their nests, coconuts and twigs[7] carried out to sea, and the clouds that tend to form over some islands in the afternoon. It is also conceivable that Lapita sailors followed the smoke from distant volcanoes to new islands.

[5] **Oral history** consists of spoken memories, stories, and songs, and the study of these as a way of discovering information about the past.
[6] An **archipelago** is a group of islands, especially small islands.
[7] A **twig** is a very small thin branch that grows out from a main branch of a tree or bush.

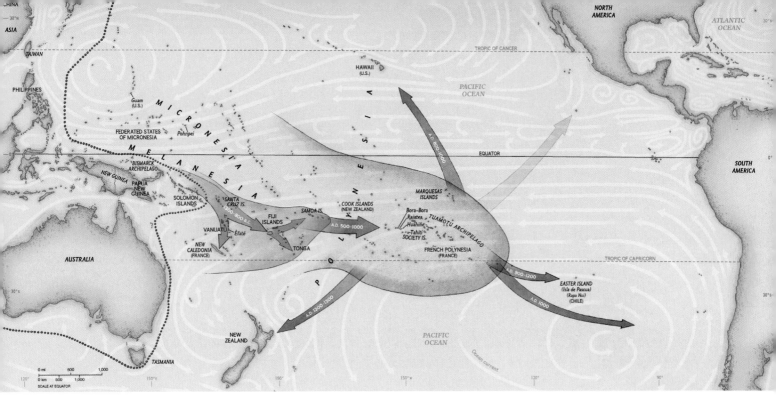

▲ The Lapita people traveled east from New Guinea some 3,000 years ago, and within a few centuries reached Tonga and Samoa. After a pause of a thousand years, their Polynesian descendants pushed even farther, eventually settling even the most remote islands.

Helped by El Niño?

100 These theories rely on one unproven point—that the Lapita and early Polynesians had mastered the skill of sailing against the wind using a sailing technique called "tacking." Rather than give all the credit to their bravery
105 and ability to tack, Athol Anderson of the Australian National University believes that they may also have been lucky—helped by a weather phenomenon known as El Niño.

El Niño occurs in the Pacific Ocean when the
110 surface water temperature is unusually high. It disrupts world weather in a variety of ways, but one of its effects is to cause trade winds in the South Pacific to weaken or to reverse direction and blow to the east. Scientists believe that
115 El Niño phenomena were unusually frequent around the time of the Lapita expansion, and again between 1,600 and 1,200 years ago, when the early Polynesians began their even more distant voyages. Anderson believes that
120 the Lapita may have been able to take advantage of trade winds blowing east instead of west, and thereby voyage far to the east without any knowledge of tacking techniques.

The success of the Lapita and their descendants
125 may have been due to their own sailing skill, to reverse trade winds, to a mixture of both, or even to facts still unknown. But it is certain that by the time Europeans came to the Pacific, nearly every piece of land, hundreds of islands
130 and atolls[8] in all, had already been discovered by the Lapita and Polynesians. Exactly why these ancient peoples set out on such giant migrations remains a mystery. However, as Professor Irwin puts it, "whatever you believe,
135 the really fascinating part of this story isn't the methods they used, but their motives. The Lapita, for example, didn't need to pick up and go; there was nothing forcing them, no overcrowded homeland. They went because
140 they wanted to go and see what was over the horizon."[9]

[8] An **atoll** is a small coral island or group of islands.
[9] The **horizon** is the line in the far distance where the sky seems to meet the land or the sea.

Reading Comprehension

A. Multiple Choice. Choose the best answer for each question.

Gist **1.** Another title for this reading could be _____.
   a. *How Ancient Pacific Peoples Explored the Pacific*
   b. *How El Niño Helped the Lapita*
   c. *The Race Between the Lapita and the Polynesians*
   d. *The Myth That the Lapita Explored the Pacific*

Reference **2.** The phrase *these amazing voyagers* on line 22 refers to _____.
   a. men who went to the moon
   b. the Lapita and early Polynesians
   c. today's Polynesians
   d. Manutea Owen and the people of Bora Bora

Inference **3.** Which of the following statements is a fact, not just a theory?
   a. Lapita canoes had triangular sails.
   b. Lapita sailors knew how to sail against the wind.
   c. The Lapita stopped exploring when the weather changed.
   d. No one has found an intact Lapita canoe.

Detail **4.** How might El Niño have assisted the Lapita and early Polynesians?
   a. by making the water temperature more comfortable
   b. by reversing the direction of the trade winds
   c. by making tacking easier
   d. by providing more wood to build canoes

Paraphrase **5.** What does Irwin mean by *they wanted to go and see what was over the horizon* on lines 140–141?
   a. They were motivated by a curiosity about new places.
   b. They hoped for greater security in faraway places.
   c. They desired better living conditions on other islands.
   d. They needed to find food and fresh water over the horizon.

Critical Thinking

Was the success of ancient sailors due to "sailing skill, reverse trade winds, a mixture of both, or even to facts still unknown"? Which do you think is most likely? Why?

B. Classification. Match each description (**a–f**) with the group it describes.

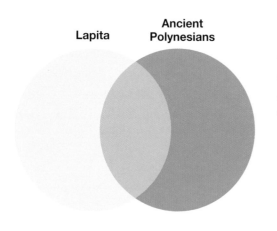

Lapita   Ancient Polynesians

   a. explored the Pacific from about 1300 to 800 B.C.
   b. reached South America around 1000 A.D.
   c. their navigation techniques are not fully understood
   d. colonized New Caledonia and Samoa
   e. colonized Easter Island and Hawaii
   f. may have been helped by El Niño

Vocabulary Practice

A. Completion. Complete the information with the correct form of words from the box. Three words are extra.

analogous	boundary	conceivable	disrupt
intact	interval	outdo	
stretch	stubborn	revere	

Ten years ago, most experts would have agreed that the first people in the Americas arrived about 14,000 years ago by walking across a land bridge that crossed the Bering Strait—the **1.** _____ between Siberia and Alaska. They then traveled south through an open area of ground between great sheets of ice that **2.** _____ across North America at that time. Today, however, this theory is being challenged.

An alternative theory suggests that instead of a single first migration, various groups of people came to the Americas at **3.** _____ spaced well apart in time. Another theory proposes that, rather than walking across a land bridge, some came by boat. According to this theory, ancient people might have kayaked[1] their way along the shoreline just as adventurous tourists do today.

▲ An archeologist examines Meadowcroft Rockshelter, U.S.A. Tools found in this cave are 19,000 years old.

Looking at ancient tools found in America, archeologist Dennis Stanford noticed that their shape is **4.** _____ to tools used by the Solutrean culture of southwestern Europe. He thinks it is **5.** _____ that people of that culture may have kayaked across the Atlantic from Europe to America perhaps 20,000 years ago or earlier.

The science of archeology often produces theories that are based on very small bits of evidence. Today's archeologists know that being **6.** _____ and holding on to one theory while shutting out the others isn't good science. They know they need to be patient as more buried pieces of the puzzle are dug out of the ground. As new evidence is discovered that **7.** _____ existing theories, they adjust those theories to explain the new facts.

[1] A **kayak** is a narrow boat like a canoe.

B. Words in Context. Complete each sentence with the best answer.

1. A person who is revered is highly _____.
   a. respected   b. feared

2. It is generally _____ to change a stubborn person's mind.
   a. easy   b. difficult

3. If an ancient tool is found intact, it is _____.
   a. broken   b. complete

4. Someone who wants to outdo others is _____.
   a. caring   b. competitive

5. Some students disrupt class by _____.
   a. talking on cell phones   b. studying hard

Word Partnership

Use **boundary** with: (*prep.*) boundary **around** places/things, boundary **between** places/things; (*v.*) **cross a** boundary, **mark/set a** boundary; (*n.*) boundary **dispute**, boundary **line**

Journey of Discovery

A. Preview. Look at the photograph of the *Mata Rangi III*, a boat constructed entirely of grass-like plants called reeds, and compare it to modern-day boats. How far do you think this boat can travel? Why do you think so?

B. Summarize. Watch the video, *Journey of Discovery*. Then complete the summary below using the correct form of words from the box. Two words are extra.

proof	revere	intact	outdo	conquer
disrupt	immense	stubborn	interval	refined

▲ This tiny ship is 20 meters (65 feet) long and only big enough for a few crew members.

Long ago, Spanish sailors traveled **1.** _____ distances in their wooden ships. Now, Kitín Muñoz, a modern-day sailor, hopes to **2.** _____ those brave adventurers by sailing a small ship made of reeds, the *Mata Rangi III*, across the Atlantic Ocean. This small ship is based on the ones used in pre-European South America, and was built by Aymara Indians from Bolivia using no modern materials.

This will be the third journey for Muñoz. The first two failed, but Muñoz is a **3.** _____ man who will not give up. This time he will leave from Barcelona, go along the coast of Africa, stop at the Cape Verde islands, and then cross the Atlantic Ocean and finish in Colombia.

One day off the North African coast, heavy winds and rough waves **4.** _____ the sailors' plans for a smooth journey. Water poured into the boat. After a while, the storm lost power, and fortunately, the ship was still **5.** _____. This experience is **6.** _____ that the reeds are strong enough for such difficult conditions. Another problem was the long **7.** _____ at sea when there was little or no wind. Such times were hard for the men, who got bored or depressed.

After more than a month at sea, the *Mata Rangi III* reached Cape Verde, where they celebrated the first part of the journey. Ahead of them still lies the wide Atlantic Ocean, which they hope to somehow **8.** _____.

C. Think About It.

1. Do you think the *Mata Rangi III* is capable of crossing the Atlantic Ocean? Do an Internet search on Kitín Muñoz to find out if his journey was successful.

2. Do you think that the *Mata Rangi III* project was worth the time and effort? Explain why or why not.

To learn more about the human journey, visit elt.heinle.com/explorer

UNIT 6

Conservation Challenges

WARM UP

Discuss these questions with a partner.

1. What places on earth are the least affected by the modern world?
2. What kinds of pressures is the natural world facing today?
3. What can we do to protect endangered forests and animals?

6A Disappearing Forests

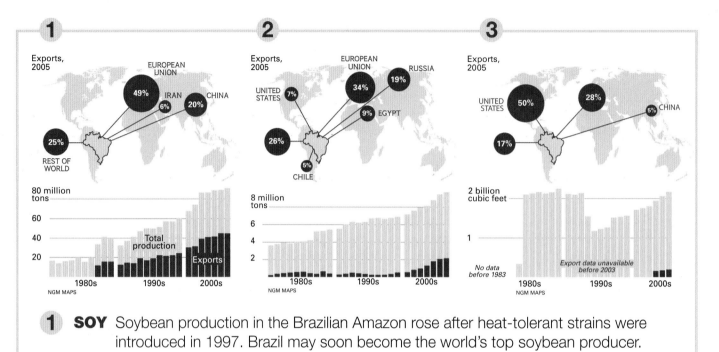

1 SOY Soybean production in the Brazilian Amazon rose after heat-tolerant strains were introduced in 1997. Brazil may soon become the world's top soybean producer.

2 BEEF The world's largest exporter of beef since 2004, Brazil now supplies nearly every country, including emerging markets such as Algeria, Romania, and Egypt.

3 TIMBER Recent years have seen rising demand for Brazilian hardwoods in Europe, the U.S., and Asia. Most timber from the Amazon is taken illegally, and stays in Brazil.

Before You Read

A. Multiple Choice. Read the information and look at the charts above. Then answer the questions.

1. In the 1990s, what percent of Brazilian beef production was exported?
   a. about 50%   b. under 10%   c. over 80%

2. What has been the overall trend in soy production in the 2000s?
   a. It has increased.   b. It has decreased.   c. It has remained the same.

3. In 2005, which of these imported the largest percentage of Brazilian beef?
   a. the U.S.   b. Russia   c. the European Union

4. When was the largest fall in Brazilian timber production?
   a. 1983–84   b. 1992–93   c. 2001–02

B. Scan. In 2005, a courageous woman lost her life in her battle to save the Amazon. What was her name? How did she die? Scan the first part of the passage to find out.

Last of the Amazon

▲ As Brazilian forest land is cut back, a single tree remains standing in an empty field.

On the morning of February 12, 2005, on a secluded path deep in Brazil's Amazon rain forest, two gunmen confronted a 73-year-old nun named Dorothy Stang. The nun[1] warned
5 the gunmen that the forest was not theirs and that they had no right to clear-cut the trees to plant grasses for their cattle.

"So, you don't like to eat meat?" one of the men taunted.

10 "Not enough to destroy the forest for it," she replied.

"If this problem isn't resolved today, it's never going to be," the man said.

According to a witness, who later appeared
15 at the two men's trial,[2] Stang saw him reach for his gun. She opened her Bible and read, "Blessed are they who hunger and thirst for justice, for they shall be satisfied." As she turned to go, one of the men aimed his gun
20 at her and pulled the trigger.

The Battle for the Amazon

"The death of the forest is the end of our lives," Stang would tell her followers, mostly poor family farmers who had settled small
25 plots of land along the Trans-Amazonian Highway, the largest road cutting through the Amazon rain forest. Stang encouraged farmers to live and work in harmony with the Amazon ecosystem, in contrast with large-scale
30 cattle ranchers and land speculators[3] whose widespread tree-cutting often results in the destruction of entire ecosystems. She worked to educate poor farmers, organizing them and encouraging them to resist the ranchers and
35 speculators who want the same land—and who are sometimes ready to use violent methods to obtain it.

▲ Brazilian women wear T-shirts with photos of Dorothy Stang, murdered for trying to protect the forest. Their shirts read "The death of the forest is the end of our life."

[1] A **nun** is a member of a female religious community.
[2] A **trial** is a formal meeting at a law court, at which a judge and jury listen to evidence, and decide whether a person is guilty of a crime.

[3] If someone **speculates** financially, they buy property, stocks, or shares, in the hope of being able to sell them again at a higher price and make a profit.

During the past 40 years, close to 20 percent of the Amazon rain forest has been cut down—
40 more than in all the previous 450 years since European colonization began. Scientists fear that an additional 20 percent of the trees will be lost over the next two decades. If that happens, the forest's ecology may begin to fall
45 apart. Intact, the Amazon produces half its own rainfall through the water it releases into the atmosphere. Eliminate enough of that rain through clearing, and the remaining trees dry out and die. The natural result is an increase in
50 forest fires burning out of control.

Much of the destruction of the Amazon is done illegally. Incredibly, there are more than 160,000 kilometers (100,000 miles) of illegal logging roads throughout the forest. Once
55 the trees have been cut down and taken away, the logging roads provide access to the forest for ranchers, farmers, settlers, and others attracted by the promise of free land. There is great competition, and gunmen are frequently
60 recruited as a way to protect settlers' claims.

The production of fake, illegal titles to Amazon land has become so common that Brazilians have a name for it: *grilagem*, from the Portuguese word *grilo*, which means
65 "cricket."[4] In order to make fake land titles look older and therefore more authentic, *grileiros*, as the people who steal land by creating false titles have come to be known, put the documents in drawers full of hungry
70 crickets. The crickets eat some of the pages and make the documents look older. The practice is certainly widespread: in just three years, the Brazilian government discovered 62,000 questionable land titles.

[4] A **cricket** is a small, jumping insect that produces short, loud sounds by rubbing its wings together.
[5] When people **clash**, they fight, argue, or disagree with each other.
[6] If the authorities **prosecute** someone, they charge them with a crime and put them on trial.
[7] A **plantation** is a large piece of land, where crops such as rubber, tea, or sugar are grown.
[8] A **chainsaw** is a tool powered by an engine used to cut down trees.

▲ Large industrial farms, like this 400-square-kilometer (150-square-mile) soybean farm in Mato Grosso, help make Brazil the world's second largest exporter of the bean.

75 ## A Clash of Ideals

"What's happening today in Amazonia is a clash[5] between two models of development," said Felicio Pontes, one of a new group of government lawyers seeking to prosecute[6]
80 land fraud and environmental crimes in the Amazon. The first model is based on logging and cutting down trees to create large cattle ranches and plantations,[7] usually undertaken by big business. It devastates
85 the forest. The alternative model, advocated by Dorothy Stang, is what Pontes calls social environmentalism. This newer model encourages small-scale family farms that work together and manage the forest in
90 sustainable ways.

Perhaps the best-known representative of the first model is Blairo Maggi, the governor of the state of Mato Grosso. Maggi is often portrayed by the environmental movement as
95 representing big business and rapid destruction of the rain forest. The non-governmental organization Greenpeace has given Maggi, who is known as "the King of Soy" because the company he founded is the world's largest
100 single producer of soy beans, its Golden Chainsaw[8] Award for leading Brazil in deforestation for three straight years.

Sawdust flies as a logger illegally ▶ cuts a hardwood tree on private land. "The Amazon is too big for police to shut down all illegal operations," says Enrico Bernard of Conservation International.

Not all environmentalists see Maggi in a completely negative light, however. He is known for respecting private property, he doesn't allow any land to be cleared illegally, he doesn't make use of slave labor, and he is careful not to use agricultural chemicals within 500 meters (0.3 miles) of a stream. "We're very responsible environmentally and socially," Maggi says.

To Maggi, deforestation is an exaggerated issue. He thinks people fear it because they do not understand how enormous the Amazon really is. "All of Europe could fit inside the Amazon," he says, "and we'd still have room for two Englands."

And what does Maggi think of Dorothy Stang's vision of small growers living and farming in harmony with the land? "*Totalmente errado*—completely wrong," Maggi says. He believes that such projects as Stang's won't succeed because they don't take the laws of business into consideration. He believes that it is useless to fight the big business model because it makes the most efficient use of the land and can maximize production. As production grows, prices fall to levels such that it is no longer feasible for small producers to compete without a great deal of financial help from the government.

A Cause for Hope

Stang would have been pleased when in February 2006, coinciding with the one-year anniversary of her death, Brazil's president announced the protection of 65,000 square kilometers (25,000 square miles) of rain forest. Although *grileiros* still operate freely over wide areas of the Amazon, they will be kept out of the protected area. Some environmentally responsible logging will be allowed, but no clear-cutting or settlements will be permitted.

Additionally, an older law that restricts farmers to clearing no more than 20 percent of their land is finally being enforced. If properly followed, this law could radically change the current patterns of deforestation. While in the past most farmers have largely ignored the law, in the years since Stang was murdered government pressure has increased on *grileiros* and farmers who have cleared too large a percentage of their land. In Mato Grosso, Governor Maggi helps such farmers by allowing them to buy up forest areas adjacent to their farms in order to supplement their percentage of forested land. Thanks to these and other efforts, recent forest surveys seem to indicate a decrease in the rate of deforestation of the Amazon. However, the fight to protect the forest is not over yet. There is a long way to go before Dorothy Stang's dream of a protected and sustainable Amazon is realized.

Reading Comprehension

A. Multiple Choice. Choose the best answer for each question.

Purpose

1. What is the author's purpose in writing the passage?
   a. to explain Brazil's economic need to exploit the Amazon
   b. to inform the reader about the struggle to save the Amazon
   c. to suggest better solutions for protecting the Amazon
   d. to celebrate the successes achieved in protecting the Amazon

Detail

2. Which of the following statements about Dorothy Stang is true?
   a. She sometimes used violent methods to obtain land.
   b. She was killed by mistake on a dark night in the forest.
   c. She encouraged farmers to resist ranchers and speculators.
   d. She wished to clear-cut the forest to allow poor farmers in.

Detail

3. What are *grileiros*?
   a. people who create and use false land titles
   b. insects used to make documents look older
   c. government investigators of questionable land titles
   d. gunmen hired to protect illegal land holdings

Gist

4. According to Maggi, why is Stang's model of development "completely wrong" (line 121)?
   a. It is too kind to farmers.
   b. It refuses to accept government help.
   c. It doesn't follow the laws of business.
   d. It causes too much anger among ranchers.

Reference

5. Which of the following does *such farmers* in line 153 refer to?
   a. farmers who follow the Stang model
   b. farmers from big businesses
   c. farmers of mainly soy beans
   d. farmers who have cleared too much land

> ## Critical Thinking
>
> Is your point of view about using the Amazon rain forest closer to Dorothy Stang, to Blairo Maggi, or do you have another point of view?

B. For and Against. Complete the chart using no more than three words from the reading in each blank.

Blairo Maggi: Socially and Environmentally Responsible?

Arguments for
1. He is careful to respect private _____.
2. He never makes use of _____ labor.
3. He never uses _____ within 500 meters of a stream.

Arguments against
4. He does not believe in Stang's vision of farmers living and working _____ the forest.
5. Greenpeace gave him its _____ award.
6. He doesn't worry about deforestation, because he thinks it is a(n) _____.

Vocabulary Practice

A. Completion. Complete the information with the correct form of words from the box. Two words are extra.

adjacent	authentic	supplement
confront	devastate	found
fraud	harmony	secluded taunt

▲ American bison have made a comeback at Yellowstone National Park.

In the early history of the United States, the impact of people on nature was **1.** _____. Wild animals of all kinds were enthusiastically hunted, and in some cases, hunted to extinction. Although nature seemed inexhaustible then, as the nation matured, it became necessary to **2.** _____ the issue of preserving the disappearing wildlife and wild places.

In 1872, the government **3.** _____ America's first national park, Yellowstone National Park. It set aside over 800,000 hectares on which no one could live, mine, log, or even hunt. Over the years, America's national parkland has been **4.** _____ with more than 33 million additional hectares, and today it accounts for 3.6 percent of the country's land area. The National Park System is very popular, attracting almost 300 million visitors a year. The immense number of visitors has led to unfortunate overcrowding in some easily accessible parks. However there are many parks that are more **5.** _____ and far from civilization. Unlike "tourist traps," these parks receive lower numbers of visitors, and thereby provide a look at totally **6.** _____ natural spaces, unchanged for centuries.

At Yellowstone and large national parks like it, wildlife has been making a comeback. Populations of American bison, brown bears, and even wolves are increasing in the parks. For the most part, wildlife and humans exist peacefully and in **7.** _____ with each other. However, bears and wolves have been responsible for killing domestic animals in areas **8.** _____ to the parks, and programs introducing such animals back into national parks are still controversial.

B. Definitions. Match the words from the box in **A** with their definitions.

1. peace rather than fighting or arguing _____

2. real, genuine _____

3. to start an institution, company, or organization _____

4. something or someone that deceives people in a way that is illegal or dishonest _____

5. add to something in order to improve it _____

6. next to _____

7. quiet and private (for a place) _____

8. say unkind or insulting things, especially about someone's weaknesses or failures _____

9. deal with a problem or task _____

Thesaurus   **taunt** Also look up: (v.) mock, provoke, tease

Animal Protectors

A

B

C

Samburu National Reserve, Kenya

Before You Read

A. Matching. Match each description below with the picture it describes (A–C).

1. Adult elephants have long, curved tusks on either side of their trunk. This eight-month-old infant calf will grow tusks later in life. ____

2. A group of elephants enjoys a mud bath. The baths are cooling and also protect against insects and the sun. ____

3. Two young elephants hold each other in a tight embrace. Physical contact between elephants ranges from emotional bonding to playful fighting to real combat. ____

B. Skim for the Main Idea. What are the first and second parts of this two-part reading about? Write 1 and 2.

____ a description of Samburu National Reserve
____ a short biography of Douglas-Hamilton
____ an elephant attack on Douglas-Hamilton and others
____ conflict between Douglas-Hamilton and African authorities

For the Love of Elephants

1 Author David Quammen writes about an extraordinary experience among the elephants of Samburu National Reserve, Kenya.

5 Late one afternoon, biologist Iain Douglas-Hamilton stopped by my tent and asked if I wanted to drive out and see some elephants before sunset. I asked him if he would like to take a walk instead. I knew that walking around the reserve could be risky, but surely

10 we could at least climb the little hill just behind camp. He agreed, and we did. The view of the river from the top was magnificent. Just north of us was a larger hill known as Sleeping Elephant. I asked him if he had ever climbed

15 that one. He told me he hadn't, but, with a mischievous[1] look in his eye, that we could.

We walked toward Sleeping Elephant: two middle-aged white men and a young Samburu man named Mwaniki. We walked only five

20 minutes before we saw a female elephant with two babies ahead of us. We paused, admiring these noble creatures from a safe distance until they seemed to withdraw, and then we went on, unable to foresee that our lives were in

25 danger. Seconds later, we looked up to see the female staring angrily at us from 70 meters (76 yards) away. Her ears were spread wide, showing us her agitation. Trumpeting loudly, she charged.

30 Mwaniki and I turned and ran, and we managed to put a safe distance between us and the elephant. Mwaniki continued to run all the way back to camp to get help. At first Douglas-Hamilton also turned and ran—then thought

35 better of it, turned back, threw his arms out, and yelled to stop the elephant. Sometimes this works, but the female kept coming. Douglas-Hamilton turned again and ran, but the elephant caught him as he tried to evade her. She lifted him and then threw him as he yelled

40 for help. She stepped forward and stabbed[2] her sharp, rigid tusks[3] downward at him. Then she backed off about ten steps and paused. This was the moment, he told me later, when he

45 had time to wonder whether he would die.

I ran back to Douglas-Hamilton, and to my surprise, he wasn't dead. After stabbing at him once and missing, the elephant had turned away. She went off to find her babies. Douglas-

50 Hamilton was scratched, but not badly hurt; his shoes, glasses, and watch were gone, but he was OK. He stood up. Then a dozen people arrived from camp, and helped retrieve his things.

[1] A **mischievous** person likes to have fun by playing harmless tricks on people or doing things they are not supposed to do.
[2] If you **stab** someone, you push a sharp object into their body.
[3] **Tusks** are the two very long, curved, pointed teeth of an elephant, wild boar, or walrus.

▲ Douglas-Hamilton's plane is a tool by which to see and know animals. After 40 years, and 6,000 piloting hours, it is also a pleasure.

55　Afterwards, Douglas-Hamilton and I hypothesized about what had triggered the attack. It was possible that we surprised her. Perhaps it was her mother's instinct to defend her calves. It was also conceivable that she had
60　recently been frightened by a lion and was in an agitated state. The more difficult question, however, was why, at the last minute, did she decide not to kill him? I suppose we will never know, but I like to think that, after confusing
65　him with an enemy, she finally recognized in Douglas-Hamilton a genuine friend of elephants.

Iain Douglas-Hamilton, Elephantologist

70　"If you had asked me when I was ten years old what I wanted to do," Douglas-Hamilton says, "I'd have said: I want to have an airplane; I want to fly around Africa and save the animals." Later, while studying zoology[4] at
75　Oxford University, he found his goals hadn't changed. "Science for me was a passport to the bush,"[5] he says, "not the other way around. I became a scientist so I could live a life in Africa and be in the bush."

80　Early in his career in Africa, he went to Tanzania as a research volunteer in Lake Manyara National Park. He bought himself a small airplane, which he could use for tracking elephants. There at Manyara, Douglas-
85　Hamilton did the first serious study of elephant social structure and spatial behavior (which includes where they go and how long they stay there) using a radio tracking system. He also became the first elephant researcher to
90　focus closely on living individual animals, not just trends within populations or the analysis of dead animals. He got to know individual elephants and their personalities, gave them names, and watched their social interactions.

95　Then came the difficult years of the late 1970s and '80s, when Douglas-Hamilton sounded the alarm against the widespread killing of African elephants. The killing was driven by a sudden sharp rise in the price of ivory[6]
100　and made easy by the widespread availability of automatic weapons. Douglas-Hamilton calculated elephant losses throughout Africa at somewhere above 100,000 animals annually. He decided to do something.

▲ The Ewaso Ngiro River, Samburu National Reserve, offers refreshment to a group of elephants.

[4] **Zoology** is the scientific study of animals.
[5] The wild, uncultivated parts of some hot countries are referred to as the **bush**.
[6] **Ivory** is a hard, cream-colored substance that forms the tusks of elephants.

▲ A guide in Samburu National Reserve sits in one of Save the Elephant's trucks, which has been destroyed by a bull elephant.

105 With funding from several conservation NGOs,[7] Douglas-Hamilton organized an immensely ambitious survey of elephant populations throughout the continent. From the results, compiled in 1979, he figured
110 that Africa then contained about 1.3 million elephants, but that the number was declining at too fast a rate. Some experts in the field disagreed, and struggle between the two sides over elephant conservation policy in the 1980s
115 became known as the Ivory Wars.

Douglas-Hamilton spent years investigating the status of elephant populations in Zaire, South Africa, Gabon, and elsewhere, both up in his airplane and on the ground. He flew
120 into Uganda during the chaos that followed the collapse of the government of the time and saw the bodies of slaughtered[8] elephants all over the national parks. "It was a dreadful time. I really spent a terrible 20 years doing
125 that," he says now. However, his work helped greatly to support the 1989 decision under the Convention on International Trade in Endangered Species to abolish the international sale of ivory.

130 In 1997, Douglas-Hamilton came to Samburu National Reserve in Kenya. By that time, he had established his own research and conservation organization, Save the Elephants. Today, he divides his time between teaching

135 a new generation of elephantologists and studying the movement of elephants using global positioning system (GPS) technology.[9] The data he acquires from elephants wearing GPS collars[10] is used by the Kenya Wildlife
140 Service to provide better wildlife-management and land-protection advice to the government. Save the Elephants now has GPS tracking projects not just in Kenya but also in Mali, South Africa, and the Democratic Republic of
145 the Congo.

Following the attack outside his camp, Douglas-Hamilton was able, using his equipment, to identify the elephant that threatened him as Diana, one of the females
150 from a herd he had been tracking for some time. Diana was just like any other elephant— sensitive, unpredictable, and complex. Although her behaviour on that afternoon had been violent, at the last moment she had made
155 a choice. And not even Ian Douglas-Hamilton, with all his modern equipment and years of experience, can know exactly why she attacked him—or why she let him live.

[7] An **NGO** (non-governmental organization) is an organization that is not run by the government.
[8] If large numbers of people or animals are **slaughtered**, they are killed in a way that is cruel or unnecessary.
[9] **GPS** (global positioning system) technology uses a network of satellites to determine exact locations on the surface of the earth.
[10] A **collar** is a band of leather or plastic that is put around the neck of an animal.

Reading Comprehension

A. Multiple Choice. Choose the best answer for each question.

Inference

1. Why did Douglas-Hamilton have *a mischievous look in his eye* when he agreed to go walking with the author (line 16)?
   a. He knew that it was a dangerous thing to do.
   b. He was really supposed to be finishing his work.
   c. He had a surprise planned for the author.
   d. He thought the author was afraid of elephants.

Vocabulary

2. In lines 34–35, what does *thought better of it* mean?
   a. decided not to do what he had intended
   b. decided it was better to do what he had intended
   c. decided not to change other people's intentions
   d. decided that he should think more about it before doing it

Paraphrase

3. Which of the following is closest to Douglas-Hamilton's meaning when he said "Science for me was a passport to the bush" on lines 76–77?
   a. My scientific education took place mostly in the bush.
   b. I took a trip to the bush to study science.
   c. The reason I studied science was to be able to work in the bush.
   d. In my opinion, science can be good preparation for the bush.

Detail

4. Douglas-Hamilton was the first elephantologist to _____.
   a. track elephants with an airplane
   b. study trends in elephant populations
   c. get to know individual elephants
   d. analyze the bodies of dead elephants

Detail

5. What is the name of Douglas-Hamilton's own research and conservation organization?
   a. Ivory Wars
   b. Kenya Wildlife Service
   c. Samburu National Reserve
   d. Save the Elephants

Critical Thinking

Why do you think Douglas-Hamilton's work is funded by conservation NGOs and not by local governments in Africa?

B. Sequencing. Number the events (**1–6**) in the order in which they happened.

   ___ **a.** The international sale of ivory was abolished.
   ___ **b.** Douglas-Hamilton did the first serious study of elephant social structure.
   ___ **c.** Douglas-Hamilton went to Samburu National Reserve in Kenya where he began studying elephant movements using GPS technology.
   ___ **d.** The results of Douglas-Hamilton's elephant population survey were compiled, leading to the so-called Ivory Wars.
   ___ **e.** Douglas-Hamilton went to Lake Manyara National Park in Tanzania as a research volunteer.
   ___ **f.** Douglas-Hamilton organized a survey of elephant populations throughout Africa.

Vocabulary Practice

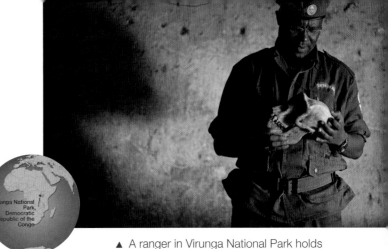

▲ A ranger in Virunga National Park holds the skull of a murdered gorilla.

A. Completion. Complete the information using the correct form of words from the box. Two words are extra.

abolish	agitated	chaos
collapse	compile	evade
genuine	instinct	weapon
withdraw		

Virunga National Park, in the Democratic Republic of the Congo, is one of the few places where one can find wild mountain gorillas. Hunting and habitat destruction have forced the roughly 720 remaining mountain gorillas to **1.** _____ to just a few protected areas. Even there, they aren't safe. On July 22, 2007, people armed with automatic **2.** _____ killed several members of a mountain gorilla family in Virunga. The largest male of the family, a 230-kilogram (500-pound) gorilla named Senkwekwe, probably smelled the killers coming near, but, used to seeing many park visitors, he would not have been very **3.** _____. However, this was the last time he would see a human. Shot through the middle of the chest, he **4.** _____ on the jungle floor, dead.

The gorillas weren't killed for their meat; their bodies were simply left on the ground. Their babies weren't taken to be sold; they were simply left to die. Finding the killers was difficult, as men with guns are everywhere—war has caused **5.** _____ in the country. Fortunately, the person who may have ordered the killing wasn't able to **6.** _____ the police. Virunga National Park's chief warden at the time of the killings was arrested. In Virunga, trees are illegally cut down to produce charcoal, an important and valuable fuel. Park rangers are frequently killed in their efforts to **7.** _____ this illegal trade. The warden was reportedly connected to illegal charcoal production in the park, and it is thought that he had the gorillas killed in order to damage the reputation of a ranger who was effectively fighting the charcoal producers. However, there is good news, too. According to the most recent numbers **8.** _____ by park rangers, the mountain gorilla population in Virunga is increasing.

B. Definitions. Match the words from the box in **A** with their definitions. One word is extra.

1. very worried or upset _____

2. not false, real _____

3. collect and put together many pieces of information _____

4. to pull back, move back, or remove _____

5. to put an end to _____

6. to avoid or escape _____

7. to suddenly fall down _____

8. natural behavior or reaction _____

9. complete disorder and confusion _____

Word **Partnership**

Use **chaos** with:
(*prep.*) **bring** chaos, **cause** chaos; (*adj.*) **complete** chaos, **total** chaos; (*n.*) chaos **and confusion**

Africa from the Air

A. Preview. You will hear these phrases in the video.
Read and match the words in bold to their definitions.

▲ Michael Fay posing next to his airplane in the African desert

1. "if you fly, you **traverse** those human boundaries . . ."
2. "their natural habitats are **losing ground** to human development . . ."
3. "eastern lowland gorillas . . . **have seen a** collapse of 70 percent . . ."
4. "Tourism has become a genuine **economic incentive** . . ."
5. "manage the impact of our **human footprint** . . ."

a. have experienced _____
b. move over or cross _____
c. development and consumption by people _____
d. financial reward _____
e. failing to keep up, declining _____

B. Summarize. Watch the video, *Africa from the Air*. Then complete
the summary below using the correct form of words from the box.
One word is extra.

harmony	chaos	confront	adjacent	authentically
compile	found	instinct	secluded	devastate

National Geographic Explorer-in-Residence J. Michael Fay has
1. _____ a remarkable collection of photographs of Africa from the
air, using a camera attached to his plane that took high quality photos as
he flew over the continent.

His photos reveal that Africa's great wild animals are in danger, their
habitats **2.** _____, some reduced to almost nothing, because of human
development. The populations of lions, elephants, and gorillas have all
declined in recent years. Today, large animals that are **3.** _____ wild,
that is, not managed by humans in parks and preserves, only exist in a few
4. _____ places where there are few humans to bother them.

In game preserves such as Mala Mala in South Africa, humans and animals
live side by side in **5.** _____. Mala Mala, which was **6.** _____ in
1927, is the largest area of privately owned land in South Africa.

Fay discovered a worrying scene in Tanzania where hundreds of hippos
crowd into a fast-drying river. They are driven there by their natural
7. _____ during the dry season, but the water is being used up by
humans for irrigation of farms **8.** _____ to the river.

Through his photos, Fay encourages people to **9.** _____ the problem
of vanishing wildlife in Africa and to take action before it is too late.

C. Think About It.

1. How do our
   actions in our
   home countries
   affect the animals
   in Africa? How
   can we reduce
   our human
   footprint?

2. Have you ever
   seen a picture
   of an abused
   animal or
   conservation
   problem, and
   been inspired to
   action?

To learn more about
conservation challenges,
visit elt.heinle.com/explorer

A. Crossword. Use the definitions below to complete the missing words.

Across

1. evidence to show something is true
3. someone in a state of _____ is nervous or upset
5. to be better than someone in the same activity
7. someone who is _____ is greatly respected and admired
9. the primary portion of land distinguished from islands
12. complete and undestroyed
13. to _____ someone or something is to face it directly and deal with it
16. to move so as to avoid something
18. stiff and does not bend easily
19. sincere and real
20. a person you work with

Down

1. easily carried or moved
2. willing to give information when asked
4. extremely large or great
6. to tease or insult someone
8. necessary or very important
10. real, not false or copied
11. an object invented for a specific purpose
13. to put together many pieces of information
14. a puzzling question or problem
15. as a result of this, because of this
17. the _____ of something means most of it
19. a space between two objects; a wide difference between sets of ideas

B. Notes Completion. Scan the information on pages 102–103 to complete the notes.

Field Notes

Site: Rapa Nui National Park

Location: Easter Island, _____

Information:
- Easter Island, or Rapa Nui to the _____ people, was formed out of an ancient _____.
- It was discovered by the Dutch on _____, but already had human settlements despite the next inhabited island being over _____ km away.
- The island is famous for its giant stone _____ called moai.
- Scientists discovered that the first settlers may have arrived as late as _____ A.D., which means it only took _____ years for the island to be completely deforested.
- According to author _____, the tragedy of Easter Island is an example of how humans can cause _____.

Island of Statues

Site: **Rapa Nui National Park**

Location: **Easter Island (Chile), South Pacific**

Category: **Cultural**

Status: **World Heritage Site since 1995**

Easter Island

A row of *moai* gaze into the night sky.

A strange stone figure stands on a cliff, his back to the ocean. His **stern** tight-lipped expression reveals nothing as he surveys the **barren** land before him.

On this tiny patch of soil in the middle of the South Pacific ocean, a Polynesian civilization once prospered enough to build hundreds of these immense stone statues called *moai*. Yet, the *moai*—and an enduring mystery—are all that remain.

Formed out of an ancient volcanic eruption, Easter Island, or *Rapa Nui* to the Polynesians, is one of the most isolated inhabited islands in the world. The first settlers must have travelled for months in canoes to reach it—a remarkable feat of navigation given that the nearest inhabited island, let alone the mainland, is more than 2,000 kilometers away.

It is believed Easter Island had some 16 million trees before humans arrived. Yet when Dutch explorers arrived on Easter Sunday 1722 (hence its name), they found the strange statues and little else—there was no tree in sight. It seems the native islanders completely wiped out the island's natural resources, using trees for agriculture, fuel, and for building boats and statues. Once the trees disappeared, so did the people—the **perpetrators** and victims of an unparalleled environmental disaster.

Glossary

barren: dry and bare, with few plants or trees

perpetrator: someone who commits a harmful act

quarry: an area dug out from the earth to get stones or minerals

stern: very serious and strict

unchecked: uncontrolled

Collapse of a Civilization

Opinions vary as to when humans first arrived, but scientists believe the native people lived on this secluded island for centuries before disaster struck. Eventually the growing population placed too much pressure on their once-abundant resources, and people began to starve. War followed and drove the island's society to destruction.

Recently, scientists have found proof that humans may have arrived in 1200 A.D., much later than previously thought. This means deforestation started almost immediately, disrupting the ecosystem and depriving species of their habitats. It took only 400–500 years for the island to reach its current barren state. According to Jared Diamond, author of *Collapse: How Societies Choose to Fail or Succeed*, Easter Island is a glaring example of how **unchecked** human activity can lead directly to environmental disaster.

Mysterious *Moai*

Most visitors to Easter Island come specifically to see the 887 *moai*, enormous statues carved out of volcanic rock, scattered around the island. *Moai* were revered by the native people as representations of their ancestors and powerful chiefs, living and dead. However, after a devastating civil war only a fraction of them remain intact, and many lie half-buried in the ground. The question remains: with the average statue weighing more than an elephant, how was it feasible to transport them? Writer Eric von Däniken claimed that the statues must have been built by aliens using materials from outer space. Unsurprisingly, historians are skeptical about this claim. It is more conceivable that the *moai* were simply dragged to their sites—an immense task, which accounts for many of them being left at their **quarry**. Not all historians agree, however, and the riddle of the statues remains unsolved.

▲ Some *moai* were 10 meters tall and weighed more than 80 tons.

Population

A Global View

The total world population has reached six and a half billion and continues to rise. For **demographers**—people who study population trends—this is a cause for concern. As food, water, and fuel resources become scarce, competition for control of those resources becomes more intense, thereby resulting in conflict and environmental damage. Demographers foresee the world's population eventually reaching a limit—but possibly not until the year 2200, when the world's population could reach 11 billion.

Most governments compile **census** data every few years to assess how their national population is changing. In developing countries, where high birthrates are the norm, over half the population may be below 20 years of age. These countries face the challenges of providing sufficient education and jobs while developing effective family-planning programs.

In developed countries with low birthrates, census **statistics** reveal shrinking populations, with growing numbers of elderly people but fewer workers able to provide tax money for health care and **pensions** (money provided to someone after he or she has retired). In these countries, immigrant labor plays a vital role in supporting national economies.

In this 3-D model, the tallest peaks represent places with highest **population density** (average number of people per square kilometer). Eastern China, Japan, Indonesia, India, and the cities of Europe and the Americas contrast with the world's highest, coldest, and driest regions, less suited for human life.

Word Link

The word root **graph**, from the Greek word meaning *to write*, is used in many words that describe fields of study, e.g., *demography/ demographer, geography/ geographer, biography/biographer*.

Critical Thinking

What are the advantages and disadvantages of a growing global population? How is your own country affected by population change?

The Population Boom

Until about two centuries ago population growth was gradual. Then improvements in health and nutrition resulted in a rapid expansion of the world's population, from one billion in 1800 to more than six billion in 2000. China and India today have more than a billion people each, making Asia by far the most **populous** continent. Over 400,000 babies come into the world every day—most in Asia, Africa, and Latin America.

104 Review 2

NG BOOK DIVISION

14 50 100 150 200 250 300 350 400 450 500 550 600 650 700 750 800 850 900 950 1000 1050 1100 1150 1200 1250 1300 1350 14
Year

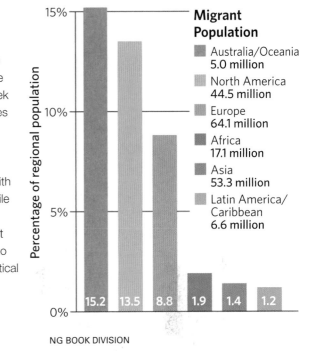

People on the Move

Migration occurs when people leave their homes to seek better opportunities abroad. **Migrant workers** provide essential labor in richer countries with low birthrates, while **refugees** flee to adjacent or distant foreign countries to escape harsh political or environmental conditions in their own.

Migrant Population

- Australia/Oceania 5.0 million
- North America 44.5 million
- Europe 64.1 million
- Africa 17.1 million
- Asia 53.3 million
- Latin America/Caribbean 6.6 million

Percentage of regional population

15.2 | 13.5 | 8.8 | 1.9 | 1.4 | 1.2

NG BOOK DIVISION

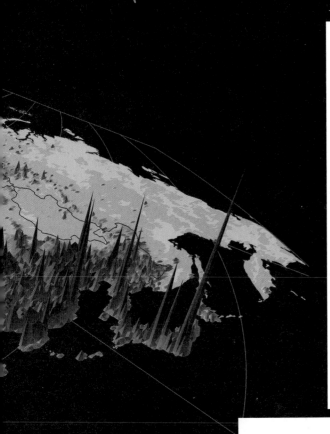

Billions of people

- Asia
- Africa
- Latin America
- Europe
- North America
- Australia/Oceania

A Different World View

This is what the world would look like if each country's size was directly related to its population. Canada, the world's second largest country, has only 32.9 million people; its size on this map is just a fraction of that of India's, which, with a population that is 34 times greater, appears to be immense.

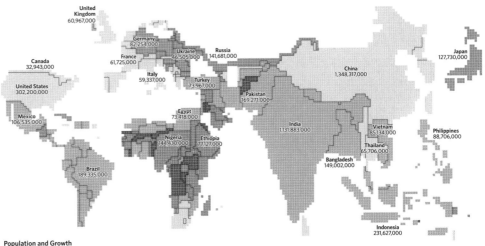

United Kingdom 60,967,000
Germany 82,254,000
Ukraine 46,505,000
Russia 141,681,000
France 61,725,000
Canada 32,943,000
Italy 59,337,000
Turkey 73,967,000
China 1,348,317,000
Japan 127,730,000
United States 302,200,000
Pakistan 169,271,000
Mexico 106,535,000
Egypt 73,418,000
India 1,131,883,000
Vietnam 85,134,000
Philippines 88,706,000
Nigeria 144,430,000
Ethiopia 77,127,000
Thailand 65,706,000
Brazil 189,335,000
Bangladesh 149,002,000
Indonesia 231,627,000

Population and Growth
3% and above | 2-2.9% | 1-1.9% | 0-0.9% | Population decline

Each square represents one million people. Colors represent growth rates, excluding migration. (2007 data)
NG BOOK DIVISION

A. Definitions. Use the correct form of words in **bold** from pages 104 to 105 to complete the passage.

1. _____ today keep careful track of human **2.** _____ density, and it is clear that some countries and regions have higher density than others. One of the tools used to count people is the taking of a regular **3.** _____ every few years. The information collected has revealed some interesting population **4.** _____. For example, the world's population may reach 11 billion in 2200. In addition, the numbers show that the populations of many developed countries are shrinking. This creates various problems. With too few young people paying taxes, there is insufficient tax money to provide older people with health care and the **5.** _____ they need to live on. This lack of younger workers can be filled, however, by **6.** _____ workers who come from nearby countries, as well as by **7.** _____ who are forced to flee their home countries. In this way, countries that are less **8.** _____ can be supported by immigrant labor from those with high populations.

B. Word Link. The root word **graph** or **graphy** (meaning *write* or *writing*) can be used to form many words. Look at the prefixes and their meanings. Then write the correct prefix in front of *graph* to make a word that completes each sentence correctly.

Prefix	Meaning	Prefix	Meaning
auto-	self	demo-	people
biblio-	book	phono-	sound
bio-	life	seismo-	earthquake
calli-	beauty	tele-	over a distance

1. _____graphy is an especially elegant style of writing.

2. The first practical _____graph was invented in 1837. It was an electrical device used to send messages by wire.

3. The _____graph, also known the record player, is an old-fashioned technology for playing music.

4. The intensity of the shaking of the ground can be measured using a(n) _____ graph.

5. A(n) _____graph is the signature of someone famous that is specially written for someone who admires the famous person.

6. A(n) _____graphy is a list of books on a particular subject, or a list of books and articles that are referred to in a particular book.

7. _____graphy is the statistical study of human populations.

8. A(n) _____graphy of someone is an account of their life, written by someone else.

C. **Thesaurus.** Write each of the six words in the box under the word they are closest to in meaning. Use your dictionary to help you. Then use the correct form of the six words to complete the sentences.

breed	erase	erect	initiate	duplicate	revoke

reproduce	abolish	found

1. Engineers have plans to _____ a bridge whose design is based on a sea sponge, a small creature that lives on the ocean floor.
2. While elephants can grow in numbers in the wild, in zoos they rarely _____ successfully.
3. Although biomimetics can make use of many parts of nature, many structures are simply too complex for scientists to _____.
4. In 2001, the Zambian government _____ all big game hunting licenses, but then, in 2003, allowed hunting again.
5. It is believed that elephants may sometimes _____ the destruction of forests by pushing down trees that later provide fuel for forest fires.
6. All physical evidence of the boats and navigation methods used by the Lapita people has been _____ from Earth over time.

D. **Word Link.** The root word **rupt** (meaning *break* or *burst*) is contained in several English words. Complete the sentences using the correct form of words from the box. Use a dictionary to help you.

abrupt	bankrupt	corrupt	erupt	interrupt	rupture

1. _____ government officials have in the past accepted money to look the other way and not investigate environmental crimes.
2. The elephant's change in direction was so _____ that we barely had time to get out of its way.
3. The migration of the Lapita people was _____ by a period of about 1,000 years before their descendants began to start exploring again.
4. It is possible that the Lapita and early Polynesians followed the smoke from _____ volcanoes to find islands in the Pacific Ocean.
5. Thousands of liters of oil spilled into the sea after the ship hit a large rock and its side _____.
6. One of the top fashion companies in Paris declared that it was _____ and would go out of business as early as next month.

E. Word Partnership. Many phrasal verbs are of the form *verb + out* (e.g., to eliminate something using logic is to *rule it out*). Complete the sentences using the correct form of the words in the box. One word is extra.

rule	carry	stamp	freak	iron	wear	max	figure	drown

1. Elephants have four large teeth for grinding that _____ out and regrow several times during their lives.
2. In some countries, elephants are used to _____ out logging in place of trucks, tractors, or horses.
3. When rangers found dead rhinoceroses in a game park in South Africa, it took them some time to _____ out that young elephants were killing them.
4. As the elephant population grows, the government won't _____ out the possibility that hundreds of elephants may need to be killed.
5. The elephants made such a loud noise that they completely _____ out the voice of the guide.
6. When the elephant came running toward the bus, all of the tourists were terrified and started to _____ out.
7. The population of elephants in the preserve has already _____ out, and there simply isn't room for any more.
8. Although great efforts have been made to _____ out the illegal hunting of elephants, the illegal ivory trade continues to operate.

F. Choosing the Right Definition. Study the numbered definitions for *gap*. Then write the number of the definition (**1–4**) that relates to each sentence below.

gap /gæp/ (**gaps**) **1** N-COUNT A **gap** is a space between two things or a hole in the middle of something solid. ❐ *There is a gap between the train and the platform.* **2** N-COUNT A gap is a period of time when you are not busy or when you stop doing something that you normally do. ❐ *He explained the two-year* gap *in his work history.* **3** N-COUNT If there is something missing from a situation that prevents it from being complete or satisfactory, you can say that there is a gap. ❐ *The papers burned in the fire left a large gap in the tax records.* **4** N-COUNT A gap between two groups of people, things, or sets of ideas is a big difference between them. ❐ *... the gap between the younger and older generations*

_____ **a.** There is a **gap** in our knowledge about how the Lapita traveled from island to island, because no Lapita boat has ever been found.
_____ **b.** A **gap** of 1,000 years exists between the last Lapita explorations and the beginning of the explorations of the early Polynesians.
_____ **c.** When the Europeans arrived in the Pacific Ocean with their large ships, the **gap** in sailing technology between them and the islanders was large.
_____ **d.** That the early Polynesians were able to reach Hawaii is amazing, as the **gap** of open ocean between Hawaii and the nearest island stretches for thousands of kilometers.

Song and Dance

Discuss these questions with a partner.

1. What do you know about how movies are made?

   Do you know any movie makers from your country?

2. What kinds of movies are popular in your country? Why are they popular?

3. What types of dancing do you know? Why do you think people dance?

▲ A member of Tsasala Cultural Group performs a traditional Native American dance on Cormorant Island, Canada.

7A Movie Makers

In the village of Sangola, southeast of Mumbai, Jaban Abdul Mulani runs a projector at the Ashok Touring Talkies, formerly a traveling tent theater.

Before You Read

A. Quiz. How much do you know about Bollywood? Complete the quiz below.

1. Where is Bollywood?
a. Los Angeles   b. Rome   c. Mumbai

2. What kinds of movies are mainly made there?
a. musicals   b. Westerns   c. documentaries

3. What language are Bollywood movies mainly in?
a. English   b. Hindi   c. Arabic

4. Compared with Hollywood movies, Bollywood movies are _____.
a. more popular   b. less popular   c. equally popular

B. Scan. Quickly scan the reading to check your answers to the quiz.

Hooray for Bollywood

Director Yash Chopra (right, legs crossed), plans a scene ▶ using 50 dancers at Film City in Mumbai.

1   The scene is a movie set outside Mumbai. It's after midnight on a hot and humid June night. A balding man shouts commands into a microphone. The camera zooms in on a group
5   of dancers as they swirl[1] in front of a beautifully decorated temple. A song slowly starts . . .

Veteran film director Yash Chopra is directing a scene from the movie *Veer-Zaara*, a story of romance between Veer, an Indian army
10   officer, and Zaara, a Pakistani woman. In this scene, Veer is taking Zaara to meet his relatives in his village during a folk festival. Yash is filming in Film City, a 200-hectare[2] (500-acre) wonderland just outside of Mumbai,
15   with make-believe temples, mansions,[3] police stations, and even entire villages. Film City is in the heart of Bollywood—as India's filmmaking industry is known—a movie industry that produces the world's most popular art form.

Yash Chopra, Filmmaker

Yash Chopra's half-century filmmaking career has produced many popular movies, and his film company, Yash Raj Films, is the most successful in Bollywood. These days, Yash and
25   his son Aditya work together—Aditya writes the stories, and Yash directs them. Aditya says he wrote the story of *Veer-Zaara* as a way for his father to return to his roots. Born in Lahore, in what is now Pakistan, Yash moved
30   with his family to India when he was a boy. He started working in the film industry in 1951.

After decades in the city, Yash still prefers the food of his native region, Punjab, and speaks with a thick Punjabi accent. He is a rustic man
35   in a glamorous[4] world.

During the 1960s and '70s, Yash introduced many elements now widely used in Bollywood films: romantic plots, beautiful costumes and sets,[5] and great songs sung in exotic places like
40   the Swiss Alps. (The Swiss have even given him an award for the contribution his films have made to tourism.) "In Hollywood they call these films musicals," he says. "Here, every film is a musical."

45   Indian films draw a global audience estimated at 3.6 billion annually—a billion more than Hollywood. The secret to Bollywood's worldwide appeal, says Yash, is that its films are "wholesome"[6] —his favorite word. The Indian
50   government has given him four national awards in the category of "Best Film for Providing Popular and Wholesome Entertainment." He won't allow kissing in his movies. "If a boy loves a girl in India," he says, "they feel shy
55   of kissing in public."

[1] If something **swirls**, it moves round and round quickly.
[2] One **hectare** (ha.) = 10,000 square meters.
[3] A **mansion** is a very large, impressive house.
[4] **Glamorous** people or things are more attractive, exciting, or interesting than ordinary people or things.
[5] The **set** for a play, movie, or television show is the furniture and scenery on the stage when the play is being performed or in the studio where filming takes place.
[6] If you describe something as **wholesome**, you think it is likely to have a positive or healthy influence on people.

▲ Bollywood actress Preity Zinta heading to the set of her film *Veer-Zaara*.

▲ Shah Rukh Khan, a Muslim who has become the largest star in largely Hindu India, is surrounded by fans eager for his autograph.

In *Veer-Zaara*, the hero and heroine[7] never even touch each other, except in a fantasy song scene. But the audience loves it. Yash tries to make sure they are moved by his love
60 stories: "The audience should leave with tears or a smile."

Appealing to a Global Market

Aditya was just a teenager in the 1980s, when Bollywood went through what is now
65 considered to be its dark period. Bollywood films lost a lot of their popularity when TV and video took customers away, and filmmakers like Yash seemed unsure of how to bring the audience back. At the age of 23, Aditya
70 stepped in to modernize Bollywood films. His first film, *Dilwale Dulhania Le Jayenge* (*The Brave Heart Will Take the Bride*), was about Indian expatriates[8] living in London who, in the end, get back in touch with their Indian
75 roots and values. The movie suggested that it was possible to remain genuinely Indian while embracing globalization. It became one of the most successful Bollywood movies of all time.

The newer Bollywood films are aimed at
80 India's urban consumers as well as the overseas market—some 20 million Indian expatriates around the world who love Hindi films even after they have forgotten Hindi and may never find the opportunity to visit India. Sanjeev
85 Kohli, CEO[9] of Yash's movie company, says,

"Their children's only connection with India is Hindi films. Hindi film is India for them." Bollywood has even changed the wedding rituals of overseas Indians, who now wear
90 costumes and dance in ways inspired by Bollywood films.

Yash also kept the overseas Indians in mind while planning *Veer-Zaara*. "It's a challenge to make a film for both the viewer in the [modern
95 American cinema] and the one in the village theater with a noisy fan," Kohli says. Yash is betting that the overseas Indian audience is just as hungry as the rural Indian viewers for a portrayal[10] of village India. The movie supplies
100 them with an image of the rural India they wish they could have grown up in before they moved to New York or London.

Bollywood Superstars

In Mumbai, a crew of hundreds works through
105 the night to complete the scene in which Veer brings his sweetheart home. Next to Yash on the set is Amitabh Bachchan, the actor who is playing Veer's uncle. A prominent star in

---

7 The **heroine** of a book, play, movie, or story is the main female character, who usually has good qualities.
8 An **expatriate** is someone who is living in a country that is not their own.
9 The **CEO** (Chief Executive Officer) of a company is the person who has overall responsibility of the management of that company.
10 A **portrayal** of someone or something is a representation of them in a book, movie, or play.

▲ Under a tent, an all-male audience—common in rural areas—watches a Bollywood movie quietly. Big-city viewers are livelier, says film expert Manjunath Pendakur. "They cheer, boo, get into fights, even get on stage and dance."

Bollywood for decades, Amitabh was ranked the "greatest star of stage or screen" in a BBC[11] online vote in 1999, winning out over the greatest Hollywood stars of all time.

The part of Veer is played by Shah Rukh Khan, who at the time of filming is 39, but has already made 49 films—always appearing in wholesome roles. Shah Rukh, the biggest star in largely Hindu India, is a Muslim. Though Muslims make up only 12 percent of India's population, three of the five biggest male movie stars have the same Muslim last name—Khan.

Khan says that he has never experienced prejudice as a Muslim in the Indian film industry: "It welcomes everybody with open arms." It certainly welcomed Javed Siddiqui, a Muslim writer who has written over 80 films. Siddiqui, who speaks Urdu, the official language of Pakistan and a similar language to Hindi, says that the ideal Hindi movie is a combination of themes taken from the stories of many different cultures—like India itself.

The Chopras stress that *Veer-Zaara* follows in that tradition. It is a love story between an Indian and a Pakistani that never mentions the politics of the India-Pakistan relationship, makes only passing references to religion, shows no poverty, and has no wars or even fighting. "If we are successful in really pulling this film off, it could go a long way towards peace," Aditya says. "Every Hindi film has an impossible dream, but you like to believe that it's possible." So the last line of the movie is: "Veer and Zaara back at the village live happily ever after." And the audience, no matter where in the world they are, can walk out with tears, or a smile.

[11] The **BBC** (British Broadcasting Corporation) is a British organization that broadcasts radio and television programs.

Reading Comprehension

A. Multiple Choice. Choose the best answer for each question.

Gist
1. What is this reading mainly about?
   a. the career of Yash Chopra
   b. the movie *Veer-Zaara*
   c. traditional Indian culture
   d. the Indian film industry

Inference
2. Which of the following would Yash Chopra NOT consider *wholesome*?
   a. Hindi movies made outside of India
   b. modern Bollywood movies
   c. movies that make people cry
   d. movies in which people kiss

> **Critical Thinking**
>
> Yash Chopra says, "Here, every film is a musical." Why are all Bollywood films musicals?

Detail
3. What caused Bollywood movies to lose popularity in the '80s?
   a. bad economic times
   b. competition from other media
   c. an increase in the number of foreign movies
   d. their wholesomeness

Vocabulary
4. In line 74, the phrase *get back in touch with* is closest in meaning to _____.
   a. connect once more with
   b. back away from
   c. reverse the direction of
   d. travel back to

Detail
5. According to Javed Siddiqui, the ultimate Hindi movie _____.
   a. is a story that can help fight prejudice in Bollywood
   b. should include ideas from different cultures
   c. can contribute to peace between India and Pakistan
   d. can be easily translated into the Urdu language

B. Summary. Complete the sentences below. Fill in each blank with no more than three words from the reading.

   1. The scene from *Veer-Zaara* in which Veer takes Zaara to meet his relatives was actually filmed in _____, a large filmmaking zone in the heart of Bollywood.
   2. The most successful filmmaking company in Bollywood is _____.
   3. Bollywood films are also popular with the _____ expatriates living outside of India.
   4. Bollywood superstar Amitabh Bachchan was ranked the "_____ of stage or screen" in 1999.
   5. Of the five most popular male Bollywood stars, three have the same Muslim last name—_____.

Vocabulary Practice

A. Completion. Complete the information using the correct form of words from the box. One word is extra.

▲ A young boy practices flips at the Shaolin Temple, a famous martial arts school in Henan, China, which has been featured in many films.

exotic	prejudice	overseas
theme	plot	folk

In recent years, Chinese films have had growing success in **1.** _____ markets, and, in 2000, the film *Crouching Tiger, Hidden Dragon* achieved immense success worldwide. In Europe and the United States, where many people had never seen a *wuxia* movie, the film presented viewers with a fascinating and **2.** _____ fantasy, of a kind they may never have experienced before. *Wuxia* stories are usually set in China's distant past. In these stories, fighting always occurs using *wushu* techniques—the many amazing fighting styles developed in China's long history. *Wuxia* stories are sometimes compared to the **3.** _____ tales of England, for example Robin Hood, as both are popular stories of heroes fighting for honor and justice.

The **4.** _____ of a *wuxia* story might begin with a young man suffering a tragedy of some kind. He then goes through a very difficult period of learning *wushu* techniques, until he becomes a great hero and uses his skills to fight evil. Another common type of story involves a great hero and his enemy. The hero slowly learns of the evil intentions of his enemy and in the end the two confront each other. Examples of **5.** _____ found in *wuxia* stories are good against evil, fate, and love.

B. Words in Context. Complete each sentence with the best answer.

1. An example of a rustic setting is _____.
   a. a farmhouse   b. a hospital

2. People frequently bet on _____.
   a. horse races   b. medical procedures

3. Someone who is online is _____.
   a. fishing   b. using the Internet

4. To hide the fact that he was balding, John _____.
   a. wore a hat   b. kept his mouth closed

5. Prejudice is a judgment we make _____.
   a. based on knowing someone for a long time
   b. before truly getting to know a person

Thesaurus   **prejudice** Also look up: (*n.*) bias, bigotry, intolerance

7B

Let's Dance

A South American man demonstrates his tango skills to a street crowd.

Before You Read

A. Categorize. All of the words below are found in the reading. Do they usually have a positive, negative, or neutral meaning? Mark them **+**, **−**, or **0**. Use your dictionary to help you.

___ enduring	___ frivolous	___ prosperous	___ grieve
___ lyrical	___ mourn	___ abused	___ melodic
___ harmony	___ struggle	___ severe	___ inspiring

B. Predict. Various foreign cultures contributed to the development of the Argentine tango. Match each culture with its contribution. Then read the passage to check your answers.

1. Italian   ___   **a.** strong rhythms
2. African   ___   **b.** a musical instrument called the *bandoneon*
3. German   ___   **c.** melodic singing

Tango: Soul of a Nation

A rainy day leaves empty tables, but the show goes on as Natalia Pastorino and Alejandro Nievas tango at a club in Buenos Aires. "There's a lot of sadness in our country," says Pastorino, "but when you dance, you forget. You focus on your partner, on the music. You dance with your heart."

1　Alicia Monti, with short black hair and high heels, is all business as she walks quickly through the Abasto shopping mall in Buenos Aires, Argentina. Shoppers step aside
5　respectfully as she passes. It is 7:25 p.m., and she is headed down the marble[1] hall past the stores to an open space in the center of the mall, where the Tuesday tango class she and her partner lead is about to begin. Already,
10　tango recordings are heard from the speaker system, and on this cool evening a couple of dozen men and women of all ages—some in pairs, some alone—are taking off their coats and scarves, smiling and eager.

15　Monti's partner, Carlos Copello, appears moments later. Pomade[2] makes his hair shine like leather, and even his walk evokes a dance. The students are very different in appearance from their instructors—most are wearing
20　sneakers. A couple of the men have dirty hands from work. Following Copello's instructions, the men pair off with their wives or friends or complete strangers. Copello places his right hand around Monti's back and brings
25　her right hand up in his left, and the students do likewise. Copello holds Monti firmly but at a distance, as if the two were squeezing a third person between them. Copello tells the students to straighten up and keep their eyes
30　off the floor. A young man and woman are smiling happily. They have just figured out the basic step, and they're circling the dance floor in harmony.

The Tango's Origins

35　The tango took over Buenos Aires nearly a century ago. Today it remains at the center of the emotional life of *porteños*—the inhabitants of the port city of Buenos Aires. This touching, expressive, and authentically Argentine music is
40　part of the essence of what it means to belong to this much abused and beautiful city. Indeed, there seemed to be a renewed interest in the tango in the difficult economic times of 2002, when the most severe economic crisis in

▲ Couples dance away the afternoon at a *milonga* (tango session) at a club in Buenos Aires.

[1] **Marble** is a type of very hard rock that feels cold and is often used to make statues or parts of buildings.
[2] **Pomade** is a pleasant-smelling cream that makes hair look smooth and shiny.

Argentina's history pushed half the population below the poverty level. Yet even as they struggled to pay their bills, many people found new meaning in a music—and a dance—that was neither easy nor frivolous. It suited the times.

A mall may seem like an odd place to learn to dance the tango. In reality, though, the Abasto shopping center is full of the dance's ghosts. It was built only a few years ago where the city's central market once was, in what is still a working-class neighborhood. Toward the end of the 19th century, a flood of European immigrants, the largest number of them from Italy, settled in Argentina, and many found work in this market. With their melodic singing, they enriched what was initially a plain music and a rough dance. By the 1920s, the tango was the accepted music of Buenos Aires. Rhythms of the dances of freed African slave communities became part of the dance, and a German instrument—the bandoneon—became part of the classic tango sound.

Carlos Gardel, Genius of the Tango

Perhaps the greatest star of the tango was Charles Gardes. He was born in 1890 in France and was brought to Buenos Aires three years later by his mother. He became known to the world as Carlos Gardel. A brilliant singer and composer, Gardel transformed the tango from its earlier racy[3] form into an enduring lament.[4] In his clear, lyrical voice he sang of what makes humans everywhere grieve: failure, loss, the passing of time, the death of love and trust.

Gardel incorporated new, refined lyrics[5] into the old tango tunes and gave them new energy, inspiring others to write new tangos. For example: *I know that life is but an exhalation,[6] that twenty years are but an instant . . . I live with my soul fixed to a gentle memory whose loss*

I mourn[7] again. He composed dozens of songs, recorded hundreds of others, and made eight feature-length movies.

Gardel's career in the early 1900s coincided with good economic times in Argentina. Buenos Aires grew in beauty, adding broad avenues and modern public buildings. The music's second golden age was in the prosperous years of the 1940s, when the great tango halls and orchestras played through the *porteño* night.

Hard Times and Hope

Argentina changed dramatically after World War II. Unemployment became chronic, government unstable, and fewer and fewer people enjoyed the night life. In the 1970s, the international popularity of rock and roll shut down most of the local tango recording studios. Tango dance halls gradually closed down, and tango orchestras almost disappeared. Although tangos were still written and recorded, nobody wanted to dance to them.

▲ José Libertella (left) and Luis Stazo of Sexteto Mayor play the bandoneon, the instrument brought to Argentina by European immigrants that gives tango its distinctive sound.

[3] If something is **racy**, it is lively, amusing, and slightly shocking.
[4] A **lament** is an expression of sadness, regret, or disappointment.
[5] The **lyrics** of a song are its words.
[6] When you **exhale**, you breathe out the air that is in your lungs.
[7] If you **mourn** something, you regret that you no longer have it.

▲ Jorge Martorello (right) practices a dance move at the well-known Rodolfo Dinzel studio in Buenos Aires.

At age 70, José Libertella can still remember those days: "A music that started out for the feet ended by being for the head." Libertella is still a master of the bandoneon. When he started the Sexteto Mayor Orchestra with fellow musician Luis Stazo in 1973, most people under retirement age considered the tango to be something of an antique. "Stazo and I each had our own groups, but neither of us could afford to keep going by ourselves any longer," Libertella says of that period. "We didn't know if we'd survive 30 days, much less 30 years."

The first years were hard, but in 1983 he and Stazo were saved by *Tango Argentino*, a show that started in Paris and was a success on Broadway. *Tango Argentino* featured the Sexteto Mayor, six couples who surprised and pleased audiences with their amazing dancing. The Sexteto have since gone on to tour Europe and have appeared often in the U.S. In recent years, an all-tango radio station, FM Tango, has introduced a new generation of Argentines to the tango. One modern practitioner is Daniel Melingo, a popular young Argentine singer and composer who has hope for Argentina's unique dance form: "What we need are new authors for new tangos, because the form has enormous potential."

Meanwhile, in Buenos Aires, the tango continues in classical style at Monti and Capello's free Tuesday tango classes at the Abasto mall, which Tulio Tochia has just recently joined after being away from the dance for 26 years. "I had stayed away from the tango all those years," he says, "and then one evening I agreed to keep a friend company while he went to a tango lesson. Just for the hell of it, I tried a few steps myself, and the next thing I knew, I was completely into the dance. I couldn't stop." It's been a century since Gardel's arrival in Buenos Aires—and still they tango.

Reading Comprehension

A. Multiple Choice. Choose the best answer for each question.

Main Idea   **1.** What is the main idea of this reading?
   a. The tango is unlike any other form of dance.
   b. After a period of disinterest, the tango's popularity is rising again.
   c. The tango is gradually becoming less important to Argentina.
   d. Today, only working-class people are interested in the tango.

Detail   **2.** According to the passage, which of the following is true about Alicia Monti?
   a. She has a full-time job in a shopping mall.
   b. She teaches an evening dance class.
   c. One of her students is Carlos Copello.
   d. She prefers to work alone, without an assistant.

Inference   **3.** Why does the author say that the Abasto mall is full of the tango's ghosts (line 53)?
   a. Tango music is played from speakers in the mall.
   b. Many shoppers learned the tango from people who have since died.
   c. It was built in a neighborhood with a long tango history.
   d. Many of the people who used to dance in the mall died a long time ago.

Detail   **4.** Which of these accomplishments was NOT attributed to Carlos Gardel?
   a. He made a number of movies.
   b. He composed many songs.
   c. He recorded hundreds of songs.
   d. He invented tango dance steps.

Paraphrase   **5.** Which of the following is closest in meaning to *A music that started out for the feet ended by being for the head* (lines 111–112)?
   a. People appreciated tango music but no longer danced to it.
   b. The tango ended by being replaced by rock and roll.
   c. The dance aspect of tango developed before the music.
   d. Although the poor started the tango, the rich enjoy it today.

Critical Thinking

What impressions of the tango does the author hope to express by describing Alicia Monti's class at the beginning of the passage?

B. Sequencing. Write the number of each event in the correct place on the timeline.

   1. *Tango Argentino* is a success on New York's Broadway.
   2. The tango becomes the dominant form of music in Buenos Aires.
   3. Charles Gardes, the future Carlos Gardel, is born in France.
   4. As the country becomes more wealthy, the tango rises in popularity again.
   5. Rock and roll's popularity forces local tango recording studios to close.

1890   1940s   1983

1920s   1970s

Vocabulary Practice

A. Completion. Complete the information below using the correct form of words from the box. Three words are extra.

chronic	enrich	frivolous	grieving
inhabitant	likewise	odd	practitioner
prosperous	rhythm		

▲ A dance student at the Fine Art Institute, Santiago de los Caballeros, Dominican Republic

A 3,400-year-old image of a person dancing—discovered in the Middle East—is proof that we, the **1.** _____ of Earth, have been dancing for a very long time. From the first kick of a baby's foot to a wedding dance, dancing is a part of our lives. Just the beat of our own heart can provide the **2.** _____ for dancing, or we can dance to the sounds of a full orchestra. So, what is this thing called dance? According to Judith Jamison, a skilled **3.** _____ of the art of the dance and artistic director of the Alvin Ailey American Dance Theater, "It is as close to God as you are going to get without words."

When we dance, we express love, hate, joy, and sorrow. We celebrate birth, death, and everything in between. We dance not only for serious reasons, but for **4.** _____ reasons too. We dance in **5.** _____ times to celebrate good fortune, but we do **6.** _____ in hard times: out of sadness, to attain peace, and, sometimes, in an attempt to heal.

"I remember a couple," says Lester Hillier, owner of a dance studio in Davenport, Iowa. "One of their sons had been killed. The **7.** _____ parents had a dance lesson scheduled the day after it happened. They insisted on coming anyway." They practiced the steps they'd learned. As the hour passed, the couple asked for one last dance. And when it ended, the wife rested her head on her husband's chest; he wrapped his arms around her shoulders. "If we just sat at home, what would we do?" he said quietly.

B. Definitions. Match the words from the box in **A** to their definitions. Two words are extra.

1. to improve something's quality, usually by adding something to it _____
2. feel very sad about someone's death _____
3. silly or light-hearted way, rather than serious and sensible _____
4. (for an illness) lasting for a very long time _____
5. strange or unusual _____
6. a person who lives in a place _____
7. rich and successful _____
8. a regular series of sounds or movements _____

Word Link

The suffix **–wise** in certain words has the meaning of *in the direction of*, *way of*, or *manner of*, e.g., clock**wise**, like**wise**, other**wise**.

Aztec Dancer

A. Preview. These phrases below will appear in the video. Match each phrase in bold with its definition.

1. The Aztec path finds **its most powerful expression** through dance
2. Cuco **sets out for** his daily ritual
3. Cuco . . . **pay[s] his respects to** the Powers of the Cosmos
4. Cuco **explains the deep significance behind** each move

a. to go somewhere with a purpose _____
b. elaborates on the importance of something _____
c. to recognize and honor _____
d. the most effective communication _____

B. Summarize. Watch the video, *Aztec Dancer*. Then complete the summary below using the correct from of words from the box. Two words are extra.

▲ A man dressed in traditional Aztec costume performs a sacred dance while tourists look on.

enrich	practitioner	theme	frivolous
rustic	likewise	inhabitant	exotic
prejudice	rhythm	prosperity	overseas

Cuco Murillo and his small family live in a(n) **1.** _____ house in the Mexican countryside that he and his father built on their own. Cuco is a modern day descendant of the Aztecs. The Aztecs were the **2.** _____ of central Mexico before invaders from **3.** _____ arrived. Like his ancestors, Cuco now reveres Ometoetl, the God of the Aztecs. Cuco celebrates Aztec beliefs, but he especially enjoys the Aztec dance. He is thankful for this dance which has greatly **4.** _____ his life.

In preparation for his dance, Cuco sings a prayer as he beats a steady **5.** _____ on a traditional drum. Cuco then puts on a(n) **6.** _____ and beautiful costume. It is the same costume design as that used by the ancient Aztec **7.** _____ of this dance. His ankle jewelry represents rain, a symbol of **8.** _____ in many cultures. As Cuco says, "Without rain, there is no life."

Cuco describes four different **9.** _____ of his dance, which celebrate water, fire, air, and earth. He says Aztec people did them to worship their god. The Olmec and Maya people, another group who lived in Mexico before the European conquest, did **10.** _____.

C. Think About It.

1. Why does the Aztec dance refer to water, fire, air, and earth?

2. Do you know any traditional dances? Does your culture feature a traditional dance?

To learn more about song and dance, visit elt.heinle.com/explorer

UNIT 8
Investigations

WARM UP

Discuss these questions with a partner.

1. What kinds of technology do police use to solve or prevent crimes?

2. Should the police be able to put surveillance cameras in any public space?

3. Do you know of any mysterious deaths or unsolved crimes?

What do you think happened?

▲ Yellow police tape protects a crime scene in Connecticut, U.S.A.

123

▲ *Napoleon Crossing the Alps*, by Jacques-Louis David (1800)

Life and Death of Napoleon

1769 Napoleon Bonaparte born on island of Corsica, France

1785 Joins the French army

1796 Achieves victories in Italy and Austria

1804 Crowned **Emperor** Napoleon I

1812 Invades Russia but retreats before reaching Moscow

1815 Defeat at Battle of Waterloo. Sent as **prisoner** to island of St. Helena

1821 Dies May 5th. Doctors' report states cause as stomach cancer

1840 Grave is reopened and body returned to Paris

1961 **Analysis** of a sample of Napoleon's hair reveals **presence** of arsenic

◄ A sample of hair supposedly belonging to Napoleon Bonaparte

A Mysterious Death

Before You Read

A. Quiz. Read the information above. Use the correct form of words in **blue** to complete the definitions.

1. _____ is used to treat and cure illnesses.
2. If you _____ something, you consider it carefully in order to fully understand it.
3. If something, such as a chemical or disease, is _____ in something else, it exists within that thing.
4. _____ is a serious disease caused by the spread of abnormal body cells.
5. A(n) _____ is a male ruler of a(n) _____.
6. A(n) _____ is someone who is kept in a(n) _____ as a punishment or because they have been captured.

B. Predict. Scan the reading to find the five headings. Each heading suggests a possible reason for Napoleon's death. With a partner, discuss what kind of information might be contained in each section. Then read the passage and check your ideas.

Arsenic Known as the king of poisons. Colorless, tasteless, and odorless. Less than 3 grams can cause low blood pressure, internal bleeding, then death. Used in small amounts as **medication** for a variety of diseases, including **cancer**.

▲ A bag of arsenate of lead, otherwise known as arsenic

What Killed the Emperor?

▲ A sketch of Napolean Bonaparte in bed at his death on the island of St. Helena.

It's a story as compelling as any murder mystery. It begins in 1821 on the remote, secluded British island of St. Helena in the South Atlantic Ocean. This is where Napoleon Bonaparte—one-time Emperor of France—is confined as a prisoner after losing his final battle at Waterloo in 1815. In February 1821, Napoleon's health reportedly begins to fail, and he dies three months later at the age of 52. An autopsy[1] performed the next morning reveals a stomach ulcer,[2] possibly cancerous.

The real cause of death, however, has been in dispute ever since. Many are convinced that, in fact, Napoleon was murdered. Historians, toxicologists,[3] doctors, and other experts, as well as amateur investigators, have considered the question of how and why he died, but so far they have not been able to reach an agreement.

Political Murder?

Ben Weider, founder of the International Napoleonic Society and head of a large body-building business based in Canada, is a proponent of the theory that Napoleon was poisoned with arsenic, a deadly chemical.

Weider has relentlessly sought the cause of Napoleon's death for more than four decades and has put considerable resources into solving the mystery. In his view, Napoleon was poisoned by the British and by French royalists,[4] who wanted him out of the way once and for all.[5]

Weider offers as the central point of his hypothesis the hair analysis done by Pascal Kintz, a French toxicologist at the Legal Medicine Institute of Strasbourg. Kintz subjected samples of Napoleon's hair to analysis and confirmed that it contained arsenic. While Kintz can't say exactly how or why the arsenic was there, Weider is convinced that "the poisoning of Napoleon was planned and deliberate."

Poisoned by His Wallpaper?

David Jones, an immunologist[6] at the University of Newcastle in England, has studied the walls at Longwood House, the building on St. Helena where Napoleon lived his last years. He found that the wallpaper

[1] An **autopsy** is an examination of a dead body by a doctor who cuts it open in order to try to discover the cause of death.

[2] An **ulcer** is a sore area on the outside or inside of your body that is very painful and may bleed.

[3] **Toxicologists** are scientists who study poisons and their effects.

[4] A **royalist** is someone who supports their country's royal family or who believes that their country should have a king or queen.

[5] If something happens **once and for all**, it happens completely or finally.

[6] An **immunologist** is a scientist who studies the body's immune system.

▲ This scrap of wallpaper comes from Napoleon's home, Longwood House. Could the arsenic in this wallpaper have been responsible for the man's death?

was painted with a substance containing the
50 deadly poison arsenic. According to Jones,
conditions on the hot and humid island
caused arsenic to be released into the air.

Then again, paint may not have been the
only source of arsenic on St. Helena. Some
55 toxicologists say that it is not uncommon for
people who eat large amounts of seafood to
have an unusually high level of arsenic in the
blood. Because St. Helena is a small island
2,000 kilometers (1,200 miles) from the
60 nearest mainland, it is likely that a large part
of Napoleon's diet was comprised of seafood.
Additionally, the doctors who examined
Napoleon's body after his death didn't find any
of the usual symptoms associated with arsenic
65 poisoning, such as bleeding inside the heart.

Doctor's Mistake?

Steven Karch, an American heart disease
expert, believes that Napoleon was killed by
his own doctors. They gave him large doses
70 of dangerous chemicals commonly used as
medicine at the time. According to Karch's
theory, the day before Napoleon's death, they
gave him a massive amount of mercurous
chloride, a chemical which was once given to
75 patients with heart disease. That and other
medications disrupted Napoleon's heartbeat
and resulted in his heart ceasing to beat.
While Karch admits that arsenic exposure was
a partial cause, he believes it was the doctors'
80 errors that actually brought on the
heart attack.

Disease?

Cancer and ulcers, as reported by doctors
who examined the body, were the cause of
85 Napoleon's death, believes Jean Tulard, the
preeminent[7] Napoleon historian in France.
Tulard remains unconvinced by Kintz's hair
analysis. In his estimation, the hair that was
tested may not even have been Napoleon's.
90 Tulard also discounts the poisoning theory
on the grounds that no one has yet found
anything linking the British or the French
royalists—or anyone else for that matter—to
any plot against Napoleon's life.

95 Still, doubts remain that cancer was one of
the main causes. One cancer specialist believes
that Napoleon probably didn't have advanced
stomach cancer, because people with that
disease always lose a lot of weight. Napoleon,
100 according to reports, had never lost any weight
during his stay on St. Helena. In fact, he had
gained a fair amount.

[7] If someone is **preeminent** in a group, they are more important, powerful, or capable than other people in the group.

▲ François de Candé-Montholon is a descendant of the Count of Montholon, the man that Candé-Montholon believes killed Napoleon.

Napoleon's remains ▶ are entombed in this monument, Hôtel des Invalides, in Paris, France.

A Case of Revenge?

"One of my ancestors did it," says François
105 de Candé-Montholon. "I'm an aristocrat.[8]
Aristocrats don't like revolution, and Napoleon made revolutions." Candé-Montholon's great-great-great-great grandfather, the Count of Montholon, was stationed with Napoleon
110 on St. Helena. Napoleon had a love affair—and fathered a child—with the count's wife. The count, it is observed, had control of Napoleon's wine cellar and food. Could he, motivated by revenge, have poisoned the wine?

115 "Everyone is right, and no one is right," says Paul Fornes of the George Pompidou Hospital in Paris. Fornes has reviewed the 1821 autopsy report and other historical records and concludes: "Napoleon may have
120 died with cancer, but he didn't die of cancer." Likewise, he says that although the hair analysis indicates the presence of arsenic, no one can say if he was intentionally given the arsenic, or if it killed him. In Fornes's opinion, evidence
125 for murder by poisoning is inconclusive and wouldn't hold up[9] in a court of law.

Napoleon Bonaparte's body was returned to France in 1840, and it has rested in a truly grand tomb in Paris for nearly 150 years.

130 Some think it is time to open the tomb and to examine the remains using modern methods. French historian and doctor Jean-François Lemaire, however, believes that serious science and history have little to do with it anymore:
135 "We are now in the world of entertainment," he says. It seems unlikely that new facts will settle the issue—people just enjoy the mystery too much.

[8] An **aristocrat** is someone whose family has a high social rank, especially someone who has a title.
[9] If an argument or theory **holds up**, it is true, even after close examination.

Reading Comprehension

A. Multiple Choice. Choose the best answer for each question.

Main Idea
1. What is the main idea of the reading?
   a. Napoleon was murdered by the British or the French.
   b. Napoleon died of either stomach ulcers or cancer.
   c. Depressed and in failing health, Napoleon killed himself.
   d. The cause of Napoleon's death is the center of a debate.

Detail
2. Which of the following do BOTH David Jones and Steven Karch believe?
   a. Napoleon's death was due to a medical mistake.
   b. Arsenic played a part in Napoleon's death.
   c. Napoleon's diet contributed to his death.
   d. The reasons for Napoleon's death cannot be explained.

Detail
3. Which person strongly believes that Napoleon was murdered?
   a. Ben Wieder   c. Jean Tulard
   b. Pascal Kintz   d. Paul Fornes

Vocabulary
4. In line 80, what does *brought on* mean?
   a. led to   c. revealed
   b. prevented   d. cured

Inference
5. Why does François de Candé-Montholon seem proud that his ancestor murdered Napoleon?
   a. Because he has a personal dislike of Napoleon.
   b. Because by murdering Napoleon, his ancestor became an aristocrat.
   c. Because his ancestor had control of Napoleon's wine cellar and food.
   d. Because Napoleon caused revolutions and had wronged his family.

> **Critical Thinking**
>
> Which of the theories in the passage do you think is the most likely? Why?

B. Matching. Match each cause (**1–5**) with the correct effect (**a–e**).
One effect is extra.

Causes
1. Hot and humid weather on St. Helena   _____
2. Hair sample analysis   _____
3. A diet including large amounts of seafood   _____
4. Advanced stomach cancer   _____
5. Mercurous chloride given in large doses   _____

Effects
   a. can reveal arsenic poisoning.
   b. usually results in significant weight loss.
   c. may have disrupted Napoleon's heartbeat.
   d. can be determined using modern methods.
   e. caused arsenic in the wallpaper to be released into the air.
   f. can cause high levels of arsenic in the blood.

Vocabulary Practice

A. Completion. Complete the information using the correct form of words from the box. One word is extra.

symptom	cease	inconclusive
proponent	dispute	compelling

Fugu, or puffer fish, is a delicacy[1] in Japan, but it can also be deadly. The skin, liver, and other internal parts of the fish contain tetrodotoxin, a powerful toxin that causes

▲ The puffer fish, or *fugu*, is a delicacy in Japan, but if prepared incorrectly, it can be deadly.

nerves to **1.** _____ functioning properly. You might think that this is a(n) **2.** _____ reason to stay away from this dangerous food, but *fugu* is in fact quite popular. In 1975, the famous Japanese kabuki[2] actor Mitsugoro Bando, who enjoyed the pleasant feeling it created on his tongue and lips, spent a night feasting on *fugu* liver. Unfortunately for him, this time, the feeling was followed by classic **3.** _____ of fugu poisoning: inability to move his arms and legs, difficulty breathing, then, eight hours later, death. There is no cure for *fugu* poisoning. For this reason, *fugu* chefs are strictly trained and must be licensed; of the 900 who took the 2008 exam, only 63 percent passed. Additionally, Japan has forbidden the public sale of *fugu* liver since 1983.

The source of the *fugu's* poison is a subject of **4.** _____. While some believe that *fugu* produce their own poison, Tamao Noguchi, a researcher at Nagasaki University, believes that the poison comes from the small animals that the fish eat. In experiments, Noguchi has raised *fugu* in a laboratory, controlled their diet, and produced toxin-free fish. Noguchi is a(n) **5.** _____ of lifting the ban on *fugu* liver, and hopes his research will help. "A great delicacy; once you eat, you cannot stop," he says.

[1] A **delicacy** is a rare or expensive food that is considered especially nice to eat.
[2] **Kabuki** is a traditional theater style in Japan.

B. Words in Context. Complete each sentence with the best answer.

1. A building described as grand is probably _____.
   a. large and impressive   b. in need of repair

2. If a test for a poison is inconclusive, the poison _____ been found.
   a. has   b. hasn't

3. An animal that is massive is very _____.
   a. dangerous   b. large

4. An attack that is relentless _____.
   a. soon finishes   b. goes on for a long time

5. A crime of revenge is carried out by someone who _____.
   a. has been wronged in some way
   b. is in great need of money

Usage

In informal American English, one thousand dollars is sometimes referred to as **a grand**. The plural form doesn't require an *s*, e.g., **three grand**, **ten grand**.

8B Watching You

▲ A security camera captures someone arriving at the National Geographic Society building in Washington, D.C., U.S.A.

They're Not Just Watching Bad Guys

Are you being watched? Chances are yes—more than ever before. Video cameras are everywhere on city streets. Marketers are analyzing our every purchase. And we can look forward to less and less privacy in decades to come.

- It's not only people nearby who can listen to your cell phone conversations. Anyone with the technical ability can listen in from a distance.
- Legal and illegal tracking of your online activity is commonplace. Wireless laptop and PDA communications can be illegally picked up by technologically skilled eavesdroppers.[1]
- If your car has a GPS system, the information on your whereabouts is available to companies, insurers, and law enforcement.

So who's watching? The government crime-fighting agencies, certainly, but you're more likely to be watched by employers, who have the legal right to read employees' e-mails, monitor Internet activity, and eavesdrop on telephone calls. Your information is also valuable to marketers who buy, sell, and share it more than ever before.

[1] If you **eavesdrop** on someone, you listen secretly to what they are saying.

Before You Read

A. Discussion. Read the information above. What do you think are the advantages and disadvantages of the forms of surveillance listed above? Make a list. Then discuss your ideas with a partner.

B. Scan. What are some other types of surveillance that the passage discusses.

High-Tech Surveillance

1 In the 18th century, legal expert Jeremy Bentham developed plans for a new type of prison. He called his prison a *Panopticon*, from the Greek word meaning "all-seeing." It

5 was designed with a central guard tower from which every prisoner could be observed 24 hours a day, seven days a week. At any given time, prisoners could never be sure if they were being watched or not, and therefore

10 they would be less likely to break prison rules. In fact, Bentham said that the guards might even leave from time to time: the prisoners, thinking that they were still being watched, would continue their good behavior. Two

15 centuries later, in 1949, British author George Orwell, in his classic novel *1984*, wrote about a future society where it is impossible to evade surveillance by the authorities. In the novel, citizens are constantly reminded of

20 the authorities' presence by the phrase "Big Brother is watching you."

In a sense, the world of surveillance predicted by Bentham and Orwell has already come to pass.[1] Public video systems are now in use

25 in many cities around the world. In Paris, for example, there are road cameras nearly everywhere to help regulate traffic, and some 2,000 cameras on city buses detect and deter crime. In Britain in the 1970s and '80s, cities

30 and towns began installing cameras to monitor streets and parks, public transportation,

▲ Computer scientist John Daugman has developed a system of identifying individuals using iris (the colored part of your eye) recognition. Here he is wearing specially made contact lenses with digital maps of his own irises.

stadiums, and shopping areas. Now, with more than four million such cameras nationwide— that's one camera for every 15 people—Britain

35 has more surveillance cameras than anywhere else in the world. British sociologist[2] Clive Norris and his colleague Michael McCahill estimate that the average visitor to London is now caught on video 300 times in a single day.

40 Having thoroughly studied surveillance trends in the United Kingdom, they have concluded that all Britons should assume that they are always being watched once they step outside their homes.

▲ In 2002, when posters started appearing on London buses reading "Secure Beneath the Watchful Eyes," many Londoners mistook the signs for a joke. But the posters were real.

[1] If something **comes to pass**, it happens.
[2] A **sociologist** studies society or the way society is organized.

▲ One of four million surveillance cameras in the United Kingdom, this one in London includes tiny wipers to clear the rain.

The Surveillance Society

When it comes to catching the bad guys, a surveillance camera is a police officer's best friend. There is little a criminal can say in his defense when the crime he is accused of committing has been caught on video. Once mainly seen in banks and government buildings, video surveillance systems have become standard equipment even for the smallest convenience stores.

Even when criminals are not actually caught on video, just the presence of video cameras can make a location safer. In the hope of deterring criminals, some people post signs saying "Video Surveillance Is in Operation" even where no video cameras exist. This deterrence is probably one of the main reasons that Britons accept such a high level of video surveillance. Although the British public seems to approve of their use, the actual effectiveness of the cameras is far from clear. Studies by Norris and McCahill show that video surveillance had "a sustained and dramatic reductive effect in some areas" but "a negligible[3] impact in others." Now, the British government is moving ahead to the next step in its surveillance program: an ambitious vehicle surveillance system designed to deter known criminals from making use of the country's roads.

Surveillance Success

Fighting crime hasn't been the only success for video surveillance. One autumn day in Brittany, France, 18-year-old Jean-Francois LeRoy was swimming in a 25-meter public swimming pool. He was practicing holding his breath for long periods of time when he suddenly lost consciousness. The human lifeguards watching the pool didn't realize what was happening as LeRoy sank slowly and quietly to the bottom of the pool. Without help, it would have taken him as little as four minutes to die.

Although no human lifeguard saw LeRoy drowning, 12 large machine eyes deep under the water were watching the whole incident, relaying the images to a central computer. Just nine months earlier, a modern electronic surveillance system called Poseidon had been installed. Poseidon covers a pool's entire swimming area, and is able to tell when swimmers are not moving the way they are supposed to. When the computer detects a problem, it instantly activates an alarm to alert lifeguards and displays the exact location of the incident on a monitor. Just 16 seconds after Poseidon noticed LeRoy sinking, the lifeguards pulled him from the pool and gave him CPR.[4] He started breathing again, and after one night in the hospital was released with no permanent damage. Poseidon had saved his life.

Rights for the Observed

Its usefulness for tackling crimes and saving lives notwithstanding, many citizens still voice their concern about public surveillance. "The cameras are not just coming—they're here now," warns New York civil rights lawyer Norman Siegel, who is concerned with the legal boundaries of surveillance. "There has

[3] An amount or effect that is **negligible** is so small that it is not worth considering or worrying about.

[4] **CPR** (cardiopulmonary resuscitation) is a medical technique for reviving someone whose heart has stopped beating by pressing on their chest and breathing into their mouth.

▲ Surveillance is the new entertainment at the Remote Lounge in New York City, where customers control cameras to spy on each other.

been an explosion of video surveillance in
115 public spaces without any real public debate about the pros and cons.[5] That's remarkable. You'd think there would be a referendum[6] somewhere."

Siegel, who doesn't fully oppose public
120 surveillance, offers a short list of policy suggestions for ethical surveillance practices: All video surveillance zones and cameras should be listed on a public register that can be easily accessed at a library or on the Internet.
125 Access to surveillance data should be strictly limited, and material that records no criminal acts should be kept only temporarily. An individual in each community should actively assure that the regulations are enforced. In
130 addition, every surveillance zone should include visible warning signs.

One place where the presence of surveillance is very clearly advertised is the Remote Lounge in New York City. This trendy bar
135 is using video surveillance in an unexpected and amusing way. The Remote Lounge is packed with video cameras and monitors, and the entrance features a brightly-lit sign: "Upon entering these premises[7] your name,
140 image, voice, and likeness may be broadcast live over the Internet." Customers must agree to give up their rights to privacy while in the bar. Inside, customers use remote control video cameras and monitors to spy on other
145 customers, whether they're aware of it or not. When customers think about being watched by others, "they're taken aback[8] by the lack of privacy," says co-owner Keven Centanni. But when they themselves watch other customers,
150 "they feel empowered." Clearly, for customers at the Remote Lounge, being watched has its discomforts, its reassurances, even its thrills—just as it does in the real world, where surveillance surrounds us all.

[5] **Pros and cons** are arguments in favor of and arguments against a particular issue.

[6] A **referendum** is a vote in which all the people in a country are asked whether they agree or disagree with a particular policy.

[7] **Premises** is a legal term referring to a piece of land and buildings on it.

[8] If you are taken **aback** by something, you are surprised or shocked by it.

Reading Comprehension

A. Multiple Choice. Choose the best answer for each question.

Purpose   **1.** Why does the author refer to *the Panopticon*?
  a. to argue that surveillance should only be used on criminals
  b. to offer a historical example of the power of surveillance
  c. to remind us of one source of inspiration for George Orwell
  d. to suggest that other prison designs are less effective

Detail   **2.** Using video surveillance warning signs without cameras _____.
  a. is ineffective
  b. is not recommended by police
  c. can still deter criminals
  d. has saved the government money

Inference   **3.** Why are people like Norman Siegel concerned about the growth of surveillance?
  a. There is no evidence at all that video cameras prevent crime.
  b. The British public is generally opposed to video surveillance.
  c. Most surveillance video images are of no value to police.
  d. There is little public discussion about ethics.

Critical Thinking

What is your opinion of the Remote Lounge as entertainment?

Detail   **4.** Which statement about the Remote Lounge is NOT true?
  a. Customers spy on each other.
  b. Customers must give up their right to privacy.
  c. Most customers don't know they are being watched.
  d. Customer information may be broadcast on the Internet.

Inference   **5.** Which of the following people might be most likely to approve of video surveillance?
  a. Clive Norris and Michael McCahill
  b. Jean-François LeRoy
  c. Norman Siegel
  d. the author of this passage

B. Completion. Complete the diagram using words from the passage. Use up to three words for each blank.

Prison Design: Jeremy Bentham's **1.** _____

Entertainment: the **5.** _____ in New York City

Uses of Surveillance

Traffic Regulation: **2.** _____ everywhere in Paris

Lifesaving: the **4.** _____ surveillance system

Authority and Control: "**3.** _____ is watching you."

Vocabulary Practice

A. Completion. Complete the information with the correct form of the words in the box. One word is extra.

relay	commit	install
oppose	alert	regulate

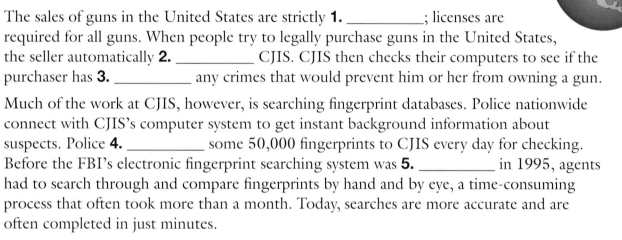
▲ An FBI employee analyzes fingerprints on a computer screen.

The Federal Bureau of Investigation, or FBI, is the top law enforcement organization in the United States. The offices of the FBI's Criminal Justice Information Services Division (CJIS), in the state of West Virginia, house the FBI's gun check headquarters, as well as the largest collection of fingerprints anywhere on Earth.

The sales of guns in the United States are strictly **1.** _____; licenses are required for all guns. When people try to legally purchase guns in the United States, the seller automatically **2.** _____ CJIS. CJIS then checks their computers to see if the purchaser has **3.** _____ any crimes that would prevent him or her from owning a gun.

Much of the work at CJIS, however, is searching fingerprint databases. Police nationwide connect with CJIS's computer system to get instant background information about suspects. Police **4.** _____ some 50,000 fingerprints to CJIS every day for checking. Before the FBI's electronic fingerprint searching system was **5.** _____ in 1995, agents had to search through and compare fingerprints by hand and by eye, a time-consuming process that often took more than a month. Today, searches are more accurate and are often completed in just minutes.

B. Completion. Complete the sentences with the correct form of the words in the box. One word is extra.

spy	ethical	oppose	deter	commit	assure

1. People who jealously protect their right to privacy are likely to _____ most forms of surveillance.
2. Satellites circling the Earth now have such powerful cameras that they can be used to _____ on individual people on the Earth's surface.
3. Many companies now sell fake surveillance cameras that look just like the real thing. These fake cameras still have the effect of _____ crime, but at a much lower price.
4. While the police and government must be _____ in their use of surveillance, individuals have been known to use it for questionable or even evil purposes.
5. Government leaders are often keen to _____ the public that information it obtains through surveillance will never be misused.

Word Partnership   Use *install* with: (*adj.*) **easy to** install; (*n.*) install **equipment**, install **machines**, install **software**

Frog Licker

A. Preview. This is a picture of Valerie C. Clark, a herpetologist whose job is to study reptiles and amphibians like frogs, snakes, and lizards. What do you think she is doing, and why is she doing it?

B. Summarize. Watch the video, *Frog Licker*. Then complete the summary below using the correct form of words from the box. Two words are extra.

symptoms	inconclusive	commit	proponent
assure	alert	cease	deter
ethical	relentless		

The island of Madagascar is home to the Mantella poison frog. Their poison originates from their diet of ants, millipedes, and mites. The frogs are brightly colored to **1.** _____ larger animals from eating the frog, as they have learned that bright colors mean poison.

Valerie C. Clark studies the Mantella and its diet. She and her team use a GPS system to **2.** _____ her to the frogs' location. They study the insects in the frogs' diet to discover which ones possess the chemicals contributing to the frogs' poison. Although tests are still **3.** _____, Clark believes a certain purple millipede may be a source of the frogs' toxic chemicals.

To test for toxins on the frogs' skin, Clark sometimes licks them. There's no need to worry—Clark **4.** _____ people who are concerned for her health that the poison will not affect her because Mantella are only mildly toxic to humans. Indeed, she shows no **5.** _____ of poisoning at all. These chemicals could actually be helpful to humans. Some scientists are **6.** _____ of the idea that chemicals from frogs could be used to make new medicines.

Frogs need to eat a variety of insects to create their chemicals. This variety is most available in untouched rainforest. This means if the **7.** _____ destruction of the rainforest doesn't **8.** _____, there will be fewer toxic chemicals with the potential to be used in making medicines.

C. Think About It.

1. What other animals use poison as a defense?

2. What do you understand by the phrase, "You are what you eat"? How does this apply to humans?

To learn more about investigations, visit elt.heinle.com/explorer

UNIT 9
Reputations

WARM UP

Discuss these questions with a partner.

1. Which historical leaders do you think did a lot of good? Which leaders did a lot of harm?

2. Which historical figures' reputations have changed over time?

3. If you could meet any historical figure, who would you choose? What would you ask him/her?

▲ A tourist in Rome, Italy, looks at the remains of an ancient statue of Constantine (emperor of Rome 272–337).

The Mongols used a variety of arrows, some of which whistled to frighten their enemies.

Mongol horsemen were skilled at shooting arrows from their horses, even to the rear. They kept plenty of extra horses—up to four for each rider.

Extent of Mongol empire in 1227

Mongols used war machines to throw rocks, fire bombs, and even diseased dead bodies at cities they attacked.

Each year a great Mongol hunt was also training for war. Horsemen surrounded all the animals in an area and were allowed only one arrow each to make a kill.

Conqueror of the World

The illustrated map above depicts the world at the time of Genghis Khan, the great military leader of the Mongols. In 1206, when he came to power, he began a string of conquests which, continued for the next 70 years by his successors, would create the largest land empire in history. The death and destruction caused by the Mongols are legendary, but there was a positive side as well. For the first time in history, Asia came under one rule, and as a result, its diverse cultures came into contact with one another. These cultures had new opportunities to trade with and learn from each other.

Before You Read

A. Discussion. Look at the map and information above. Then answer the questions below.

1. What was one way the Mongols trained themselves for war?
2. What was special about some of the arrows used by the Mongols?
3. What present-day countries did the Mongol Empire cover?
4. In what way was the Mongol empire beneficial to Asia?

B. Predict. Look quickly at the title, headings, photos, and captions on pages 139–141. Check (✔) the topics you think you'll read about.

1. ❒ destruction caused by Mongol armies   3. ❒ a critical look at Genghis Khan's image
2. ❒ Mongol defeats by powerful enemies

Who Was Genghis Khan?

A horseback herder rides across the Mongolian plains.

1 In the 1160s, on the floodplains of the Onon River in northeastern Mongolia, a boy named Tamujin was born. As a young man, he organized an alliance of rival tribes among
5 those of the grasslands north of the Gobi desert. Years later, as the fierce warrior-leader Genghis Khan, he led a vast army of nomads out of the grasslands, across deserts and against societies who had the misfortune[1] to share time
10 and space with the all-powerful Mongols . . .

1220. Samarkand, Central Asia. From the city's northwest gate, the inhabitants of Samarkand could only watch in terror as the enormous army approached. Perhaps 80,000 riders could be seen. According to one writer,
15 they appeared "more numerous than ants or locusts, [more than] the sand in the desert or drops of rain." Before them, the approaching riders drove thousands of captured civilians as a human shield.
20

The city they approached was the capital of Shah Muhammad of the Khwarezm, the center of an empire that included parts of modern-day Afghanistan and Iran. Earlier, the Shah had executed the Mongol ambassador and
25 had sent back the man's head to Genghis Khan, infuriating the Mongol leader. Shah Muhammad had 110,000 troops[2] in the city, but most were poorly disciplined and fled even before the Mongol army arrived. After just a
30 day's fighting, the city gates were opened, and the Shah's people were forced to beg the Mongols for mercy, which they did not receive.

Today, there is barely anything left of the
35 once-powerful city of Samarkand. The city was once famed for its copper and silver artisans.[3] An advanced aqueduct system once brought water to the city, making gardens bloom in the dry lands. Today, there is only grass and some
40 occasional bricks. A modern-day Samarkand has grown in its place, but of the original city's great workshops and palaces, nothing remains.

The Mongols destroyed every building in the city, killing most of its citizens and
45 taking away many of the survivors to serve as slaves. A city of over 200,000 was erased from the earth. Where the city's mosque once was, archeologist Yuri Buryakov has found the burnt bones of the mosque's defenders.
50 "[T]here were soldiers who did not want to surrender,"[4] he says. A thousand withdrew to the mosque, hoping that the Mongols would not kill them there. "But to Mongols it didn't make any difference. They would
55 kill anywhere."

[1] A **misfortune** is something unpleasant or unlucky that happens to someone.
[2] **Troops** are soldiers, especially when they are in a large organized group doing a particular task.
[3] An **artisan** is someone whose job requires skill with their hands.
[4] If you **surrender**, you stop fighting or resisting someone and agree that you have been beaten.

▲ The Ark of Herat was one of the few structures to survive when Genghis Khan ordered the slaughter of the city's inhabitants.

A bronze plaque in Mongolia shows the face of Genghis Khan. ▲

Similar stories can be told of other great cities of Central Asia: Bukhara, Balkh, Herat, Ghazni. One after another, they fell to the horsemen who burst from the grasslands of
60 Mongolia. In Afghanistan, even after 750 years, people speak of the Mongol attack as if it happened yesterday. "Only nine!" exclaims one old man in the once elegant city of Herat. "That is all that survived here—nine people!"

65 The name of Genghis Khan brings to mind the most completely ruthless and murderous of history's conquerors. Accounts like that of Samarkand and Herat, rich in poetic exaggeration, seem to be part myth and part
70 history. Experts on 12th-century sources, however, find that some writings need to be critically interpreted to produce a more balanced view of the man and his times.

Genghis Khan's love of conquest appears
75 evident in a quotation attributed to him: "Man's greatest good fortune is to chase and defeat his enemy, seize his total possessions, leave his married women weeping⁵ . . ." In 1215, in the early days of Mongol empire-
80 building, Genghis Khan's armies surrounded the city of Zhongdu (modern-day Beijing). Years later, a traveler who noticed a white hill was told it was the bones of Zhongdu's

inhabitants. It is said that even on his death
85 bed, Genghis Khan ordered the killing of the entire population of Xi Xia, a neighboring state that had defied him.

Yet the reputation of Genghis Khan as an utterly ruthless warrior may be worse than
90 the reality. Much of our information comes from chroniclers⁶ of the time who often exaggerated the facts. It is possible they were encouraged by their Mongol employers to exaggerate the tales of cruelty so that the
95 Mongols appeared more frightening to their enemies. In the city of Nishapur, a chronicler wrote that the Mongols were brutal to the extent that even the city's dogs and cats were killed. "There's no question that there was a
100 great deal of destruction," says Mongol expert Morris Rossabi. "[But] not all the cities were butchered." *The Secret History of the Mongols*, an account of Genghis Khan's early life and the oldest surviving literary work in the Mongolian
105 language, may also have bent the truth so as to enhance his reputation. "It is full of myths and legends," says historian Larry Moses, although "some of it can be [supported by] Chinese sources."

⁵ If someone **weeps**, they cry.
⁶ A **chronicler** is someone who writes an account or record of a series of events.

◄ Shepherds watch their sheep near the ruined tombs of Xi Xia royalty. The Tangut people who built these structures were the first to fall when Genghis Khan began his foreign conquests.

110 In his homeland, Genghis Khan's reputation needs little enhancement. There he is revered as the first ruler of a united Mongolia, and his face can be found on paper currency. Mongolian historian Shirendev Bagaryn
115 interprets Genghis Khan's conquests in a more positive light: "When you are eating," he says, "your appetite grows. Once you are strong you want to go find out how other people live. . . . He needed their knowledge
120 to develop his country"— for example, by borrowing the written script that his neighbors used in western China. Other historians believe that Genghis was driven less by a thirst for land than by a need to feed his people:
125 "I don't think he consciously set out to be a conqueror," says Rossabi. "In general, he didn't try to hold on to territory, except for Mongolia."

At the age of about 60, after conquering
130 much of continental Asia, Genghis Khan died, possibly after falling from his horse. His body was taken back to Mongolia for burial. Of his grave, like much of the societies he conquered, nothing remains. According to one Persian
135 historian, Genghis Khan was "possessed of great energy . . . a genius . . . a butcher, just, resolute[7] . . . and cruel," which might serve as a fair epitaph.[8] It is true that the Mongols

under Genghis Khan committed ruthless acts,
140 killing armies as well as peaceful citizens and forcing millions to accept their rule. But the 13th century saw many wars where cruelty was the norm. It could be argued that Genghis Khan was simply a man of his time, a man
145 who happened to be a brilliant military leader, and who gave to his descendants the greatest empire—and the most powerful army—the world had ever seen.

▲ A stone tortoise is one of the few things that remain of Genghis Khan's once great capital city of Karakorum.

[7] Someone who is **resolute** is very determined not to change their mind or give up a course of action.
[8] An **epitaph** is a short piece of writing about someone who is dead, often written on their grave.

Reading Comprehension

A. Multiple Choice. Choose the best answer for each question.

Main Idea

1. What is the author's central theme about Genghis Khan in this passage?
   a. He was one of history's most evil men.
   b. He is actually a hero and to be admired.
   c. His reputation may not match the reality.
   d. His chroniclers mostly exaggerated.

Inference

2. What motivated Genghis Khan to attack Samarkand?
   a. The Shah had built a mosque larger than Genghis Khan's.
   b. The Shah's well-trained army was a threat to Genghis Khan.
   c. The Shah decided to hide inside his city walls.
   d. The Shah had attacked and killed an important Mongol.

Sequence

3. What was Genghis Khan's final act of ruthlessness?
   a. burning down Samarkand's great mosque
   b. destroying the Afghan city of Herat
   c. killing the population of Xi Xia
   d. killing dogs and cats at Nishapur

> ## Critical Thinking
>
> What do you think Shirendev Bagaryn means when he says, "When you are eating, your appetite grows"? Do you agree?

Detail

4. What is Genghis Khan's reputation in Mongolia?
   a. He continues to be greatly respected by Mongolians.
   b. Few people in Mongolia know who he is.
   c. Mongolians admire his writings.
   d. He is regarded as a criminal.

Inference

5. Which of the following historians is most likely to believe that Genghis Khan's conquests improved Mongolian culture?
   a. Yuri Burgakov
   b. Morris Rossabi
   c. Larry Moses
   d. Shirendev Bagaryn

B. Matching. Match the descriptions (**1–4**) with the correct place (**a–e**). One place is extra.

1. Was once well known for its metal craftsmen. _____
2. A white hill nearby was said to be made of the inhabitants' bones. _____
3. Only nine people were said to have survived the Mongol attack here. _____
4. The Mongol army supposedly killed this city's animals. _____

   a. Herat
   b. Nishapur
   c. Samarkand
   d. Zhongdu
   e. Xi Xia

Vocabulary Practice

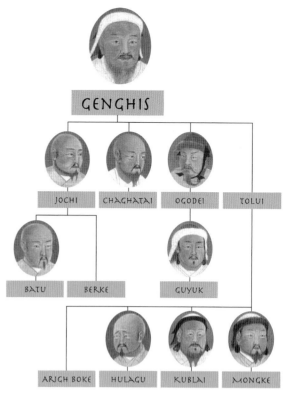

GENGHIS

JOCHI   CHAGHATAI   OGODEI   TOLUI

BATU   BERKE   GUYUK

ARIGH BOKE   HULAGU   KUBLAI   MONGKE

▲ Genghis Khan family tree

A. Completion. Complete the information with the correct form of words from the box. Two words are extra.

discipline	elegant	extent	fierce
infuriated	numerous	quotation	reputation
seize	utterly		

By the time Genghis Khan died in 1227, he had fathered **1.** _____ children by several wives, but it was his son Ogodei who was chosen to rule his empire as Great Khan. Under Ogodei, who ruled from 1229 to his death in 1241, the **2.** _____ of the already immense Mongol Empire stretched into Europe, Russia, the Middle East, and China. Ogodei proved that he and his armies were just as **3.** _____ as those of his father, killing great numbers of enemies without mercy.

Ogodei loved food and drink. He built a palace in the Mongol capital which had a(n) **4.** _____ silver fountain decorated with animals. Instead of water, the fountain poured out wine and other strong drinks. In fact, some believe it was his excessive drinking that killed him.

Ogodei's son Guyuk was next to became Great Khan, but ruled only for two years before his death. There followed a power struggle; it was finally decided in 1251 that Mongke, a grandson of Genghis, would be the next Great Khan. However, at the celebration, Shiremun, a competitor for power, arrived to kill Mongke, hoping to **5.** _____ power for himself. The threat was discovered, and Mongke, who was of course **6.** _____, killed many involved in the plan, including some of his own family members.

Mongke wished to rule in the same style as his grandfather Genghis. The following **7.** _____ is attributed to him: "I follow the laws of my ancestors." Unfortunately, after Mongke died, the Mongol Empire broke into pieces. Mongke's brother Kublai, who followed him as Great Khan, directly controlled only the eastern empire, including China. Unlike the previous Great Khans, Kublai has a(n) **8.** _____ for being not only a great wartime leader, but also a great peacetime leader. He encouraged China to trade with other countries, and it was Kublai who would meet Marco Polo when he came to China.

B. Definitions. Match the correct form of words in the box in **A** to their definitions.

1. present in large numbers   _____
2. made extremely angry   _____
3. pleasing and graceful in appearance or style   _____
4. the length, area, or size of something   _____
5. very aggressive (for example, a wild animal)   _____
6. a sentence or phrase taken from a book, speech, etc., that is repeated by someone else   _____
7. take control of something quickly and suddenly, using force   _____

Thesaurus

elegant Also look up: (adj.) chic, exquisite, luxurious, stylish

9A Conqueror of the World   **143**

9B The Mother Empress

▲ A statue of Empress Catherine II of Russia, St. Petersburg, Russia

Before You Read

A. Discussion. Look at the map and photo above and answer the questions below.

1. Why do you think Empress Catherine II of Russia is known as "Catherine the Great"?

2. What other great leaders of Russia (past or present) do you know?

3. Look at the map of Russia from the time of Catherine II. Which modern country names do you see? Which names have disappeared from today's maps?

B. Predict. How do you think Catherine II came to power in Russia? Check (✓) your answer. Then read the passage to find out.

1. ❑ She married a future Tsar.
2. ❑ She led a revolution.
3. ❑ She followed her mother, Catherine I.

Catherine the Great

▲ Two women approach St. Basil's Cathedral, Moscow.

1　One night in 1744, a 14-year-old girl arrived in Moscow with her mother, hoping to marry the future tsar[1] of Russia. She wrote, "I had in my heart a strange certainty that one day

5　I should, by my own efforts, become Empress of Russia." Years later, she would become Empress Catherine II, one of Russia's most controversial rulers.

From Princess to Empress

10　The woman who would be known to history as Catherine the Great, ruler of the Russian Empire, was actually not from Russia, nor, in fact, was her name Catherine. Born Princess Sophie Friederike Auguste on April 21, 1729,

15　in a town in what is now Poland, she was the first child of a relatively unknown German prince. As a girl, she was not especially beautiful, but she did have a quick mind and plenty of charm. At age 15 she was engaged to

20　be married to a sickly and weak-minded man who, as grandson of Peter the Great, was next in line to the Russian throne.[2]

The marriage, however, was not to be a happy one. "My heart predicted nothing agreeable;

25　only ambition sustained me," she later wrote. Catherine (who changed her name after joining the Russian church) was constantly ignored by her husband, and their relationship grew distant. She wrote of her loneliness and sense

30　of isolation: "Had it been my fate[3] to have a husband whom I could love, I would never have changed towards him." Instead, Peter cared little for her and insulted her whenever he could. To flee such treatment, Catherine

35　would go riding in the country, sometimes for 13 hours a day. "The more violent this exercise was," she admitted, "the more I loved it."

In December 1761—16 years after the start of their painful marriage—Catherine's husband

40　finally became Tsar Peter III. However, when it became known that he was planning to choose another woman to become his empress, Catherine was ready to strike. With the help of friends, Catherine seized power from her

45　husband, and he was soon after murdered by her supporters. Though monarchs abroad were horrified, Catherine realized her ambition and became recognized as empress of Russia.

Reform and Rebellion [4]

50　"A Russian tsar wasn't just the head of a big government," explains Russian art historian Sergei Letin, "but the head of a big family." Russian rulers at the time were usually referred to as "Little Father" or "Little Mother."

[1] A **tsar** is an emperor of Russia.
[2] The **throne** is a way of referring to the position of king, queen, or emperor.
[3] **Fate** is a power that some people believe controls and decides everything that happens.
[4] A **rebellion** is a violent organized action by a large group of people who are trying to change their country's political system.

▲ Catherine the Great's coronation dress (the dress she wore when she became queen) is displayed beside her portrait in Moscow.

▲ The Winter Palace, St. Petersburg, was the place from which Catherine oversaw the expansion of the Russian Empire.

55 Catherine assumed this role instinctively. What Russia needed, she believed, was a strong parental hand. As ruler, she was diligent and tireless. She got up early, drank strong black coffee, rubbed her face with a piece of ice,
60 and wrote for several hours. Her rule was characterized by a quiet seriousness: "Speak with moderation," she wrote, "and not too often, in order to avoid being troublesome to others."

65 Catherine began her reign[5] full of great ideas. She was heavily influenced by the Enlightenment in Europe, and was keen to reform Russian society. She introduced a popular inoculation[6] program to fight
70 dangerous outbreaks of smallpox. Moscow's water supply was cleaned up, and institutions were set up for parentless children. She founded a system of free public schools and encouraged the best minds of Europe to visit
75 Russia. Agricultural production increased, and she worked industriously to create new building projects throughout Moscow, inspiring the saying, "When she came [it] was of wood, when she left it was of stone."

80 But for the poorest Russians, life did not improve. By the end of her rule, serfs—poor farm workers— comprised more than half the male population of Russia. As Catherine increased the power of the nobility,[7] whose
85 support she needed for her reforms, the rights of serfs disappeared. In 1773, rebellion broke out. Several nobles were murdered, and their estates were destroyed. Catherine had to rely on her military to put down the
90 rebellion, preventing the serfs from marching into Moscow. The incident affected Catherine deeply, and she abandoned any further serious attempts at social reform.

◄ In the 1770s, Catherine's unpopular policies led to a rebellion by peasants, which was put down with the help of loyal Cossacks, like this man's ancestors.

[5] A **reign** is the period of time that a king, queen, or other leader rules a country.
[6] **Inoculation** is the introduction of a small amount of a disease into a person's body to prevent him or her actually catching the disease.
[7] The **nobility** of a society are the people who belong to a high social class.

▲ Artists compete for admission to the famous Repin Institute in St. Petersburg, the arts academy Catherine expanded in an effort to promote Western learning.

Affairs of the Heart

95 Perhaps today, though, even more than for her reforms, it is for her passionate love affairs that Catherine is most remembered. The number of her affairs was wildly distorted by European nobility, who attacked her for political reasons. 100 In reality, it is estimated that Catherine had between 12 and 20 romances, each lasting between one and 12 years. While some of the objects of her affection (officially known as her "favorites") were officers and nobility, others 105 weren't famous at all. Her love letters show her eagerness to abandon herself completely: "My misfortune," she wrote, "is that my heart cannot be happy, even for an hour, without love."

110 Her great dependence on lovers left her emotionally vulnerable.[8] When one favorite, Alexander Lanskoi, passed away, Catherine described her symptoms of lovesickness: "My happiness is gone. I have thought of dying 115 myself. . . . My room, which until now was so pleasant, has become an empty cavern into which I drag myself like a ghost." Her vulnerability was further affected by a series of family disappointments in the last years of 120 her life. Her daughter Anna died as a baby. Her heir, her son Paul, whose personality resembled Peter III's, hated her. When the king of Sweden insulted Catherine by breaking

125 his promise to marry her granddaughter Alexandra, she suffered a stroke.[9] Her health continued to decline until, at the age of 67, Russia's "Little Mother" passed away.

Was Catherine Great?

Most historians today would agree that 130 Catherine's legacy[10] was decidedly mixed. On the one hand, she drove her country deep into debt for the first time in its history and created more serfs than ever before. This led to the greatest Russian uprising ever before the 1917 135 Revolution. On the other hand, during her rule of 34 years—one of the longest in Russian history—she attempted to reform many aspects of Russian life, and this gained her huge support. Not long after her death, a Russian 140 historian wrote that "virtually all [Russians] would agree that Catherine's [reign] was the happiest for Russian citizens; virtually all would prefer to have lived then than at any other time."

145 Since Catherine, Russia hasn't had another woman leader. For some modern-day Russians, such as Lyubov Sogurenko, this is a shame. "I think it would be better for the country," Sogurenko explains. "I feel a woman is more 150 serious. You understand, a woman thinks as a mother; a woman knows the problems of the family, all the pains, more than a man. It seems to me that [a female ruler] would live more for the people, the same way she does 155 for her family." Perhaps that is how Catherine herself would most like to be remembered—as a strong woman who cared passionately about her family and the Russian people.

---

[8] Someone who is **vulnerable** is weak and without protection, with the result that they are easily hurt physically or emotionally

[9] If someone has a **stroke**, a blood vessel in their brain bursts or becomes blocked, which may kill them or make them unable to move one side of their body.

[10] A **legacy** of a historical event or period is something which is a result of it and continues after it is over.

Reading Comprehension

A. Multiple Choice. Choose the best answer for each question.

Gist **1.** According to the passage, what primarily motivated Catherine the Great to become empress of Russia?
   a. love
   b. duty
   c. ambition
   d. greed

Detail **2.** Which of the following statements about Catherine is true?
   a. She was born in Russia.
   b. Her father chose the name Catherine.
   c. She enjoyed physical activity.
   d. Foreign royalty were pleased when she became empress.

Critical Thinking

Do you agree with the opinion of Lyubov Sogurenko expressed in the last paragraph of the reading? Why or why not?

Inference **3.** What is the significance of rulers being called "Little Father" or "Little Mother"?
   a. They were expected to have many children.
   b. They were also heads of the state religion.
   c. Their relationship with the Russian people was parental.
   d. The names referred to their strict discipline.

Detail **4.** Which event caused Catherine to abandon societal reform?
   a. the serf rebellion
   b. the death of Lanskoi
   c. the death of her daughter
   d. a change in her health

Inference **5.** Which of the following statements about Catherine is true?
   a. She was more motivated by self-interest than love of her country.
   b. She greatly improved the lives of Russian peasants.
   c. During her reign, she achieved all of her original goals.
   d. Today, she is probably known more for her romances than her achievements.

B. Classification. According to the passage, was Catherine's effect in the following areas mostly positive (**P**) or mostly negative (**N**)? Circle the best answer.

1. public health   **P**   **N**
2. public education   **P**   **N**
3. the rights of serfs   **P**   **N**
4. Russia's finances   **P**   **N**
5. new building projects   **P**   **N**

Vocabulary Practice

A. Completion. Complete the information with the correct form of words from the box. Two words are extra.

ambition	charm	controversial	distort	industrious
institution	insult	moderation	personality	reform

▲ Tsar Ivan IV (1530–1584)

Ivan Vasilyerich was the first tsar of Russia. His Russian nickname, Ivan Grozny, has been translated as Ivan the Terrible, but the true meaning of *grozny* has been **1.** _____: its meaning is closer to *fearsome* or *formidable*. Ivan IV was a(n) **2.** _____ figure; although he did many terrible things, he also achieved many important accomplishments for Russia.

In 1533, when Ivan was three years old, his father died, making Ivan the official Grand Prince of Moscow. However, his mother actually ruled Russia until her death when Ivan was only eight. At that time, members of the Russian nobility ruled the country, and while they treated Ivan with respect in public, they disrespected him in private, ignoring and often **3.** _____ him. Meanwhile, Ivan read widely, educating himself for the position of tsar; he would become an excellent writer and public speaker.

In 1547 Ivan achieved his **4.** _____ and was proclaimed Tsar Ivan IV. His first years were promising. He was an active and **5.** _____ leader who worked hard to make all kinds of **6.** _____ to improve the legal system, the government, the army, and to generally modernize the country. An effective military leader, he expanded Russia's borders.

Things changed in 1553, when Ivan became ill and nearly died. The illness seemed to change his **7.** _____. He seemed to lose his sense of **8.** _____ and began acting in an extreme way, whether partying, practicing religion, or committing violent acts. He ordered killings of his own people on a large scale. In an argument, Ivan even accidentally killed one of his two sons. When Ivan IV died in 1584, he left Russia to be ruled by his remaining son, Feodor.

B. Definitions. Match the correct form of words from the box in **A** to their definitions. Two words are extra.

1. subject to intense public argument, disagreement, or disapproval _____
2. one's whole character and nature _____
3. do something that is rude or offensive _____
4. the quality of being pleasant and attractive _____
5. a large important organization, such as a university, church, or bank _____
6. the desire to be successful, rich, or powerful _____
7. acting in a way that is reasonable and not extreme _____
8. report or represent a statement, fact, or idea in an untrue way _____

Word Partnership Use *reform* with: (*adj.*) **economic** reform, **political** reform; (*n.*) **education** reform, **election** reform, **health care** reform, reform **movement**, **party** reform, **prison** reform, **tax** reform

Egypt

EXPLORE ☉ MORE

Queen of Egypt

A. Preview. Cleopatra (69 B.C.–30 B.C.) has been the inspiration for many works of art and movies. What do you know of the Egyptian queen? Why do you think we are still talking about her today?

B. Summarize. Watch the video, *Queen of Egypt*. Then complete the summary below using the correct form of words from the box. One word is extra.

seize	personality	charmed	insulted
numerous	utterly	extent	reputation
fiercely	ambition		

▲ Glamorous actress Elizabeth Taylor stars as the tragic queen in a 1963 production of *Cleopatra*.

Cleopatra ruled Egypt with her brother Ptolemy until he forced her from power. Nonetheless, she still had a strong **1.** _____ to rule Egypt, and waited for her opportunity.

When Julius Caesar arrived in Egypt, he was completely **2.** _____ by her, and they soon fell in love. He defeated Cleopatra's rivals and helped her take back power. She soon after had a boy named Caesarion, whom she claimed was Caesar's son.

Cleopatra was **3.** _____ determined to keep her country independent of Rome. Her relationship with Julius Caesar helped her to achieve this until his murder. After that, her **4.** _____ as a rich and beautiful woman reached Roman general Marc Antony. He went to Egypt and also fell in love with her.

They married, and Marc Antony worked to increase the **5.** _____ of Egypt's lands by taking over some Roman ones. He also declared Cleopatra's son Caesarion to be the true successor to Julius Caesar. That was a great **6.** _____ to Julius Caesar's successor in Rome, Octavian, and he went to war against them. Antony and Cleopatra were **7.** _____ defeated at the Battle of Actium in 31 B.C. After the battle, there were **8.** _____ false reports of Cleopatra's death. Marc Antony believed them, and killed himself.

Cleopatra was unable to make peace with Octavian, and the Romans **9.** _____ control of her country. The queen couldn't bear the pain and allowed a poisonous snake to bite her, ending her life.

C. Think About It.

1. Do you think Cleopatra was an admirable woman? Why or why not?

2. Cleopatra's nose was rumored to be her most attractive feature. The French philosopher Pascal wrote that, had Cleopatra's nose been shorter, the whole face of the world would have been changed. What do you think he meant?

To learn more about reputations, visit elt.heinle.com/explorer

A. Crossword. Use the definitions below to complete the missing words.

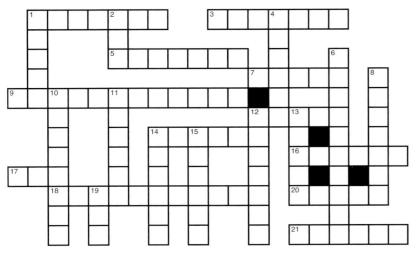

Across
1. to report or represent something in an untrue way
3. pleasing and graceful in appearance
5. an argument or disagreement between people or groups
7. to _____ something is to take hold of it quickly and firmly
9. a doctor is sometimes called a medical _____
12. to stop doing something
14. to add something to improve its quality
16. to talk about the _____ of something is to emphasize how serious it is
17. to _____ on something is to hope or expect that it will happen
18. an important and established organization
20. a main idea developed in a work of art
21. simple, usually related to the countryside

Down
1. to make someone not want to do something
2. strange or unusual
4. when you _____ over something, you feel very sad about it
6. very determined and never giving up
8. to take _____ is to harm someone who has harmed you
10. the desire to be successful, rich, or powerful
11. to say something rude or offensive to someone
12. very severe, lasting a long time
13. to warn someone; to be fully aware
14. unusual and interesting, usually from a distant country
15. a regular series of sounds or movements
19. to watch someone secretly

B. Notes Completion. Scan the information on pages 152–153 to complete the notes.

Field Notes

Site: Kremlin and Red Square

Location: Moscow, Russia

Information:
- Red Square in the heart of Moscow is the _____ and _____ center of Russia.
- The Tsar's Bell is the world's largest bell and weighs _____ tons.
- From a small _____, Ivan the Terrible once spied on _____ taking place near the cathedral.
- At the restaurant One Red Square, people can enjoy dishes from the _____ to _____ centuries.
- St. Basil's Cathedral is so beautiful that its _____ is said to have been _____ by the Tsar to prevent him from designing anything better.

Red Square

Sites: **Kremlin and Red Square**

Location: **Moscow, Russia**

Category: **Cultural**

Status: **World Heritage Site since 1990**

Moscow, Russia

The Biggest Bell

Lying next to Tsar Ivan III's Tower is the world's largest bell. At more than six meters high and weighing an immense 202 tons, the massive **Tsar's Bell** has never been rung. A great fire in 1737 caused a large piece to crack off while it was still being formed. The resulting crack is large enough to fit a grown man.

Krasnaya Ploshchad is neither red nor square (*krasnaya* meant "beautiful" in Old Russian), but Moscow's **Red Square** is still center stage for Mother Russia. The most important square in the largest city in the world's largest country is truly impressive—and, when covered by gently falling snow—utterly romantic.

In Moscow, all roads lead to Red Square. Major streets branch out from here in all directions, making it the administrative and cultural center of the country. Over the years, Red Square has witnessed some of the most dramatic scenes in Russia's noble but troubled history, from joyous **coronations** to bloody **executions**.

Despite its struggles, the country has been successful in embracing its past while looking to the future—the magnificent State Historical Museum, for example, sits adjacent to the modern architecture of GUM, Moscow's top department store. Priests and soldiers of previous eras have been replaced by tourists and stylish Muscovites (Moscow's inhabitants) navigating the vast public square. Although people and scenery have changed with the times, Red Square remains, as it has been for centuries, the heart and soul of Russia.

Glossary

coronation: the act or ceremony of crowning a king, queen, or other royal person

crypt: a room underground commonly used as a burial place

execution: the act of putting someone to death as punishment

sturgeon: a type of fish valued as a source of caviar (very expensive fish eggs)

A Tower for the Tsar

Tsarskaya, or **"Tsar's Tower,"** is the smallest tower in Red Square. It was built in 1680 to replace a wooden tower from which the young Ivan the Terrible—who was renowned for his fierce personality—was rumored to throw dogs to their death; he also used it to spy on executions taking place behind the cathedral. The new tower, however, bears no trace of its terrible past and instead resembles a Russian fairytale with its decorative **weathervane** and tiny flags.

A Fallen Leader

Close to the Lenin Mausoleum—the monument devoted to the renowned leader of Russia's 1917 revolution—lies a more humble one for a leader no less famous or ambitious. Josef Stalin, former ruler of the Soviet Union (Russia's name before 1991), was an integral, if controversial, figure in the Russian revolution. Later, he was both revered and despised during his rule. Notwithstanding his reputation as a cruel dictator, Stalin has enduring appeal among older Russians, many of whom still regard him as a great reformer. Some still grieve at Stalin's grave and place flowers to honor him on his birthday (December 21).

A Royal Dining Experience

Housed in the grand State History Museum, **One Red Square**, the restaurant with "the best address in the world," embraces history in a unique way—by allowing visitors to eat like a Tsar. Menus and recipe books of the 17th to 19th centuries were discovered intact in the museum's **crypts**, and the exotic recipes, including such luxurious dishes as **sturgeon** in cherry sauce, are now cooked and presented to diners exactly how they would have been hundreds of years ago.

A Russian Icon

Thanks to its elegant onion-shaped domes and eye-catching colors, **St. Basil's Cathedral** is the most prominent landmark on Red Square. According to legend, Tsar Ivan IV ("Ivan the Terrible"), who built the cathedral to celebrate his military victories, admired St. Basil's to the extent he had the architect blinded to prevent him designing anything better. (Skeptics have since disproved this story, however.) During the Soviet era, Stalin felt it obstructed his soldiers' battle route and ordered it torn down. One brave architect, Yuri Baranovsky, threatened to cut his own throat in opposition. This eventually deterred Stalin, but the architect was confined for five years in the *gulag*, the harsh Russian prison camp, for his defiance.

A Global View

The **technological** revolution that began in the 1950s has given rise to a new Information Age in which global communications **networks** affect every aspect of modern life. Each day trillions of dollars worth of goods and services are traded worldwide electronically, via **satellites**, under the seas, beneath our feet, and in the air around us.

Enabling this **electronic** exchange is the global Internet, a vast collection of **interconnected** computer networks carrying everything from financial data to phone calls. The huge volume of "traffic" and the complexity of **links** make monitoring and measuring the Internet a challenging task. However, attempts have been made to map the Internet at specific moments in time (see map on next page).

Increasingly, as everyday objects around us become part of this network, an intelligent "Internet of things" is evolving in which information is exchanged without the need for human intervention. Tiny electronic tags now use radio frequencies to track goods from manufacturer to consumer; soon they could provide information about a person's identity, buying habits, medical history, and much more.

The Digital World

This map reveals the extent of the "**digital** divide" between the industrialized and developing worlds. It uses the International Telecommunication Union's Digital Opportunity Index (a composite of indicators such as cell phone coverage and number of Internet users) to compare international levels of digital access. Whereas digital information is commonplace in industrialized countries, information and communication technologies (ICTs) remain far out of reach for up to a billion people in the developing world. Among the **information-rich** nations, South Korea, Japan, and Denmark have the highest index, while countries in sub-Saharan Africa—due to a combination of geographic isolation and poverty—are the least connected. Asia is the world's fastest-growing region for ICT—particularly China, which now has the world's largest number of cell phone users.

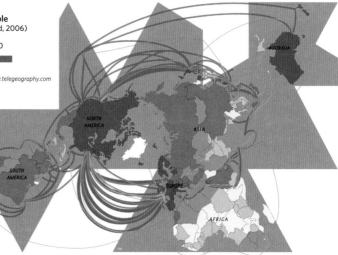

Digital Opportunity Index
(index value, 2005-2006)

- 0.6-0.8
- 0.45-0.59
- 0.3-0.44
- 0.15-0.29
- 0.01-0.14
- No data

Source: International Telecommunication Union
NG BOOK DIVISION

Fiber-Optic Submarine Cable
(capacity in gigabits per second, 2006)

10-49   50-499   >500

Source: TeleGeography Research, www.telegeography.com

Critical Thinking

How do you think the Internet will evolve in the future? What do you think people will be able to do that they can't do now?

Word Link

The prefix **com-** or **con-** can mean *with* or *together*, e.g., *compare, complex, composite, combine, compound, convene, contemporary, concurrent.*

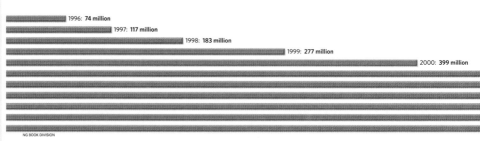

1996: **74 million**
1997: **117 million**
1998: **183 million**
1999: **277 million**
2000: **399 million**

NG BOOK DIVISION

Internet Users Worldwide (estimated), 1996–2006

A Map of the Internet

This model provides a "snapshot" of the entire Internet, based on data collected from January 1 to January 17, 2008. Internet Service Providers (ISPs) are represented by squares, with the best-connected near the center. Volume of Internet traffic is represented by color, from lowest (blue) to highest (yellow).

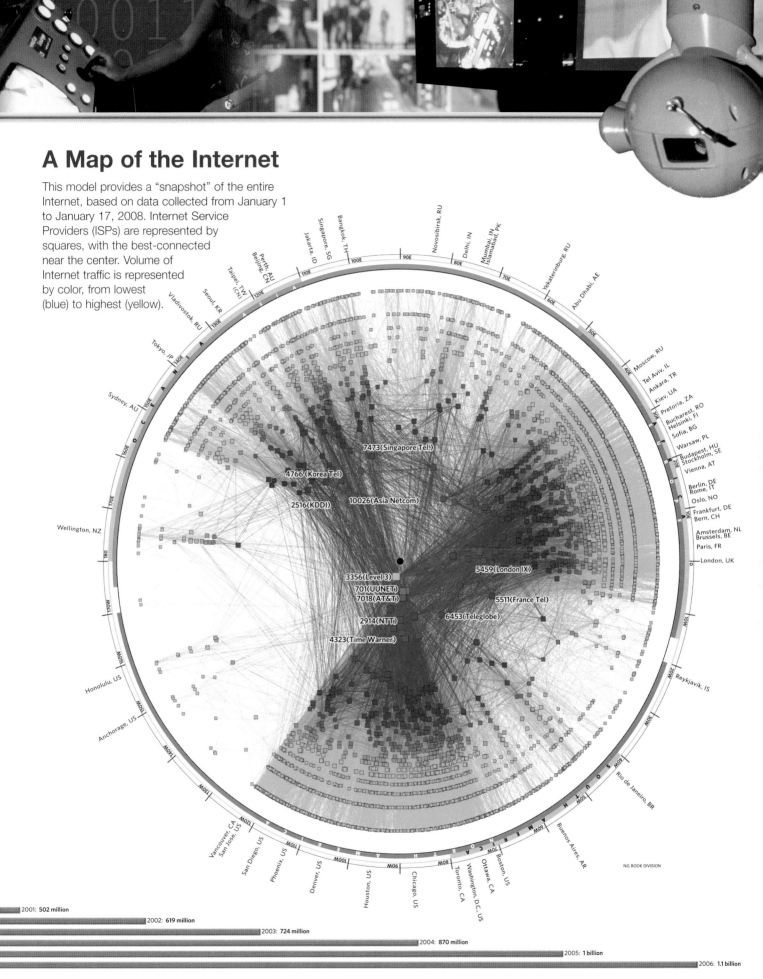

7473 (Singapore Tel.)

4766 (Korea Tel)

2516 (KDDI)

10026 (Asia Netcom)

5459 (London IX)

3356 (Level 3)
701 (UUNET)
7018 (AT&T)

5511 (France Tel)

6453 (Teleglobe)

2914 (NTT)

4323 (Time Warner)

2001: **502 million**

2002: **619 million**

2003: **724 million**

2004: **870 million**

2005: **1 billion**

2006: **1.1 billion**

NG BOOK DIVISION

A. Completion. Use the correct form of words in **bold** from pages 154 to 155 to complete the passage.

Over the last half-century, a(n) **1.** _____ revolution has radically changed our world. Today, paper communication is decreasing while **2.** _____ communication is increasing, with or without wires, or even via **3.** _____ that circle the earth. The Internet makes most of this communication possible. The Internet is a collection of computer **4.** _____, and through the Internet all of our computers can be **5.** _____. We are communicating via the Internet every time we send an e-mail or click on a(n) **6.** _____ on a website.

The developing world has far less access to cell phones and the Internet compared to the industrialized world. This difference in level of access has been called the "**7.** _____ divide." While countries like South Korea, Japan, and Denmark have high levels of electronic communication and are therefore **8.** _____, others such as some countries in sub-Saharan Africa have less overall access to electronic information.

B. Word Link. The prefixes **con–** and **com–** have the meaning of *with* or *together* in many English words. Complete the passage using the correct form of words from the box. Use a dictionary to help you. Two words are extra.

communicate	comprise	convention	contemporary	constrain
complement	convince	conversation	commit	consider

TANGO TREND **INTERLEADING**

When men and women dance, there has been a longstanding **1.** _____ that the man leads and the woman follows. Today, however, some people practice a **2.** _____ form of tango in which the lead is passed back and forth between partners, sometimes referred to as interleading. In interleading, partners **3.** _____ with each other using eyes and bodies about how the dance will continue. Although it may be difficult to **4.** _____ a traditional male tango dancer to allow his female partner to lead, some are trying to explore and promote the idea. "Tango is still evolving, forever changing," says Virginia Kelly, an Argentine native who teaches classes on interleading in New York City. She explains that interleading is not about reversing men's and women's roles in tango and having women lead all the time. A woman is free to interact with her partner and to make a proposal for the man to **5.** _____: he may either accept or refuse it. There is an exchange of the lead back and forth just as there is in a **6.** _____. In the traditional tango, the woman usually walks backwards, meaning that her actions are somewhat **7.** _____. However, more flexible steps and styles are being created to better **8.** _____ the practice of interleading.

C. Thesaurus. Write each of the six words in the box under the word they are closest to in meaning. Use your dictionary to help you. Then use the correct form of the six words to complete the sentences.

supplement	revise	misrepresent	disfigure	decorate	rehabilitate

reform	distort	enrich

1. The sultan of Khwarezm infuriated Genghis Khan by killing the Khan's messenger and _____ the faces of the people traveling with him.
2. During the reign of Catherine the Great, the Russian nobility _____ their palaces and mansions with works of art made in Europe.
3. Historians often have to _____ their attitudes towards historical figures as new information comes to light.
4. The Mongols frequently _____ their armies with soldiers from the lands they conquered.
5. Many people believe that our prison system should aim to _____ criminals, not simply punish them.
6. A new book argues that Genghis Khan was a great and effective leader who has been _____ in history books as a ruthless killer.

D. Word Link. The suffixes **–al**, **–(t)ic**, and **–ous** are added to certain nouns and verbs to create adjectives. Complete the chart with the correct adjective forms. Use your dictionary to help you. Then use the adjectives to complete the sentences below.

Noun or Verb	Adjective (-al, -ic, -ous)	Noun or Verb	Adjective (-al, -ic, -ous)
1. analogy	*analogous*	1. tradition	
2. constitution		2. fame	
3. culture		3. economy	
4. academy		4. danger	
5. envy		5. norm	
6. specify		6. drama	

1. Although Amitabh Bachchan is possibly the most _____ actor in the world with millions of fans, many in the West have never heard of him.
2. New businesses are developing increasing wealth for India, and many believe that the success of Bollywood movies is linked to this _____ success.
3. For Indian immigrants in countries around the world, Bollywood movies provide an important _____ connection with the Indian language and way of life.

4. Bollywood moviemakers must be _____ of Hollywood's profits. Despite making fewer movies, Hollywood movies bring in several times the earnings of Bollywood's.

5. While filming a particularly _____ scene for a movie in 1982, Amitab Bachchan was injured and nearly died.

6. Actors and actresses in Bollywood movies are frequently filmed wearing _____ Indian clothes such as the *sari*, *kurta*, *pajama*, or *dhoti*.

E. Word Partnership. Many phrasal verbs are of the form *verb + in* (for example, to enter a computerized system is to *log in*). Complete the passage using the correct form of the words in the box. One word is extra.

step	rake	build	tie	end	break	zoom	fill

One type of place where surveillance plays an important role is the modern casino, and the largest casino in the world is the Foxwoods Resort Casino in Connecticut in the United States. When constructing the new casino, architects **1.** _____ in a variety of surveillance systems and other crime-prevention features. The casino cashier rooms and safes are so well constructed that thieves have very little chance of being able to **2.** _____ in. At the center of the surveillance system are three monitor rooms, which are **3.** _____ in to over 4,000 cameras aimed at customers throughout the casino 24 hours a day. When a casino customer seems to be **4.** _____ in an unusual amount of money at one of the games, one of the cameras **5.** _____ in on him or her to get a closer look. If all is well, no further action is required. If, however, something illegal or against casino rules is going on, security officers on the casino floor are ready to **6.** _____ in and stop the game. In fact, a recent plot to cheat the casino out of millions of dollars was discovered and prevented. Thanks to modern surveillance methods, most attempts to cheat the casino **7.** _____ in failure for the cheaters.

F. Choosing the Right Definition. Study the numbered definitions for *plot*. Then write the number of the definition (**1–5**) that relates to each sentence below.

plot /plɒt/ (**plots, plotting, plotted**) **1** v-т/v-ı If people plot to do something or plot something illegal or wrong, they plan secretly to do it. ❏ *They plotted to kill the president.* **2** N-VAR The plot of a movie, novel, or play is the connected series of events that make up the story. ❏ *I already know the plot of that movie.* **3** N-COUNT A plot is a small piece of land, especially one that is intended for a purpose, such as building houses or growing vegetables. ❏ *That plot of land is too small to build a house on.* **4** v-т When people plot a strategy or a course of action, they carefully plan each step of it. ❏ *...their strategy for winning the election.* **5** v-т When someone plots something on a graph, they mark certain points on it and then join the points up. ❏ *The teacher plotted twenty points on the graph.*

_____ **a.** The general **plotted** the number of soldiers remaining on a chart which showed the decline in the army's strength.

_____ **b.** I'm going to see that film tomorrow night, so please don't tell me about the **plot**!

_____ **c.** Napoleon created gardens on **plots** of land around his house on St. Helena.

_____ **d.** During his life, a number of people **plotted** to kill Napoleon Bonaparte.

_____ **e.** Napoleon's strategy in that battle was extremely well **plotted**.

UNIT 10

Science Frontiers

WARM UP

Discuss these questions with a partner.

1. What are some ways in which science has improved our lives?

2. What are some things that science so far cannot explain?

3. Do you think it is important to know about space? Why or why not?

▲ A team of technicians uses microscopes to process parts for computers in Dallas, Texas, U.S.A.

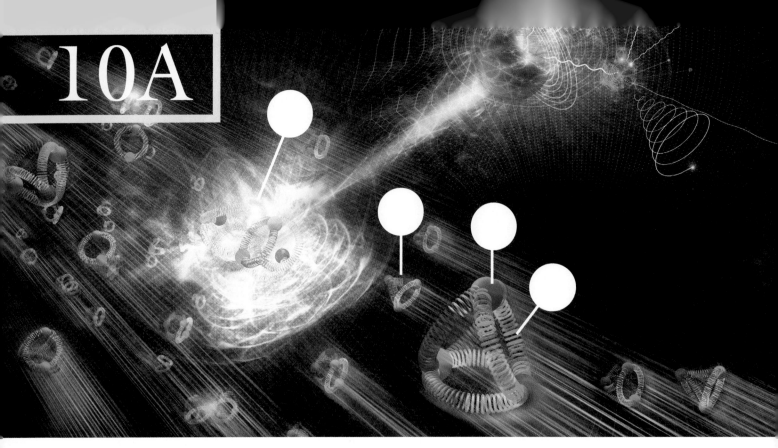

The Science of Small

Scientists have known for a long time that atoms are made of smaller objects—such as **(a) protons** and electrons—called *particles*. A *collider* is a device that causes two particle beams traveling in opposite directions at very high speeds to smash into each other. These **(b) collisions** then produce other particles, some unexpected or never seen before, which helps physicists gain new insight into the structure of the material world. The Large Hadron Collider, which is discussed in the reading passage, is the largest collider ever built.

By examining the results from experiments in colliders, physicists have learned that protons are composed of even smaller particles: a *blue* **(c) quark**, a *red quark*, and a *green quark*, all connected by **(d) gluons**. (Quarks aren't actually colored—that is just the naming system that physicists use.) In the illustration, two beams of protons are smashing into each other. The resulting high-energy collision produces other particles. To date, 57 types of particles have been detected.

Before You Read

A. Labeling. Read the information above. Then label the picture with the words in **blue**.

B. Scan. What does the word *Hadron* in Large Hadron Collider mean?
Scan the reading passage to find out.

The Great Atom Smasher

Covered with sensors, components of one of the Large Hadron Collider detectors near completion. As particles collide, detectors will track a flood of data that could provide evidence of the tiny secretive particles that scientists are looking for.

Crozet, France

1 If you were to dig a hole 100 meters (300 feet) down from the center of the charming French village of Crozet, you'd find yourself in a strange, brightly lit tunnel three meters
5 (ten feet) in diameter and 27 kilometers (17 miles) long, forming a perfect circle. Every few kilometers, the tunnel opens up into large rooms full of heavy steel structures, pipes, wires, magnets,[1] and lots of other equipment.

10 Although workers and scientists sometimes ride bicycles around the tunnel, this is no traffic tunnel. It is the largest and most complicated scientific instrument ever built, and it was made with a simple but ambitious
15 goal: to figure out what the universe is made of. Called the Large Hadron Collider (LHC), the machine sends particles[2] zooming around its circle, moving near the speed of light. At chosen points, these fast moving particles
20 collide head on. Scientists can then analyze the collisions to get information about matter, energy, and the universe.

The project will cost billions of dollars, and most of the engineering is being done by
25 European companies. Many scientists feel it has made Europe dominant once again in physics research, overtaking the United States. According to Jürgen Schukraft, an LHC project supervisor, "The brain drain that used
30 to go from Europe to the States definitely has reversed."

On September 10, 2008, the LHC's first experiment was successful when a beam[3] of particles called protons was sent completely
35 around the path in the tunnel. For the people who built the machine, the launch was a great relief. "Things can go wrong at any time," says Lyn Evans of CERN, the European research center that built the device, "but luckily this
40 morning everything went smoothly."

[1] A **magnet** is a piece of iron or other material that attracts iron toward it.
[2] A **particle** is a very small piece of matter.
[3] A **beam** is a line of light that shines from an object such as a lamp.

◀ An engineer works on one of more than a thousand magnets that steer the high speed particles toward their collision.

The Smallest Things

Scientists and even non-scientists know things today that the great physicists[4] of a century ago couldn't have imagined. For example, physicists in those days believed that the smallest things in the universe, the foundation of all matter, were atoms, a word derived from a Greek word meaning "uncuttable." Nowadays, however, we are simply not sure what the smallest particle in the universe is.

Atoms are made of particles called protons, neutrons, and electrons. Protons and neutrons (the "hadrons" that give the collider its name) are made of even smaller particles named quarks and gluons, which have been detected in collider experiments; experimental proof for the existence of quarks came in 1968 and for gluons in 1979.

To date, 57 particles have been found, challenging theoretical physicists to come up with a description of reality that includes them all. American physicist Michael Peskin believes that the LHC will be a great help in finding even more particles. "It might turn out to be like the 1950s, when we were discovering many new particles and had no clue about how they fit into a coherent picture." He adds, "I hope it will turn out like that. This is what makes science fun."

[4] **Physicists** are scientists who study the physical world of matter and energy.

By creating hundreds of thousands of head-on particle collisions each second, physicists hope to reproduce the awesome energies and temperatures of the universe near the time of its theoretical beginning, the so-called Big Bang. Scientists hypothesize that the Big Bang, a massive explosion, resulted in our universe. Among questions scientists hope to learn more about is the riddle of dark matter, the invisible material thought to make up perhaps 80 percent of the universe. Scientists are also optimistic that experiments in the LHC will reveal an intriguing particle called the Higgs boson, which theory predicts exists but whose existence has never been confirmed in an experiment. The Higgs is thought to be responsible for giving all matter its mass.

Bigger Is Better

To have a chance at achieving these goals, the LHC needed to be built larger than any previous particle accelerator ever built. By contrast, the first one, made in the early 1930s, could fit in the hand of its inventors. Along the LHC's 27-kilometer circumference are 1,600 massive magnets, most half the length of a basketball court and weighing 30 tons. To record evidence of the tiniest particles on Earth, detecting machines must be immense. The largest, called ATLAS, has a detector that's seven stories tall. The heaviest, known as CMS, is heavier than the Eiffel Tower.

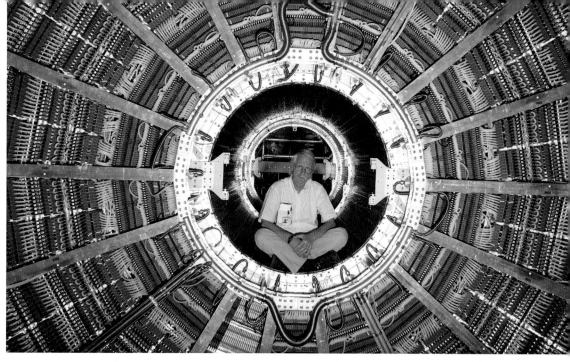

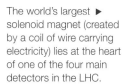
The world's largest ▶ solenoid magnet (created by a coil of wire carrying electricity) lies at the heart of one of the four main detectors in the LHC.

A machine of this incredible size and power can be dangerous, so building the LHC in a tunnel was prudent. The intense particle beam could drill a hole in just about anything. There are also concerns that the LHC experiments could create unwelcome discoveries, such as particles and other strange phenomena that could destroy Earth or even the universe. For example, one nightmare scenario is that the collisions could pack matter together so tightly that it collapses to form miniature black holes. Black holes are unimaginably dense points in space whose gravity is so strong it can pull in entire planets or even stars. The black holes could pull in our entire planet, eventually crushing it down to a size smaller than a pea.

At CERN and elsewhere, however, scientists feel that such concerns are absurd. A statement from the American Physical Society explained that collisions just like those that will take place in the LHC have taken place daily on the surface of the Earth for billions of years. There, high energy particles zoom in from outer space to smash into the earth, creating collisions of even higher energy than those in the LHC.

Why Does It Matter?

The cynic[5] might say that there's no practical use for any of this, that there might be other uses for all the money and brainpower going into these machines. But we live in a civilization shaped by physics. Computers use microprocessors, devices that would not exist without the discoveries of modern physics. The World Wide Web was invented thanks to research at CERN by computer scientist Tim Berners-Lee. The iPod couldn't exist without something called "giant magnetoresistance," discovered by physicists in the late 1980s without much thought of how it might eventually be used. Of course, many discoveries in physics have applications that are less beneficial for humanity. We know, for example, that the forces within an atom are so powerful that, unleashed and directed against humankind,[6] they can obliterate[7] cities in an instant.

But, beyond just practical uses, the LHC also represents how human beings constantly try to understand things. Peter Jenni, a Czech scientist who works on the LHC, argues that the project is important for more fundamental reasons: "Humankind differs from a collection of ants. We have intellectual curiosity. We need to understand the mechanisms of life and the universe."

[5] A **cynic** is someone who believes that people usually act selfishly or dishonestly.
[6] You can refer to all human beings as **humankind** when considering them as a group.
[7] If something **obliterates** an object or place, it destroys it completely.

Reading Comprehension

A. Multiple Choice. Choose the best answer for each question.

Gist

1. Another title for this reading could be _____.
   a. *A Coherent Theory of Particles*
   b. *A Short History of Physics*
   c. *A Giant New Machine for Particle Hunting*
   d. *Dangers of the Large Hadron Collider*

Detail

2. What was the LHC's first experiment?
   a. to send a beam of particles in a complete circle
   b. to find proof of quarks and gluons
   c. to cause two beams of particles to collide
   d. to show that atoms are not uncuttable

Vocabulary

3. In line 59, the phrase *to date* means _____.
   a. to assign a date   c. in total
   b. up to the present   d. approximately

Detail

4. What are black holes?
   a. holes drilled by the LHC
   b. points with incredibly powerful gravity
   c. places where Higgs particles are found
   d. points of entry into the LHC

Reference

5. When Michael Peskin says, "This is what makes science fun," what does *this* mean?
   a. having the opportunity to use large, very expensive machines like the LHC
   b. explaining the riddle of dark matter
   c. understanding the Higgs boson for the first time
   d. finding lots of new particles, without knowing how they fit together

Critical Thinking

In the last paragraph, Peter Jenni says, "We need to understand the mechanisms of life and the universe." What does he mean? Do you agree?

B. Supporting Ideas. Match each of the topics (**1–3**) from pages 162–163 with two of the supporting ideas (**a–f**).

Topics
1. We know more today than physicists of 100 years ago.   _____ _____
2. The LHC can be a dangerous machine.   _____ _____
3. The work of the LHC matters to people's lives.   _____ _____

Supporting Ideas
a. Unlike animals, humans have a need to understand the universe.
b. We no longer believe that atoms are the smallest things.
c. The LHC has the potential to create black holes.
d. Many popular technologies are based upon discoveries in physics.
e. The LHC's particle beam can drill a hole in almost anything.
f. Fifty-seven particles have been discovered over the course of the last century.

Vocabulary Practice

A. Completion. Complete the information with words from the box. Four words are extra.

awesome	**coherent**	**collide**	**foundation**
intellectual	**intriguing**	**overtake**	**prudent**
scenario	**unleash**		

▲ The chance to work with machines like the LHC often attracts students to the sciences.

The Large Hadron Collider (LHC) may help scientists to treat diseases, to improve the Internet, and to travel faster—perhaps even to surpass the speed of light, according to physicists.

According to Andy Parker, physics professor at Cambridge University, proton beams similar to those used in the LHC can destroy cancer tumors[1] deep inside bodies. "What you can do there is send a beam of protons into the patient, which does essentially no damage at all . . . on the way in," he explains. "All the damage is done at the point where the protons stop [i.e., at the tumor]."

Parker is also involved with a company which is using technology inspired by the LHC's computer network, set up to process the information created when particles **1.** __________. The company uses the LHC's network technology to improve the search process for images on the Internet.

Although it is a very unlikely **2.** __________, one particularly **3.** __________ possibility is that the LHC may find extra dimensions (layers of space and time). If so, the discovery could **4.** __________ powerful technologies to allow people to travel faster than the speed of light.

According to physicist Lawrence Krauss of Arizona State University, **5.** __________ curiosity is the driving force behind the research that is the **6.** __________ to support our current standard of living[2] for generations into the future. "It will help create innovation and enhance the economic future of our children in ways that we don't know," he says.

[1] A **tumor** is an unusual mass of diseased or abnormal cells in the body of a person or animal.
[2] Your **standard of living** is the level of comfort and wealth that you have.

B. Definitions. Match the correct form of the words from the box in **A** with their definitions.

1. well planned, so that it is clear and all parts go well with each other __________
2. suddenly release a powerful force or feeling __________
3. involving a person's ability to think and to understand ideas and information __________
4. interesting or strange __________
5. sensible and careful __________
6. crash into something __________
7. the things on which a belief or way of life are based __________
8. the way in which a situation may develop __________
9. pass someone ahead of you and moving in the same direction __________

Usage

Awesome is most commonly used today as a slang expression of approval.
A: *Have you heard? The boss gave us the rest of the day off.* **B:** *Awesome!*

SUDBURY
155 miles (248 kilometers) wide
1.9 billion years ago

METEOR CRATER
0.73 miles (1.17 kilometers) wide
50,000 years ago

CHESAPEAKE BAY
53 miles (85 kilometers) wide
35 million years ago

CHICXULUB
106 miles (170 kilometers) wide
65 million years ago

VREDEFORT
186 miles (298 kilometers) wide
2 billion years ago

GOSSES BLUFF
14 miles (22 kilometers) wide
143 million years ago

Width of Crater
- More than 100 miles (160 kilometers)
- 51–100 miles (82–160 kilometers)
- 11–50 miles (17–81 kilometers)
- 5–10 miles (8–16 kilometers)
- Less than 5 miles (8 kilometers)

The Threat from Space

The 174 colored dots in these images of Earth are places where **meteorites** have struck our planet and left a **crater** as evidence. These craters vary in **diameter** from less than 8 kilometers (5 miles) across to over 160 kilometers (100 miles) across. The largest craters mean that the meteorite that hit the Earth must have caused a catastrophe that changed the land, climate, and life of our planet. Today, **astronomers** are scanning the sky trying to find the next object on a collision course with our planet, in hopes of giving us the time we need to do something about it.

Before You Read

A. Definitions. Read the information above and match each word in **blue** with its definition.

1. a very large hole in the ground, that has been caused by something hitting it or by an explosion _____

2. a piece of rock or metal from space that enters the Earth's atmosphere, usually burning up but sometimes reaching the ground _____

3. a person who studies the stars, planets, and other natural objects in space _____

4. the length of a straight line that can be drawn across a circle or sphere, passing through the middle of it _____

B. Scan. Quickly scan the reading to find the people on the left. Then match each person with a description (**a–d**). Then read again to check your answers.

1. David Tholen ___   **a.** is a former astronaut.
2. Ann Hodges ___   **b.** noticed an object heading for earth.
3. Ed Lu ___   **c.** thinks nuclear bombs could be the solution.
4. Vadim Simonenko ___   **d.** was hit by a meteorite.

Target Earth

It was just after 9 p.m. on June 18, 2004, at an observatory[1] in Arizona, U.S.A. David Tholen, an astronomer from the University of Hawaii, was scanning the sky for asteroids[2] when he
5 noticed an object headed in the direction of Earth. He and his colleagues hoped to take a closer look later that week but were unfortunately prevented by rain. By the time astronomers finally got another look at it in
10 December of that year, they realized they had a problem. The object was a large asteroid, which they named Apophis after the Egyptian god of evil. Bigger than a sports arena, it comes frighteningly close to our planet every
15 few years. By Christmas, Tholen had calculated that the chance Apophis would smash into Earth on April 13, 2029, was one in 40.

Alarm about the threat started to spread to the public. Then, on December 26, 2004, a real
20 catastrophe struck: the Indian Ocean tsunami, which claimed hundreds of thousands of lives. The public forgot about Apophis. Meanwhile, astronomers[3] had found earlier images of the asteroid. The extra data enabled the scientists
25 to calculate its orbit, and they discovered that it would actually fly safely by Earth in 2029. However, this alarming scenario started a race among scientists to find solutions to the threat of large objects striking Earth.

Near Misses

30 Every day, tons of dust from comets and tiny pieces of asteroids burn up in the Earth's upper atmosphere. Most days, a piece or two of rock or metal, the size of an apple or bigger, actually
35 makes contact with the earth. Yet it's unlikely you'll ever see a meteorite[4] hit the ground, let alone be struck by one. Only one meteorite is known to have ever hit a person. The rock, about the size of a grapefruit, bounced off
40 Ann Hodges's radio and hit her as she lay on her sofa near Sylacauga, Alabama, U.S.A., in November 1954. Somehow, she escaped with only a bruised hip and wrist.

Since then, there have been some spectacular
45 near misses. On August 10, 1972, an object around five meters (16 feet) across and weighing 150 tons traveled through the upper atmosphere. Hundreds of people saw its bright trail that sunny afternoon as it crossed the
50 sky from Utah to Alberta before flying back out into space. On March 22, 1989, a rock as big as 300 meters across came within several hundred thousand kilometers of Earth, which, in astronomical terms, is uncomfortably close.

[1] An **observatory** is a building with a large telescope from which you can study the stars and planets.
[2] An **asteroid** is a large rock moving through outer space.
[3] **Astronomers** are scientists who study the stars, planets, and other natural objects in space.
[4] A **meteorite** is a large piece of rock or metal from space that has landed on Earth.

▲ A meteor impact crater near the town of Halls Creek, Australia.

▲ On June 30, 1908, an asteroid or comet exploded above Tunguska, Siberia, flattening trees across 2,000 square kilometers (800 square miles).

Smash Hits

There is evidence that, in the past, massive comets[5] or asteroids have struck Earth's surface. Thirty-five million years ago, a three-kilometer-wide (two-mile-wide) rock smashed into the ocean floor, 160 kilometers (100 miles) from what is now Washington, D.C., leaving an 85-kilometer-wide (50-mile-wide) crater buried beneath Chesapeake Bay. Another giant rock, called Titan, ten kilometers (six miles) in diameter, smashed into the Gulf of Mexico around 65 million years ago, unleashing thousands of times more energy than all the nuclear weapons on the planet combined. "The whole Earth burned that day," says Ed Lu, a physicist and former astronaut. The chaos and devastation were unimaginable. Three-quarters of all life forms, including the dinosaurs, went extinct.

Astronomers have identified numerous asteroids big enough to cause a catastrophe for the entire planet. None is on course to do so in our lifetimes, but there are many smaller asteroids that could strike in the near future, with devastating effects. On June 30, 1908, an object the size of a 15-story building fell in Tunguska, a remote part of Siberia. The object—an asteroid or a small comet—exploded several kilometers before impact, burning and blowing down trees across 2,000 square kilometers (800 square miles). Clouds of tiny particles of dust and ice filled the sky. The particles reflected the sun's light onto the Earth, and for days people in Europe could read newspapers outdoors at night.

The next time a large object falls out of the sky, we may be taken by surprise—currently, there is no early warning system for near-Earth objects. However, over the next decade, sky surveys, like the one being done by Tholen, should begin filling that gap. Astronomers are compiling a list of thousands of asteroids to help us anticipate the next strike. "Every couple of weeks," says former astronaut Lu, "we're going to be finding another asteroid with, like, a one-in-a-thousand chance of hitting the Earth."

What Can Be Done?

Within decades, the world's leaders may be faced with a dilemma: what to do about an incoming object. Few experts are giving this much thought, according to NASA astronomer David Morrison "The number would roughly staff a couple of shifts[6] at McDonalds," he says. Ed Lu, the former astronaut, is one of them.

◄ Scientist Peter Schultz studies impact zones by firing tiny pieces of aluminium into a sandpit at 20,000 kilometers an hour (12,000 miles per hour). "Standing downrange you'd be broiled [cooked] by the hot blast . . ." he says. "Think of it as a hot landslide, without a mountain."

[5] A **comet** is a bright object with a long tail that travels around the sun.

[6] A **shift** is a group of workers who work for a set period before being replaced with another group.

▲ An artist's impression of one proposal for moving asteroids. The spacecraft's gravity pulls the asteroid to a new position.

110 He is working on a plan that employs a spaceship to deflect asteroids headed for Earth. "We were originally thinking about how you would land on an asteroid and push it," he says. "But that doesn't work well." If the

115 surface isn't solid, you have trouble landing or keeping anything on it. Moreover, asteroids are always rotating. "If you're pushing and the thing is rotating, the pushing just cancels out,"[7] Lu says.

120 Pulling the asteroid along would be much easier. "Rather than having a physical line between you and the thing you're towing,[8] you're just using the force of gravity between them," Lu says. A nearby spacecraft would pull

125 the asteroid off course very slowly but steadily, using only gravity. And over the long distances of space, just a slight change in course could mean missing Earth by tens of thousands of kilometers.

130 ## An Asteroid Bomb?

The drawback to Lu's plan is that it would work only for asteroids up to a few hundred meters across that could be engaged far from Earth. If the rock is small, we could try hitting

135 it with a spacecraft. When all else fails, and for large asteroids and comets, only one strategy has a chance of working: nuclear bombs.

Russian scientist Vadim Simonenko and his colleagues concluded that the best way to

140 deflect an asteroid up to 1.5 kilometers (one mile) or so wide would be to explode a nuclear bomb nearby. The explosion would destroy smaller rocks. For larger ones, the explosion would burn a layer of rock off the asteroid's

145 surface. The expanding gas would act as a rocket motor, pushing the asteroid onto a new course.

Apophis may pose a great challenge for world leaders. As it swings past Earth in 2029, there's

150 a slim chance that Earth's gravity will deflect the asteroid just enough to put it on a certain collision course with our planet on the next pass, in 2036. The odds are currently estimated at one in 45,000, so a strike is very unlikely.

155 Meanwhile, astronomers will continue to track Apophis to learn if it will merely taunt us again, or actually strike.

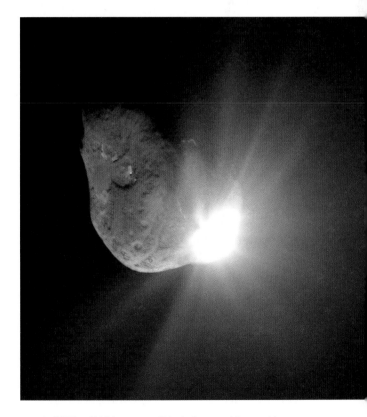

▲ In 2005, a NASA spacecraft tested a comet by crashing into it, yet barely shifted its path.

[7] If one thing **cancels out** another thing, the two things have opposite effects, so that when they are combined no real effect is produced.
[8] If a vehicle **tows** something, it pulls it along behind it.

Reading Comprehension

A. Multiple Choice. Choose the best answer for each question.

Purpose   **1.** What is the purpose of this reading?
- a. to explain the problem of objects hitting Earth and to explore solutions
- b. to give reasons why an impact from space is very unlikely
- c. to convince the reader that Apophis will probably strike the Earth
- d. to encourage the reader to get involved in saving the Earth

Sequence   **2.** Which of the following impacts is the oldest?
- a. Chesapeake Bay
- b. The Gulf of Mexico
- c. Tunguska
- d. Sylacauga

Reference   **3.** In line 95, *filling that gap* means _____.
- a. covering the space between the sun and the Earth
- b. adding to our knowledge about objects that could strike the Earth
- c. measuring the gap between the ground and a falling object
- d. completing our understanding of why objects explode above the Earth

Detail   **4.** Which method of deflection wouldn't work well on a rotating asteroid?
- a. exploding a nuclear bomb nearby
- b. hitting it with a spacecraft
- c. pulling it using gravity
- d. landing on it and pushing it

Detail   **5.** What might change the course of Apophis so that it hits the Earth within the next 30 years?
- a. its own gravity
- b. a spacecraft's gravity
- c. the Earth's gravity
- d. a comet's gravity

Critical Thinking

Which of the methods suggested in the passage do you think would be most effective in preventing a catastrophe? Can you think of any other options?

B. Sequencing. Number each event in the correct place on the timeline.

1. A large object explodes above Tunguska, destroying a vast number of trees.
2. Sports-arena-sized asteroid Apophis is predicted to pass safely by Earth.
3. Ten-kilometer-wide Titan smashes into Earth, killing three-quarters of life on Earth.
4. A three-kilometer-wide rock impacts the Earth near Washington, D.C.
5. A 150-ton meteorite burns brightly as it streaks through Earth's atmosphere.
6. A grapefruit-sized meteorite hits Ann Hodges after bouncing off her radio.

65 million years ago   1908   1972

35 million years ago   1954   2026

Vocabulary Practice

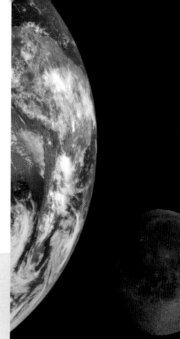

A. Completion. Complete the information below using the correct form of words from the box. One word is extra.

former	deflect	atmosphere	drawback	spectacular	pose

How did the Earth's moon form? This question has been
1. _____ by scientists for many years, and four main theories have been proposed.

> **1.** The moon is a piece of the Earth which broke off long ago.
> **2.** The Earth's gravity captured the moon as it traveled by.
> **3.** The Earth and moon simply formed together from the same cloud of material.
> **4.** The moon was formed when another object collided with the Earth.

2. _____, the first three theories were each taken seriously, but, one by one, these three theories became unpopular as researchers exposed their **3.** _____. Today, the fourth theory is the most widely accepted. This theory maintains that another planet collided with Earth, and that pieces of rocky material were **4.** _____ into space. That material became our moon.

▲ Scientists today believe the moon formed after a planet-sized object collided with the Earth.

Thanks to new powerful computers, scientists have been able to learn the size of the planet that struck the Earth, and exactly how the resulting **5.** _____ crash could have helped form the moon. They hypothesize that in order to create a moon that has the size and speed of the Earth's, the object which struck Earth 4.5 billion years ago would have had to have been about the size of the planet Mars.

B. Completion. Complete the sentences below using the correct form of words in the box. One word is extra.

atmosphere	catastrophe	dilemma	drawback	engage	motor

1. In many science fiction novels, spaceships are sent to _____ enemy aliens before they reach Earth.

2. Governments face a(n) _____: whether to spend money on the space program or to use the money to improve life here on Earth.

3. Without enough gravity, a planet or moon cannot hold on to gases that could form its _____.

4. To help robot vehicles navigate the rough surface of Mars, each of their six wheels has its own _____.

5. Although at various times in history people have predicted a great _____ that would bring an end to human civilization, they have so far been wrong.

> **Word Link** The prefix **di–** can have the meaning of *two* in certain words, e.g., *di*lemma—*a situation involving a difficult choice between two or more things*; *di*alog—*a conversation between two people*; *di*atomic—*involving two atoms*.

Solar System

A. Preview. You will hear the names of these planets in the video in order of their distance from the sun, starting with the closest planet. Match the planets (**1–8**) with their names (**a–h**).

___ a. Venus   ___ d. Earth   ___ g. Jupiter
___ b. Uranus   ___ e. Mercury   ___ h. Mars
___ c. Neptune   ___ f. Saturn

B. Summarize. Watch the video, *Solar System*. Then complete the summary below using the correct form of words from the box. Two words are extra.

intriguing	intellectual	foundation	awesome
scenario	atmosphere	pose	cohere
dilemma	unleash	engaged	formerly

Scientists believe that our solar system formed four and a half billion years ago according to the following **1.** _____. First, the huge cloud of dust and gas that forms the **2.** _____ of our solar system collapsed into a dense mass. It began to rotate and flatten into a disc. Over time, the center grew hotter and hotter until it became our sun.

Over millions of years, the remaining dust and gases **3.** _____ to form planets and moons. Mercury is closest to the sun, and is known for its extremes of temperatures. Next is Earth-sized Venus, whose **4.** _____ traps the sun's heat and raises the surface temperature to nearly 480 degrees Celsius (900 degrees Fahrenheit) The third planet is Earth, an active planet that is constantly **5.** _____ in change. Mars is a dry planet with red soil, deep canyons, and polar ice. The fifth and largest planet is Jupiter. Its great red spot is a(n) **6.** _____ storm twice as wide as Earth. After Jupiter comes Saturn, the second largest planet, famous for its rings. Seventh from the sun is Uranus, a planet which is **7.** _____ because it alone rotates on its side. Neptune, the eighth planet, is perhaps the windiest place in the solar system, with winds of over 2,000 kilometers per hour (1,200 miles per hour).

Farther on is Pluto, which was **8.** _____ considered to be a planet, but that opinion has changed. Pluto's small size **9.** _____ a rather difficult **10.** _____ for astronomers—whether to continue to call it a planet or to reclassify it. In 2006 they solved the problem by reclassifying it as a "dwarf planet."

C. Think About It.

1. Which of the planets do you think is the most interesting? Why?

2. Why does life only seem to exist on Earth and not on any of the other planets in our solar system?

To learn more about science frontiers, visit elt.heinle.com/explorer

UNIT 11
Green Living

Discuss these questions with a partner.

1. Think about items you own. What will happen to them when you no longer need them?

2. Do you recycle? What items are recyclable?

3. What do you think the expression "Waste not, want not" means?

▲ A thermal image (showing heat) of a young girl standing in front of an open refrigerator door.

173

11A A Precious Resource

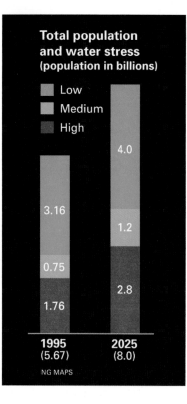

Total population and water stress (population in billions)

- Low
- Medium
- High

1995 (5.67): High 1.76, Medium 0.75, Low 3.16
2025 (8.0): High 2.8, Medium 1.2, Low 4.0

NG MAPS

◀ **A Stressful Future**

Between 1995 and 2025, a billion more people will join those already living under a high level of water stress. Add the people who face a medium level of water stress, and four billion people—half the planet's population—will have an insufficient supply of water.

A Thirstier World ▶

Because of irrigated agriculture, the industrial revolution, and a population explosion, humans use 45 times as much water as they did three centuries ago. Irrigation, which accounts for 70 percent of water use, grows 40 percent of the world's food and makes it possible to feed the planet's 6.2 billion people.

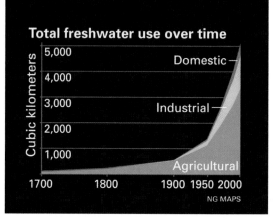

Total freshwater use over time

Cubic kilometers: 1,000–5,000

Domestic
Industrial
Agricultural

1700 1800 1900 1950 2000

NG MAPS

Before You Read

A. Multiple Choice. Read the information and look at the charts above. Then answer the questions.

1. Which of the following accounted for the smallest percentage of world water use in 2000?
   a. agricultural   b. industrial   c. domestic

2. In 1995, how many people were living under high water stress?
   a. 1.76 billion   b. 3.16 billion   c. 5.67 billion

3. Between the years 1925 and 2000, about how much has total freshwater use increased?
   a. two times   b. five times   c. ten times

4. How many more people will suffer high water stress in 2025 compared with 1995?
   a. 0.84 billion   b. 1.04 billion   c. 2.8 billion

B. Predict. The Indian village of Goratalai has suffered years of drought. What do you think they plan to do about it? Circle **a**, **b**, or **c**. Then read the passage to check your ideas.

   a. They plan to truck in bottled water.
   b. They plan to build a dam to catch rainwater.
   c. They plan to stop using water for agriculture.

Water Worries

▲ Cupping his hands to drink from a new well, Soti Sotiar is among a lucky few. Only 10 to 20 percent of rural Ethiopians have access to clean drinking water.

1 In the Castile-La Mancha region of south central Spain, Julio Escudero, a 74-year-old former fisherman, fondly[1] recalls an area on the Guadiana River called Los Ojos—"the eyes."
5 Large underground springs bubbled up into the river, where Escudero and his community fished for carp and crayfish. "I would sit in my boat six or seven meters away and just watch the water coming up," Escudero says. "Now
10 it looks like the moon." Los Ojos doesn't exist anymore: that stretch of the river dried up in 1984. Additionally, 46,000 acres of surrounding wetlands[2] —vital not only to the local people but also to countless species of
15 plants and wildlife—have disappeared.

As farming in the region has increased, La Mancha has witnessed an explosion of well[3] digging in the past 40 years that has lowered the water table and diverted water from rivers
20 and streams. The number of wells has grown from 1,500 in 1960 to an official count of 21,000 today, and some experts say the real number, including illegal wells, could surpass 50,000.

A Global Problem

25 La Mancha is just one of many places facing water shortages. This century, many countries will face the same dilemma that has confronted the people of Spain: how to balance human
30 needs with the requirements of natural systems that are vital for sustaining life on Earth. The United Nations recently outlined the extent of the problem, saying that 2.7 billion people would face severe water shortages by 2025 if
35 consumption continues at current rates. Today, an estimated 1.2 billion people drink unclean water, and about 2.5 billion lack proper toilets or waste disposal systems. More than five million people die each year from diseases
40 related to unclean water. All over the globe, humans are pumping water out of the ground faster than it can be replenished. In this difficult situation, water conservationists, such as Rajendra Singh in India and Neil MacLeod
45 in South Africa, are working to find solutions to the water crisis. Both have found innovative ways to improve their local water situations.

[1] If you remember something **fondly**, you remember it with pleasure.
[2] A **wetland** is an area of very wet, muddy land with wild plants growing in it. You can also refer to an area like this as wetlands.
[3] A **well** is a hole in the ground from which a supply of water is extracted.

▲ An Indian woman fills a bowl of water from a canal near the Hooghly River, in Kolkata.

India: A Hero in a Thirsty Land

On arriving at the Indian village of Goratalai, Rajendra Singh was greeted by a group of about 50 people. He smiled and addressed the villagers:

"How many households[4] do you have?"

"Eighty."

"It's been four years without much rain," interjected[5] a woman. "And we don't have a proper dam to catch the water."

"Do you have any spots where a dam could go?" asked Singh, 43, who has a full head of black hair and a thick beard, both with a touch of gray.

"Yes, two spots."

"Will the whole village be willing to work there?"

"Yes," they all replied together.

"I would like to help you," Singh told them, "but the work has to be done by you. You will have to provide one third of the project through your labor, and the remaining two thirds I will arrange."

The villagers clapped, the women started to sing, and the group hiked to a place in the nearby rocky hills. Singh examined the area, and after a few minutes declared, "This is an ideal site." His organization would provide the engineering advice and materials; the villagers would supply the work. The 30-foot-high earthen dam and reservoir,[6] known as a *johad*, could be finished in three months, before the start of the rainy season. If the rains were plentiful, the reservoir would not only provide supplemental surface water for drinking and agriculture, but would also replenish dry wells. "You will not see the results immediately. But soon the dam will begin to raise the water level in your wells," Singh told the villagers.

Soon Singh was gone, heading to a nearby village that had also requested help building a johad. In recent years, Singh's johads have sprung up all over Rajasthan—an estimated 4,500 dams in about 1,000 villages, all built using local labor and native materials. His movement has caught on, he says, because it puts control over water in the hands of villagers. "If they feel a johad is their own, they will maintain it," said Singh. "This is a very sustainable, self-reliant system. I can say confidently that if we can manage rain in India in traditional ways, there will be sufficient water for our growing population."

South Africa: Waste Not, Want Not

In South Africa, Neil MacLeod took over as head of Durban Metro Water Services in 1992. The situation he found was a catastrophe. Durban had one million people living in the city and another 1.5 million people who lived in poverty just outside it. Macleod and his engineers determined that the entire city was rife[7] with broken water pipes, leaky toilets, and faulty plumbing[8] whereby 42 percent of the region's water was simply being wasted. "We inherited 700 reported leaks and bursts.

The water literally just ran down the streets," recalled Macleod. "Demand for water was growing four percent a year, and we thought we'd have to build another dam by 2000."

---

[4] A **household** is all the people in a family or group who live together in a house.

[5] If you **interject**, you interrupt someone else who is speaking.

[6] A **reservoir** is a lake that is used for storing water before it is supplied to people.

[7] If you describe something bad as **rife** in a place, it is very common.

[8] The **plumbing** in a building consists of the water and drainage pipes, bathtubs, and toilets in it.

▲ With a growing population, and breaking water pipes, Mexico City must truck water to many residents. Leaking pipes claim nearly a third of the city's water.

▲ Residents of Las Vegas, in Nevada, the United States's driest state, use more than double the water most Americans do. At the Bellagio Hotel, 100 million liters (27 million gallons) of water dance to music every night.

Macleod's crews began repairing and replacing water pipes. They put water meters on residences, replaced eight-liter toilets with four-liter models, and changed
120 wasteful showers and water taps. To ensure that the poor would receive a basic supply of water, Macleod installed tanks in homes and apartments to provide 190 liters (50 gallons) of water a day free to each household.

125 Water consumption in the city of Durban is now less than it was in 1996, even as 800,000 more people have received service. Through sensible water use, Durban's conservation measures paid for themselves within a year.
130 Macleod has assured the city that no new dams will be needed in the coming decades, despite the expected addition of about 300,000 inhabitants.

In Durban, Macleod has also turned to
135 water recycling. At the water recycling plant, wastewater is turned into clean water in just 12 hours. Most people are unable to discern a difference between the usual city drinking water and the treated wastewater, although
140 it is actually intended for industrial purposes. Macleod boasts, "Go to many areas of the world, and they're drinking far worse water than this."

Some people still hope that new technology,
145 such as the desalination[9] of seawater, will solve the world's water problems. "But the fact is, water conservation is where the big gains are to be made," says Sandra Postel of the Global Water Policy Project. The dedication
150 and resourcefulness of people like Rajendra Singh and Neil Macleod offer inspiration for implementing timely and lasting solutions to the world's water concerns.

▲ A girl swims at Dubai's Wild Wadi Water Park. Oil-rich Dubai can afford to do what most water-scarce nations can't—desalinate seawater for all its freshwater needs.

[9] If you **desalinate** seawater, you remove all the salt from it.

Reading Comprehension

A. Multiple Choice. Choose the best answer for each question.

Gist **1.** Another title for this reading could be _____.
   a. *Water for the Rich, Not for the Poor*
   b. *Why We Waste Water: Two Points of View*
   c. *Water Shortages and Problem Solvers*
   d. *Politics and Water: Fighting for a Drink*

Critical Thinking

Which of the water conservation strategies in the reading do you think would be most effective in your country? Why?

Detail **2.** Which of these statements about Castile-La Mancha is NOT true?
   a. Its situation is common to many places around the world.
   b. Over-fishing has caused a great deal of environmental damage.
   c. Illegal well digging is a significant problem.
   d. The Los Ojos area has been dry for over 20 years.

Detail **2.** What is Rajendra Singh's solution to water shortages?
   a. build dams and reservoirs
   b. pump more groundwater
   c. fix leaky pipes
   d. desalinate seawater

Detail **4.** Which of these methods did MacLeod NOT make use of in Durban?
   a. repairing water pipes
   b. replacing toilets
   c. installing water meters
   d. building a new dam

Paraphrase **5.** Which of the following did Sandra Postel mean by "water conservation is where the big gains are to be made" (lines 147–148)?
   a. Water conservation is an opportunity for large profits for businesses.
   b. Water conservation is the most effective method to address water shortages.
   c. Water conservation technology is still in need of many improvements.
   d. Water conservation is required by law in order to ensure large gains.

B. Summary. Complete the information with words from the reading.

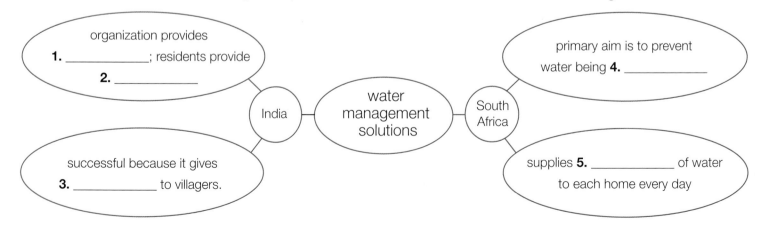

organization provides
1. _____; residents provide
2. _____

India — water management solutions — South Africa

primary aim is to prevent water being 4. _____

successful because it gives
3. _____ to villagers.

supplies 5. _____ of water to each home every day

Vocabulary Practice

A. Completion. Complete the information with the correct form of words from the box. Two words are extra.

dam	dedicated	discern	divert	inherit
whereby	leak	replenish	surpass	willing

▲ Backyard swimming pools in Phoenix, Arizona—one of the United States's driest states

Reports indicate that rising global water consumption rates, poor water management, and increased global temperatures could mean that our children and grandchildren will **1.** _____ a world in which two out of every three people in the world are affected by water shortages. By the year 2025, the world population will **2.** _____ 8 billion, 3 billion of whom could, according to the World Resources Institute, face chronic water shortages.

Some scientists say that success or failure will depend on whether people can **3.** _____ the seriousness of the situation and take action to use less water. One problem is that when water is cheap, people don't see the need to conserve. The European Environment Agency found, for example, that 75 percent of the water that households in Albania pay for is wasted because of **4.** _____ in their pipes.

If water becomes more expensive, people might be **5.** _____ to use water more efficiently. For example, during the 1993 droughts, an average farmer in California paid about ten cents a ton for water, compared to three cents a ton after rain had **6.** _____ the supply. At ten cents, many farmers in California started growing crops that require less water. When the price of water was raised in Chile, the average amount of water **7.** _____ for use in irrigation decreased by nearly 26 percent.

One notable success story is the Working for Water program in South Africa. In the past, water was priced at a similar rate for all users. However, the program has changed the way individuals are charged for water, instituting a system **8.** _____ people who conserve water pay less. Their new system is an important example for a world in which, as the population continues to grow, water becomes more important every day.

B. Definitions. Match the words from the box in **A** with their correct definition.

1. be better than, or have more of a particular quality than _____
2. a wall that is built across a river in order to make a lake _____
3. giving a lot of time and effort to something important _____
4. receive something from the people who used to have it _____
5. be aware of something and know what it is _____
6. to cause money or resources to be used for a different purpose _____
7. make something full or complete again _____
8. a crack or hole that a substance such as a liquid or gas can pass through _____

Thesaurus   **leak** Also look up: (*v.*) drip, ooze, seep, trickle; (*n.*) crack, hole, opening

11B

The Trouble with E-Waste

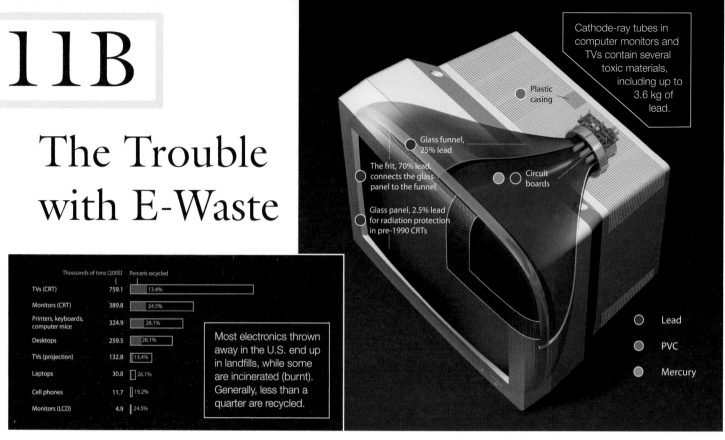

Cathode-ray tubes in computer monitors and TVs contain several toxic materials, including up to 3.6 kg of lead.

Plastic casing

Glass funnel, 25% lead

The frit, 70% lead, connects the glass panel to the funnel.

Glass panel, 2.5% lead for radiation protection in pre-1990 CRTs

Circuit boards

	Thousands of tons (2005)	Percent recycled
TVs (CRT)	759.1	13.4%
Monitors (CRT)	389.8	24.5%
Printers, keyboards, computer mice	324.9	26.1%
Desktops	259.5	26.1%
TVs (projection)	132.8	13.4%
Laptops	30.8	26.1%
Cell phones	11.7	19.2%
Monitors (LCD)	4.9	24.5%

Most electronics thrown away in the U.S. end up in landfills, while some are incinerated (burnt). Generally, less than a quarter are recycled.

○ Lead
○ PVC
○ Mercury

TVs, personal computers, and other electronics contain parts that pose no danger in daily use but become toxic without proper disposal. This electronics waste (or **e-waste**) contains dangerous substances such as:

Lead A toxin that can harm the nerves, kidneys, and reproductive system.

PVC A plastic material used to make cases for electronic goods. When burned, it releases toxic chemicals called dioxins that can cause cancer.

Mercury The only metal that is liquid at normal temperatures. Mercury has been linked to brain and kidney damage.

Before You Read

A. Quiz. Look at the information above. Then read the sentences and circle true (**T**) or false (**F**).

1. Lead makes up one quarter of the material in a CRT monitor's glass funnel. **T** **F**
2. Mercury is found in the plastic casing that surrounds a CRT monitor. **T** **F**
3. In the U.S., a larger percentage of desktops are recycled than laptops. **T** **F**
4. Fewer than one in four televisions are recycled. **T** **F**

B. Predict. The reading passage describes a project called "David." What do you think it is? Check (✔) your answer. Then read the passage to see if you were right.

❏ a program of free clinics for children poisoned by e-waste

❏ a giant machine that recycles electronics

❏ a political movement to control e-waste exports

Technology as Trash

▲ Hi-tech waste floats in a canal in Accra, Ghana.

1 As the morning rain stops in Accra, the capital city of Ghana, and the sun heats the humid air, a terrible-smelling black smoke begins to rise above the vast Agbogbloshie Market. Past the

5 vegetable and tire merchants is a scrap[1] market filled with piles of old and broken electronics waste. This waste, consisting of broken TVs, computers, and smashed[2] monitors, is known as "e-waste." Further beyond the scrap market

10 are many small fires, fueled by old automobile tires, which are burning away the plastic covering from valuable wire in the e-waste. People walk through the smoke—a highly poisonous mixture of chemicals—with their

15 arms full of brightly-colored computer wire. Many of them are children.

Israel Mensah, 20, explains how he makes his living here. Each day scrap sellers bring loads of old electronics. Mensah's friends and family

20 buy a few computers or TVs. They break them apart to remove valuable metals and wires, as well as any parts that can be resold. Then, they burn the plastic covering off the wire and sell it to replenish their supply of e-waste. The key

25 to making money is speed, not safety. "The gas goes to your nose and you feel something in your head," Mensah says as he knocks his fist against the back of his head. "Then you get sick in your head and your chest." Broken

30 computer and monitor cases are unwanted and thrown in a nearby lagoon.[3] The next day, the rain will wash them into the ocean.

The problem of e-waste

E-waste is being produced on a scale never

35 seen before. Computers and other electronic equipment become obsolete in just a few years, leaving customers with little choice but to buy newer ones to keep up. Tens of millions of tons of computers, TVs, VCRs, monitors, cell

40 phones, and other equipment are discarded each year.

▲ A boy carries copper wires from old electronic devices at a market in Ghana. Power plugs in his bundle point to Europe—where laws ban shipping such waste to poor nations—as a likely origin.

[1] **Scrap** is material from old, damaged cars or machines.
[2] If you **smash** something or if it smashes, it breaks into many pieces.
[3] A **lagoon** is an area of calm sea water that is separated from the ocean by a line of rock or sand.

◄ Poisonous smoke surrounds a young man watching piles of burning computer wire in Accra, Ghana. Metal buyers won't accept copper wire until the plastic is burned off.

Unfortunately, in most of the world, the bulk of all this waste ends up in landfills,[4] where it poisons the environment—e-waste contains a variety of toxic substances such as lead, mercury, and arsenic that leak into the ground. Recycling is in many ways the ideal solution to the problem. E-waste contains significant amounts of valuable metals such as silver, gold, and copper that make it attractive to recycle. In theory, recycling gold from old computers is far more efficient—and less environmentally destructive—than digging it from the earth. The problem is that a large percentage of e-waste that is dropped off for recycling in wealthy countries is sold and diverted to the developing world—to countries like Ghana. As quantities of e-waste increase worldwide, it poses an increasing threat to the health of people living in the developing world

To address the problem of the international trade in e-waste, 170 nations signed the 1989 Basel Convention, an agreement that requires that developed nations notify developing nations of hazardous waste shipments coming into the country. Then, in 1995, after pressure from environmental groups and developing nations, the Basel Convention was modified to ban hazardous waste shipments to poor countries completely. Although the ban hasn't yet taken effect, the European Union, where recycling infrastructure is well developed, has already written it into their laws. One law holds manufacturers responsible for the safe disposal of electronics they produce.

David and Goliath

Companies like Creative Recycling Systems in Tampa, Florida, are hoping to profit from clean e-waste recycling. The key to their business is a colossal, building-size machine that is able to separate electronic products into their component[5] materials. Company president Jon Yob called his project "David," because it has to do battle with a "Goliath"[6] in the form of the awesome quantity of e-waste in the United States.

David is able to avoid the contamination occurring in places like the market in Accra. As the machine's steel teeth break up computers, TVs, and other e-waste, toxic substances are naturally released, but there are machines installed inside David whereby all the toxic

[4] A **landfill** is a large, deep hole in which large amounts of garbage are buried.
[5] The **components** of something are the parts from which it is made.
[6] In a well-known story from the Bible, a small, young man named **David** fights a very large, strong one named **Goliath**. Surprisingly, David defeats Goliath.
[7] **Ambient** air is air that surrounds you.

▲ In Karachi, Pakistan, Salman Aziz, 11, harvests bits of metal from computer mice.

▲ Workers at a disassembly line in Austria sort smashed electronics. European laws require electronic manufacturers to cover recycling costs when their products are discarded.

dust is removed from the process. "The air that comes out is cleaner than the ambient[7] air in
95 the building," explains vice president Joe Yob (Jon's brother).

David can handle some 70,000 tons (150 million pounds) of electronics a year. Although this is only a fraction of the total, it wouldn't
100 take many more machines like David to process the entire U.S.A.'s output of high-tech trash. Unfortunately, under current policies, domestic processing of e-waste is not compulsory, and while shipping waste abroad is
105 ethically questionable, it is still more profitable than processing it safely in the U.S.A. "We can't compete economically with people who do it wrong, who ship it overseas," says Joe Yob. The company is hoping that the United
110 States government will, some time in the near future, create laws deterring people from sending e-waste overseas.

Ultimately, shipping e-waste overseas may actually come back to harm the developed
115 world. Jeffrey Weidenhamer, a chemist at Ashland University in Ohio, bought some jewelry made in a developing country for his class to analyze. It was distressing that the jewelry contained high amounts of lead,
120 but not a great surprise, as jewelry with lead has turned up before in U.S. stores. More revealing were the quantities of metals such as copper and tin mixed in with the lead. Weidenhamer argued in a scientific paper that
125 the proportions of these metals suggest that the jewelry was made from recycled computer parts.

Since the developed world is sending large quantities of materials containing lead to
130 developing nations, it's to be expected that those countries will make use of them in their manufacturing processes. "It's not at all surprising things are coming full circle and now we're getting contaminated products back,"
135 says Weidenhamer. In a global economy, it's no longer possible to get rid of something by sending it to other countries. As the old saying goes, "What goes around comes around."

Reading Comprehension

A. Multiple Choice. Choose the best answer for each question.

Main Idea **1.** What is the main idea of the reading?
   a. E-waste provides business opportunities for very few people.
   b. E-waste is enriching the developing world.
   c. The world is facing a serious e-waste problem.
   d. Recycling of e-waste should be stopped.

Critical Thinking

What steps not mentioned in the passage can people or government take to address the problem of e-waste in the world?

Detail **2.** Why are there fires at the Agbogbloshie market?
   a. to burn unwanted computer and monitor cases
   b. to burn off the covering from metal wires
   c. to keep people warm as they recycle e-waste
   d. to signal to scrap sellers that e-waste is available

Vocabulary **3.** In line 38, what does the phrase *keep up* mean?
   a. to keep the computer they already have
   b. to get educated about computers currently sold
   c. to maintain a positive attitude toward computers
   d. to obtain the latest, best-performing computers

Inference **4.** Which problem does Creative Recycling Systems have?
   a. It takes too long to build large recycling machines.
   b. They can't handle all the e-waste produced in the U.S.
   c. It costs more to use their service than to ship e-waste abroad.
   d. They are breaking current laws by shipping e-waste overseas.

Paraphrase **5.** In line 138 it says, "What goes around comes around." What does this mean?
   a. Your actions have consequences that will eventually affect you.
   b. Whether or not your actions are correct, bad things will happen to you.
   c. No matter how unfairly you are treated, continue to treat others fairly.
   d. Don't worry about the actions of others because you can't control them.

B. Completion. Complete the flow chart. Fill in each blank with up to three words from the reading.

The E-Waste Trail
1. In theory, the best way to deal with e-waste is to _____ it.
2. E-waste from the developed world is often diverted to Ghana and other countries in the _____.
3. Precious metals removed from e-waste have been found to have high amounts of _____, such as arsenic.
4. The Basel convention aims to completely stop _____ to poor countries.
5. Products made from the contaminated metals are sold back to developed countries, for example in _____ sold in American stores.

Vocabulary Practice

A. Completion. Complete the paragraphs below using the correct form of the words in the box. One word is extra.

hazardous	discard	pile
substance	notify	infrastructure

Reuse and recycle: these well-known ideas for dealing with trash are being employed to handle e-waste such as old computers, cell phones, and televisions. Many companies send used electronic items from the United States and the European Union to developing nations. They claim to be recycling, and also helping the developing world modernize its **1.** _____. However, the reality may be quite different.

▲ Customers shop for used televisions at a secondhand electronics market in Lagos, Nigeria.

The Basel Action Network of Seattle, Washington, recently reported that three-quarters of the supposedly reusable electronics shipped to Lagos, Nigeria, are in fact broken. Consequently, **2.** _____ of e-waste end up being **3.** _____ along rivers and roads. Often it's picked apart by the desperately poor, who come in contact with toxic **4.** _____—such as lead—in the broken equipment. Lead is known to be especially **5.** _____ to the health of growing children.

Richard Guttierez of the Basel Action Network believes companies in developed nations pay lip service[1] to recycling while actually disposing of their e-waste as cheaply as possible, leaving the developing world to deal with the problems it causes.

[1] **Paying lip service** is agreeing with or supporting something using words, but not really meaning it.

B. Words in Context. Complete each sentence with the best answer.

1. A computer described as colossal must be extremely _____.
   a. large   b. small
2. The word distressing is commonly used to describe _____.
   a. problems   b. gifts
3. If a file on your computer has been modified, it has been _____.
   a. lost   b. changed
4. If you are notified about something, you are _____ about it.
   a. told   b. angry
5. Technology that is obsolete is _____.
   a. very new   b. no longer useful

Word Partnership	Use **substance** with: (adj.) **banned** substance, **chemical** substance, **natural** substance

Droughts

A. Preview. You will hear these words in the video. Match each word with its definition.

1. ___ drought	**a.** to ruin the land by planting too many vegetables and fruits in an area
2. ___ famine	**b.** a relatively short period of time during which no rain falls
3. ___ overgraze	**c.** a situation in which large numbers of people have little or no food, and many of them die
4. ___ overcrop	**d.** a long period of time during which no rain falls
5. ___ dry spell	**e.** to allow too many farm animals to eat and destroy plants in an area

B. Summarize. Watch the video, *Droughts*. Then complete the summary below using the correct form of words from the box. One word is extra.

colossal	willing	divert	hazardous
whereby	infrastructure	modify	replenish
surpass	distress		

▲ Farmer and ox work in a rice field cracked by drought in Cambodia.

The causes of droughts can be natural. Droughts are sometimes caused by long-term high pressure systems **1.** _____ rain clouds are prevented from forming. Long droughts are **2.** _____ to all living things including crops, animals, and people.

Human causes of droughts include **3.** _____ water away from areas that need it for agricultural purposes or to **4.** _____ city water supplies. Overcropping and overgrazing can worsen the effects of a drought. Such effects include soil erosion, dead crops, and forest fires. Droughts can result in high food prices, causing financial **5.** _____ for many. Famine caused by droughts killed over 40 million people in the 20th century alone.

The 1930s drought in the central United States caused widespread crop failures. The clouds of dust in the air were so **6.** _____ that it became known as the Dust Bowl. In some places, the drought lasted eight years. Other droughts, though, have **7.** _____ the Dust Bowl's severity, lasting for decades or even centuries.

It may be possible to avoid some droughts in the future if we humans can **8.** _____ the ways we use land and water. However, even if we are **9.** _____ to change our ways, there is little we can do to stop droughts which are caused by natural processes.

C. Think About It.

1. How much water do you think you use in a day?

2. Which areas of the world suffer from droughts? Why are those areas most affected?

To learn more about green living, visit elt.heinle.com/explorer

UNIT 12
Quality of Life

Discuss these questions with a partner.

1. Where in the world do you think people have the highest quality of life?

2. Do you think your lifestyle is better or worse than your grandparents'? How?

3. Who is the oldest person you've met? Why do you think some people can live to a very old age?

12A

The Kingdom of Happiness

▲ Four Bhutanese farmers take a lunch break from working in the rice fields.

The Last Shangri-la

Shangri-la is the mythical permanently happy land deep in the Himalayas that features in British author James Hilton's 1933 novel Lost Horizon. There, completely isolated from the outside world, people live in health and harmony.

The country of Bhutan has often been called "the last Shangri-la." It is a small mountain nation situated in the Himalayas, which, until the 1960s, was cut off from the outside world. But, unlike Shangri-la, a policy of isolation meant that Bhutan's health care system, school system, roads, and other areas of infrastructure remained backward.

In recent years, Bhutan has been steadily opening itself up to the modern world. Its previous and current kings have tried to carefully manage Bhutan's modernization and engagement with the outside world, hoping to avoid the problems of change through *Gross National Happiness*, a concept of development that puts the well-being of Bhutan's people first.

Before You Read

A. Discussion. Look at the information about Bhutan above. Then answer the questions below.

Bhutan allowed television to be broadcast for the first time in 1999. If it had been your decision, which television programs would have been broadcast first (in translation, if necessary)? Which would have been broadcast later or not at all? Give reasons for your choices.

B. Scan. The government's plan for the Gross National Happiness of the Bhutanese people has four parts, or "pillars." Try to guess one or more of them. Then scan the reading passage to check your ideas.

Bhutan's Great Experiment

▲ Morning studies done, monks at Kurjey Lhakhang monastery head out for lunch.

1   First come the high, clear notes[1] of a ceremonial trumpet, then the Buddhist pilgrims[2] move toward the sound. The sun has set behind the mountains over Thimphu, capital of the
5   Himalayan kingdom of Bhutan, and the day's final ritual is set to begin. Along the edges of the crowd stand peasants, some of whom have taken three days to get here from their remote villages. For many, this is their first visit to the big city,
10 likely the only capital in the world without a single traffic light. A group of Buddhist monks,[3] arms linked and wearing wine-colored robes, has assembled in the central plaza. Everyone presses forward to get a look at a small boy, dressed in
15 cool, urban clothing, standing in the center of the circle.

As the rhythm accelerates, the boy—seven-year-old Kinzang Norbu—throws himself to the ground, spinning[4] around rapidly on his back.
20 The music from the speakers is not Buddhist chants but rather pop star Shakira's song "Hips Don't Lie" playing from a white Macintosh laptop computer. And when Norbu spins to a stop in a no-hands headstand, his bright orange,
25 knee-length shirt rides up to reveal a temporary tattoo that spells out—in English letters—"B-Boyz." In one spectacular performance, Norbu

has displayed the essence of a country that is attempting the impossible: to jump from the
30 Middle Ages to the 21st century without losing its balance.

Opening Up Shangri-la

For more than a thousand years, this tiny, intriguing kingdom has survived in isolation,
35 a place the size of Switzerland hidden in the mountains between two adjacent giants, India and China. Closed off from the outside world both by geography and government policy, the country had no roads, electricity, motor vehicles,
40 telephones, or postal service until the 1960s. Ancient temples sit high on misty cliffs; sacred, unconquered mountains rise above untouched rivers and forests; a grand wooden chalet[5] is inhabited by a kind, fatherly king and one of his
45 four wives, all sisters. For many visitors Bhutan brings to mind analogies to Shangri-la, the exotic, isolated Himalayan paradise[6] from James Hilton's 1933 novel *Lost Horizon*.

[1] In music, a **note** is a sound of a particular pitch.
[2] **Pilgrims** are people who make a journey to a holy place for religious reasons.
[3] A **monk** is a member of a male religious community.
[4] If something **spins**, it turns quickly around a central point.
[5] A **chalet** is a small wooden house, especially in a mountain area.
[6] You can refer to a place or situation that seems beautiful or perfect as **paradise** or a paradise.

▲ A village school in Bhutan draws 55 children from three villages. In remote areas, access to school remains a problem, so the government recently called for more than 120 more community schools to be built.

But even Shangri-la must change. When King Jigme Singye Wangchuck became king in 1972, Bhutan suffered from chronic poverty, and its illiteracy[7] and infant mortality[8] rates were among the highest in the world. These were consequences of a stubborn policy of isolation. "We paid a heavy price," the king would say later. His father, Bhutan's third king, began opening up the country in the 1960s, improving infrastructure by building roads, establishing schools and health clinics nationwide, and pushing for United Nations membership. King Jigme Singye Wangchuck would go much further. He tried to dictate the terms of Bhutan's opening—and in the process redefined the very meaning of development. The phrase he invented to describe his approach is "Gross National Happiness." In November 2008, his son, Jigme Khesar Namgyel Wangchuck, took over from him, becoming Bhutan's fifth king.

Gross National Happiness

Guided by the "four pillars of Gross National Happiness"—sustainable development, environmental protection, cultural preservation, and good government—Bhutan has pulled itself out of terrible poverty without exploiting its natural resources. Nearly three quarters of the country is still forested, with more than 25 percent designated as national parks and other protected areas—among the highest percentages in the world. Rates of illiteracy and infant mortality have fallen dramatically, and the economy is booming.

Among the reforms of 1999, Bhutan granted its citizens access to television—the last country on the planet to do so. Some Bhutanese started to go online in the same year. Next came the daring final step of Bhutan's experiment: the move to democracy. In 2006, abolishing much of his own power, the king set up a democratic government, betting his country's future on its success.

The real test of Gross National Happiness, then, is just beginning. Bhutan's new leaders face many distressing dilemmas, not least of which is a public that loves its kings and is skeptical of democracy. Can Bhutan maintain its identity in the face of globalization? How can it engage the modern world and enjoy its benefits, while making sure the drawbacks are minimal? How can tradition and development be compatible?

Cultural Collisions

Karma Jigme, 26, recently returned to the traditional rural town of Nabji (still without television and electricity) after working in more developed towns. Jigme's tales from the modern world have all the magic of Bhutan's traditional legends. The first time he saw television, he says, he hid under his bed, fearing that the angry pro wrestlers on screen "would jump out of the box and hurt me." While painting a monastery,[9] Jigme heard an extremely loud sound, and then, "I saw a house in the shape of a fish flying through the air." The airplane terrified him so much he almost fell off his ladder.

---

[7] **Illiteracy** is the inability to read and write.
[8] The **infant mortality rate** is the percentage of babies who die in a particular place.
[9] A **monastery** is a building in which monks live.

▲ Actors and crew on the set of *Bakchha* (*A Ghost's Attachment*). It's a horror film and a musical, says screenwriter Tshering Penjore. "A hit song almost always guarantees success."

It is not only the Bhutanese who are being exposed to a new culture; the outside world is also being introduced to Bhutan—through its movies. Two decades ago, Bhutan had never produced a feature film,[10] but in 2006 this tiny nation released 24 films, perhaps the highest rate per person for any country in the world. Khyentse Norbu is a film director who has enriched Bhutan's film industry. He makes movies with themes that explore the playful encounters of tradition and the modern world. He followed his surprise hit about soccer-loving monks, *The Cup* (1999), with a Bhutanese tale, *Travelers and Magicians* (2003). "Movies," says Norbu, 47, "are our modern-day thangkas"—the ancient Tibetan religious stories decorated with colorful illustrations. "Rather than fear modernization," he says, "we should see it as a tool that can help us express our culture . . ."

Bhutan's defenders of tradition, however, are agitated by these controversial changes and grieve the loss of their folk ways. They oppose what they see as invasion by a frivolous, materialistic global culture that is eroding their values and institutions. Sonam Tshewang, a junior high school teacher in Thimphu, believes something vital has already been lost. "Some kids have become so Westernized[11] that they've forgotten their own cultural identity," he says. One girl in his class even changed her name to Britney, after the American singer Britney Spears.

Kinzang Norbu, meanwhile, seems unconcerned. A day after his break-dancing performance, Norbu walks home from school in neatly combed hair and dressed in a gray *gho*, the traditional clothing of Bhutan. When he arrives home—his mother runs a bar decorated with photos of Bhutanese kings next to a large picture of another king, Elvis Presley—Norbu changes into a T-shirt and discusses, in English, internationally famous basketball and soccer stars.

His vote for the world's coolest person? It's a contest between American rap singer 50 Cent and Bhutan's fourth king. As a child of Bhutan's great experiment, Norbu sees no need to give up one or the other. Flashing a smile, he says: "I like them both!"

[10] A **feature film** is a film distributed to theaters for public viewing.
[11] If something is **Westernized** it is influenced by the culture and civilization of the West, i.e. Europe and the Americas.

Reading Comprehension

A. Multiple Choice. Choose the best answer for each question.

Purpose

1. What point does the author wish to illustrate through the opening scene of monks watching the boy dance?
   a. Bhutan is a country with a great degree of artistic freedom.
   b. Bhutan's monks are very curious and open-minded.
   c. Bhutan's capital city of Thimphu attracts a wide range of people.
   d. Bhutan is a country where the modern and the traditional mix.

Paraphrase

2. On line 55, what did the king mean when he said, "We paid a heavy price."
   a. Modernizing the country cost a lot of money.
   b. The policy of isolation had painful consequences.
   c. Opening up the country caused serious problems.
   d. Bhutan lost its identity in opening up to the world.

> **Critical Thinking**
>
> Do you think "Bhutan's great experiment" will likely succeed or fail? Why?

Sequence

3. Which of these events occurred last?
   a. Bhutan's first democratic government was set up.
   b. Bhutan's third king began opening up the country.
   c. Jigme Singye Wangchuck became king of Bhutan.
   d. Bhutan's citizens were allowed access to television.

Inference

4. What do Karma Jigme's tales from the modern world illustrate?
   a. He has a rich imagination.
   b. He had never seen an airplane before.
   c. He likes to play jokes on his friends.
   d. He is afraid of flying.

Main Idea

5. What is the main idea of the 9th paragraph (from line 113)?
   a. Movies are an aspect of modernization that can benefit Bhutanese society, not threaten it.
   b. Rather than make movies, Bhutanese people should focus on more traditional cultural activities.
   c. It was beneficial for Bhutan that modern technology was introduced so late.
   d. Bhutan is likely to become one of the world's major film-making centers.

B. True or False. Read the sentences below and circle **T** (true), **F** (false), or **NG** (not given in the passage).

1. *Lost Horizon* is a very popular novel in Bhutan.   **T   F   NG**
2. Bhutan's poor economy is preventing the nation's development.   **T   F   NG**
3. In 2006, Bhutan's people decided to remove their king from power.   **T   F   NG**
4. *The Cup* is a movie about monks who love soccer.   **T   F   NG**
5. More young people are leaving Bhutan than ever before. **T   F   NG**

Vocabulary Practice

A. Completion. Complete the information using the correct form of words in the box. Three words are extra.

compatible	booming	assemble
democracy	designate	erode
exploit	minimal	rural
sacred		

▲ In spite of its plans to modernize, Bhutan hopes to keep 68 percent of its land covered in forests.

Gross Domestic Product, or GDP, is an economist's term for the total value of goods and services produced by a country each year. A high GDP indicates a wealthy nation, but it may or may not indicate a happy one. That is why Bhutan prefers to measure its success using GNH—Gross National Happiness—instead. Bhutanese GNH seems to be increasing in various areas:

In 2006, Bhutan chose **1.** _____ as its system of government, believing that its inherent freedom is the most **2.** _____ with the GNH approach to development.

In 1960, Bhutan had no public school system. Today it has schools at all levels, and in all areas, both in cities and towns, and in **3.** _____ areas.

Bhutan has been able to **4.** _____ the power of its mountain rivers to produce electricity, much of which is sold to neighboring India, whose economy is **5.** _____.

Bhutan protects its natural environment. The government has **6.** _____ large areas of forest as protected areas. They hope to keep 68 percent of the country covered in forests.

Of course not every person in Bhutan is happy. Recently, reports of violence among young people have been increasing. However, Bhutan is being as careful as possible to make sure the negative effects of internationalization are **7.** _____.

B. Definitions. Match the correct form of words from the box in **A** with their definitions. Two words are extra.

1. come together in a group _____
2. believed to be holy and to have a special connection with God _____
3. to develop resources or raw materials and use them for commercial activities _____
4. working well together or existing together successfully _____
5. gradually weaken or lose value _____
6. in the country, away from cities or large towns _____
7. having increased economic activity _____
8. select and set aside for a particular purpose _____

Word Link

The root **minim** has the meaning of *the least* or *the smallest* in words such as: **minimize**—*to make as small as possible*; **minimum**—*the smallest amount.*

12B

In Search of Longevity

Squatting effortlessly on a slippery embankment, 89-year-old Kame Ogido inspects a pinch of seaweed, part of a low-calorie, plant-based diet that may help give Okinawans an average life expectancy of 82 years, among the longest in the world. These "super seniors," and others in Italy and California, share a number of habits that may be the secrets of living longer.

Before You Read

A. Discussion. Read the information above. What healthy habits do you think Okinawans and other long-lived seniors have that help them live longer? For each of the categories below, write down one or two healthy habits.

Food	
Drink	
Family	
Social Life	
Activity	

B. Scan. The Okinawans' longevity may be partly due to *ikigai* and *moai*. Quickly scan the reading to find out what these two Japanese words mean.

The Secrets of Long Life

When she turned 100, Marge Jetton ▶ of Loma Linda, California, renewed her driver's license for another five years.

A long healthy life is no accident. It begins with good genes inherited from your family, but it also depends on good habits. So what's the formula for success? In a recent study, funded in part by the U.S. National Institute on Aging, scientists have focused on groups living in several regions where exceptional longevity is the norm: Sardinia, Italy; Loma Linda, California; and the islands of Okinawa, Japan. Groups living in these three areas of longevity offer three sets of guidelines to follow.

Sardinians

Taking a break from farm work in the village of Silanus, 75-year-old Tonino Tola tickles the chin of his five-month-old grandson, Filippo, who watches from his mother's arms. "Goochi, goochi, goo," Tonino whispers. For this strong, healthy, 1.8-meter-tall (six-foot-tall) man, these two things—hard work and family—form the foundation of his life. They may also help explain why Tonino and his neighbors live so long.

A community of 2,400 people, Silanus is located on the edge of a mountainous region in central Sardinia, where dry fields rise suddenly into mountains of stone. In a group of villages in the heart of the region, which scientists call the "Blue Zone," 91 of the 17,865 people born between 1880 and 1900 have lived to their hundredth birthday—a rate more than twice as high as the average for Italy.

Why do they live so long? Lifestyle is part of the answer. By 11:00 A.M. on this particular day, the industrious Tonino has already milked four cows, chopped wood, slaughtered[1] a calf, and walked four miles with his sheep. Now, taking the day's first break, he gathers his grown children, grandson, and visitors around the kitchen table. Giovanna, his wife, unties a handkerchief containing a paper-thin flatbread called *carta da musica*, pours some red wine, and cuts slices of homemade pecorino cheese.

These Sardinians also benefit from their genetic history. According to Paolo Francalacci of the University of Sassari, 80 percent of them are directly related to the first Sardinians, who arrived in the area 11,000 years ago. Genetic traits made stronger over generations may favor longevity. Nutrition, too, is a factor. The Sardinians' diet is loaded with fruits and vegetables, milk and milk products, fish, and wine. Most of these items are homegrown.

[1] To **slaughter** animals such as cows and sheep means to kill them for their meat.

▲ 103-year-old Giovanni Sannai regularly dines with his family in Sardinia. Scientists say that older people who live near loved ones tend to live longer.

Adventists

It's Friday morning, and Marge Jetton is
55 speeding down the highway in her purple Cadillac.[2] She wears dark sunglasses to protect her eyes from the sun's glare, though her head is barely higher than the steering wheel. Marge, who turned 101 in September, is late for one of
60 several volunteer commitments she has today. Already this morning she's eaten breakfast, walked 1.6 km (1 mile), and lifted weights. "I don't know why God gave me the privilege of living so long," she says, pointing to herself.
65 "But look what he did."

Marge, like many other residents of Loma Linda, California, surrounded by orange trees and polluted air, is a Seventh-day Adventist. The Adventist Church has always practiced and been
70 a proponent of healthy living. It forbids smoking, alcohol consumption, and foods forbidden in the Bible, such as pork. The church also discourages the consumption of other meat, rich foods, caffeinated drinks, as well as most spices.
75 Adventists also observe a sacred day of the week on Saturday, assembling and socializing with members to relieve stress.

A study found that the Adventists' habit of consuming beans, soy milk,[3] tomatoes, and other
80 fruits lowered their risk of developing certain cancers. It also suggested that eating whole wheat bread, drinking five glasses of water a day, and, most surprisingly, consuming four servings of nuts a week reduced their risk of heart disease.
85 And it found that not eating red meat had been helpful in avoiding both cancer and heart disease.

In the end, the study reached a surprising conclusion, says Gary Fraser of Loma Linda University: the average Adventist's lifespan
90 surpasses that of the average Californian by four to ten years. That compelling evidence makes the Adventists one of the most-studied cultures of longevity in the United States.

Okinawans

95 The first thing you notice about Ushi Okushima is her laugh. It fills the room with pure joy. This rainy afternoon she sits comfortably wrapped in a blue kimono. Her thick hair is combed back from her suntanned[4] face, revealing alert, green
100 eyes. Her smooth hands lie folded peacefully in her lap. At her feet sit her friends, Setsuko and Matsu Taira, cross-legged on a tatami mat,[5] drinking tea.

Ushi has recently taken a new job. She also tried
105 to run away from home after a dispute with her daughter, Kikue. A relative caught up with her in another town 60 kilometers (40 miles) away and notified her daughter. Not long ago she started wearing perfume too. When asked about the
110 perfume, she jokes that she has a new boyfriend. Predictable behavior for a young woman, perhaps, but Ushi is 103.

▲ 102-year-old Okinawan Kamada Nakazato joins her family and friends for a cup of tea several times a week.

With an average life expectancy of 78 years for men and 86 years for women, Okinawans
115 are among the world's longest-lived people. This is undoubtedly due in part to Okinawa's warm and inviting climate and scenic beauty. Senior citizens living in these islands tend to enjoy years free from disabilities. Okinawans
120 have very low rates of cancer and heart disease compared to American seniors. They are also less likely to develop dementia[6] in old age, says Craig Wilcox of the Okinawa Centenarian[7] Study.

125 A lean diet of food grown on the island and a philosophy of moderation—"eat until your stomach is 80 percent full"—may also be factors. Ironically, this healthy way of eating was born of hardship. Ushi Okushima grew
130 up barefoot[8] and poor; her family grew sweet potatoes, which formed the core of every meal. During World War II, when the men of the island joined the army, Ushi and her friend Setsuko fled to the center of the island
135 with their children. "We experienced terrible hunger," Setsuko recalls.

▲ 84-year-old Okinawan Fumiyasu Yamakawa practices yoga every day, in training for an annual decathlon. His favorite events are the high jump and the pole vault.

Many older Okinawans belong to a *moai*, a mutual support network that provides financial, emotional, and social help throughout life.
140 *Ikigai* may be another key to their success. The word translates roughly to "that which makes one's life worth living," and it is something that is different for each person. "My *ikigai* is right here," says Ushi with a slow sweep of her
145 hand that indicates her friends Setsuko and Maira. "If they die, I will wonder why I am living."

[2] **Cadillac** is an American brand of car.
[3] **Soy milk** is a drink made from soy beans.
[4] If you are **suntanned**, the sun has turned your skin an attractive brown color.
[5] **Tatami mats**, made of woven straw, are the traditional material for floors in Japanese houses.
[6] **Dementia** is a serious illness of the mind.
[7] A **centenarian** is someone who is a hundred years old or older.
[8] Someone who is **barefoot** is not wearing anything on their feet.

Reading Comprehension

A. Multiple Choice. Choose the best answer for each question.

Purpose

1. What is the purpose of the reading?

   a. to revise the lifespan estimates for three cultures with high longevity
   b. to compare three cultures, and rank them in terms of longevity
   c. to investigate three cultures with high longevity and discover their habits
   d. to expose the myths about three famous cultures with high longevity

Paraphrase

2. Which of the following is NOT mentioned as a factor in Sardinian's longevity?

   a. quality of medical treatment   c. lifestyle
   b. nutrition   d. genetic history

Detail

3. Which of the following statements about Marge Jetton is NOT true?

   a. She has strong religious beliefs.
   b. She is careful about what she eats and drinks.
   c. She has an active social life.
   d. She is unable to do physical exercise.

Inference

4. In line 91, *that compelling evidence* refers to _____.

   a. Adventists' reduced rates of heart disease
   b. Adventists' life span compared to average Californians
   c. Adventists' avoidance of eating red meat and drinking of soy milk
   d. Adventists' reduced risk of certain cancers.

Detail

5. Which of the following is NOT mentioned as a reason for the Okinawans' longevity?

   a. their social relationships   c. their religious beliefs
   b. their diet   d. their natural environment

Critical Thinking

The reading presents a variety of guidelines to help in living longer. Which do you think would work best for you? Why?

B. Classification. According to the article, do these sentences describe the Sardinians, the Adventists, or the Okinawans? Write each answer (**a–f**) in the correct place in the chart.

   a. Religion is an important factor in their longevity.
   b. Most of their food is homegrown.
   c. They have strong friendships and family relationships.
   d. They drink red wine and eat cheese.
   e. They drink five glasses of water a day.
   f. They eat until they are 80 percent full.

Sardinians   Adventists

Okinawans

Vocabulary Practice

A. Matching. Read the information below and match each word in **red** with its definition.

Food is necessary for all living things. The body requires good nutrition to function well. Therefore, it seems quite ironic that starving animals that eat barely enough to survive are the ones who live the longest. For more than 70 years, scientists have known that animals such as dogs and mice show increased longevity with decreased food intake. In other words, mice fed 40 percent fewer calories[1] than what is considered to be a healthy diet will live, on average, 40 percent longer than mice fed normal diets.

Could eating less food be a useful guideline to help slow the aging process in humans as well? Donald Ingram at the National Institute of Aging investigates the effects of a lean diet (which is 30 percent reduced in calories) on monkeys. It's too soon to tell if the animals will live longer; the study began in 1987, and the monkeys typically live for 40 years, but so far, the animals do seem to be somewhat healthier. "But we just don't know enough yet about how much longer large animals might live on a calorie-restricted diet," Ingram said.

[1] **Calories** are units used to measure the energy value of food.

▲ An elderly Okinawan woman picks her homegrown vegetables. Could eating less help you live longer?

1. long life _____
2. low in fat _____
3. odd because it is the opposite of what one might think _____
4. only just _____
5. advice about how to do something _____

B. Words in Context. Complete each sentence with the best answer.

1. If your doctor forbids you to eat fish, you _____ eat it.
   a. should   b. shouldn't

2. It's always discouraging when you _____ a test.
   a. fail   b. pass

3. After you _____, your lifestyle usually changes.
   a. get married   b. go shopping

4. An employee might be given a privilege as a form of _____.
   a. punishment   b. reward

5. You may feel relief when something bad _____.
   a. happens   b. doesn't happen

Word Partnership

Use **relief** with: (v.) **express** relief, **feel** relief, **bring** relief, **provide** relief; (n.) **sense of** relief, **sigh of** relief, **pain** relief, relief **from symptoms**, **disaster** relief

▲ Running is an excellent way to relieve stress.

EXPLORE MORE

The Science of Stress

A. Preview. Read the passage below and match each word in **blue** with its definition. You will hear these words in the video.

It is important to get exercise on a daily basis as it helps improve our psychological and **physiological** functions. For example, running on a **treadmill** is a great way to **boost** your mood. This is because the "happy hormones" produced by your brain **kick in** even though your energy is being **depleted**.

1. to reduce the amount or supply of something   _____
2. to begin to take effect   _____
3. an exercise machine that allows you to run while staying in one place   _____
4. help to increase, improve, or be more successful   _____
5. having to do with the way the body works physically   _____

B. Summarize. Watch the video, *The Science of Stress*. Then complete the summary below using the correct from of words from the box. One word is extra.

exploiting	lifestyle	guideline	longevity	lean
assembled	relieve	erode	minimal	compatible

Without at least a(n) **1.** _____ amount of stress to give us energy, we could not get through the day. However, a very stressful **2.** _____ can have a negative effect on our bodies. Dr. Kathy Matt and her colleagues are investigating what stress does to a body, and proving that stress is not just psychological, but physiological as well.

When our body experiences physical stress, it produces two hormones that give us energy: adrenaline and cortisol. It also produces them in cases of psychological stress. Dr. Matt and her team have **3.** _____ a series of tests to show the effects of stress on the body.

While running on a treadmill, the woman's body releases a lot of stress hormones, but she's also **4.** _____ every bit of energy they create. However, when she is stressed psychologically instead of physically, the same hormones are created. The problem is that the type of energy they provide is not **5.** _____ with the situation of test-taking at a desk, because the physical energy cannot be used.

Too much cortisol **6.** _____ the bones, weakening them and making them more likely to break. This could create problems that have an impact on **7.** _____, perhaps taking years off a person's life. Therefore, it is important to exercise regularly. Putting the body through the stress of exercise is one way to **8.** _____ psychological stress, thereby preventing its harmful effects. And, it keeps a body **9.** _____ by burning off extra calories, too!

C. Think About It.

1. What causes you physical stress? What causes you psychological stress?

2. What do you do to help relieve stress?

To learn more about quality of life, visit elt.heinle.com/explorer

200   Unit 12 Quality of Life

A. Crossword. Use the definitions below to complete the missing words.

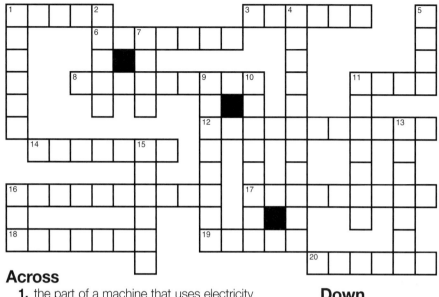

Across
1. the part of a machine that uses electricity or fuel to produce movement
3. holy, connected to God
6. to release something, usually a destructive force
8. dangerous to one's health or safety
11. a number of things placed one on top of the other
12. very impressive or dramatic
14. through which, by which
16. to try to prevent by showing disapproval
17. to make full or complete again
18. very small in quantity, value, or degree
19. gradually destroy or remove over a long period of time
20. previous, having been in the past

Down
1. to change slightly in order to improve it
2. far away from large towns or cities
4. an unexpected event that causes great damage or suffering
5. to _____ a question is to put it forward to someone
7. a _____ occurs when liquid or gas escapes through a crack or hole
9. out of date and no longer in use
10. a possible way
11. sensible and careful
13. very impressive and often frightening
15. only just
16. a wall built across a river to stop water from flowing

B. Notes Completion. Scan the information on pages 202–203 to complete the notes.

Field Notes

Site: Pantanal Conservation Area

Location: _____, Brazil

Information:
- The Pantanal is the world's largest _____ and is situated in _____ Brazil next to the country of _____.
- Over _____ of the land is underwater during the annual floods. Water levels can rise up to _____ meters in some areas.
- The Pantanal has exotic animal species like _____ (small alligators), giant snakes called _____, and carnivorous fish called _____.
- The habitat of many of these animals is under threat from pollution and _____.
- Cattle ranches called _____ sometimes engage in _____ to make a living and conserve the Pantanal.

Sites: **Pantanal Conservation Area**

Location: **Mato Grosso, Brazil**

Category: **Natural**

Status: **World Heritage Site since 2000**

Pantanal Conservation Area

Pantanal floods can cause water levels to rise up to five meters in some areas, creating lakes filled with aquatic plants and fish.

In a corner of western Brazil, adjacent to the Bolivian border, lies one of South America's great natural wonders. Although less famous than the Amazon rainforest, the Pantanal nonetheless has the distinction of being the world's largest wetland, measuring up to 195,000 square kilometers (75,000 sq mi)—or almost twice the size of England. It also has the greatest concentration of wildlife in South America.

The Pantanal is renowned for its annual floods, or what locals call the "full." Heavy rain and swollen rivers **submerge** over 80 percent of the Pantanal, replenishing the land after the dry season and allowing an immense variety of plants to take root in the fertile soil. The wetland is also home to a spectacular range of wildlife, including alligator-like caimans, **elusive** jaguars, huge anacondas, and large mouse-like creatures called capybaras. Like the Amazon, this wildlife **sanctuary** is under threat from deforestation and pollution. In the 1980s, a booming trade in exotic animal skins saw wildlife numbers decline, until stricter regulations were introduced.

Much of the Pantanal's land today is privately owned and is populated with numerous cattle ranches called *fazendas*. To help conserve the Pantanal, some *fazendas* are turning to ecotourism: tourists pay to live on a ranch and experience its way of life. However, this poses a dilemma to the ranchers, as they need money and support but many dislike the intrusion into their lives.

Glossary

elusive: difficult to find
infested: present in large and unwanted numbers
notorious: to be well known for something bad
sanctuary: a place where people, or wildlife, can live freely

Wetland Cowboys

Life on a *fazenda* is often tough and hazardous. Due to the annual floods, the Pantanal cowboys, or *pantaneiros*, must learn to farm in waist-deep water and train horses to cross caiman-**infested** water. They also lead hundreds of cattle to dry land while defending them against jaguars on the hunt. Long distances and secluded locations ensure a very lonely life.

Not everyone is willing to be a *pantaneiro*. The hard labor and secluded lifestyle has discouraged the young from staying and this traditional way of life, passed down for generations, is slowly dying out. Yet a small group remains behind, dedicated to saving the Pantanal. As one cowboy says: "Your spirit would die if you weren't out in the open, with the long, beautiful view."

▲ According to records, the biggest anaconda ever found was a colossal 11 meters (37 ft) long.

Fearsome Fish

Meet the red-bellied piranha, the most **notorious** fish in South America. Pantanal waters are full of these fierce carnivores. Although mostly scavengers, large groups of hungry piranha have been known to attack young or sickly animals by seizing them and dragging them into the water. Tourists to the Pantanal can go on piranha fishing tours, although they are warned to be careful when unhooking the fish—many experienced Pantanal fishermen have lost fingers to these awesome predators.

A Global View

Home galaxy of our Earth, the Milky Way is a rotating mass of gas, dust, stars, and other objects, held together by the forces of **gravity**.

A Tour of Our Galaxy

In the year 1054 A.D., Chinese and Arab **astronomers** were startled by the appearance of a new star, so bright that it was visible in broad daylight for several weeks. Although they did not realize it at the time, they had witnessed a supernova—the explosion of a dying star. The catastrophic event, occurring about 6,500 light-years* from the Earth, resulted in the formation of an interstellar cloud of dust and gas known today as the Crab Nebula.

The Crab Nebula is just one of many spectacular features that populate the Milky Way, the **galaxy** in which the solar system—and our own planet—is located. The Milky Way is a spiral-shaped system of a few hundred billion stars. Bright regions of recently formed stars highlight its arms, while older stars explode and fade as beautiful nebulae.

All objects in the Milky Way—including our **solar system**—**orbit** (move around) the galactic center, much like planets in Earth's solar system revolve around the sun. But our solar system is tiny compared to the Milky Way: light from a star at one end of the galaxy would take 100,000 years to reach the opposite side. And our galaxy is small compared to the vastness of space: astronomers estimate there are at least a hundred billion galaxies scattered throughout the **universe**.

*One **light-year** is the distance that light can travel in one year, approximately 9.5 trillion (9,500,000,000,000) kilometers.

Interstellar Twisters

A pair of twisted structures at the heart of the Lagoon Nebula—5,000 light-years away— have a tornado-like appearance. These "twisters" are much larger than storms on earth: each one is half a light-year long (about 5,000,000,000,000 kilometers).

1

Twin Jet Nebula

Stellar "wind" rushes outward in opposite directions from the hot core of Nebula M2-9. The wind travels 200 miles in a single second, like high-speed gases escaping from back-to-back jet engines.

2

The Cat's Eye

Discovered by astronomer William Herschel in 1786, NGC 6543, known as the Cat's Eye Nebula, is one of the most complex—and most beautiful—nebulae ever seen.

3

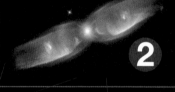
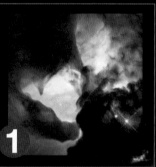

30°

20,000

60°

30,000

P E R S E U S   A R

40,000

50,000 light-years

Direction of rotation

120°

O   U

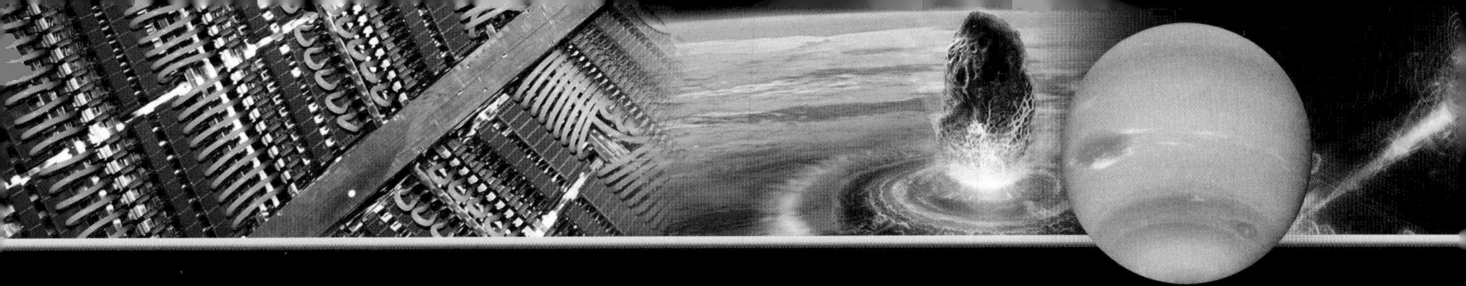

A Star Is Born

4

Astronomers believe these columns in the Eagle Nebula may contain "EGG"s (Evaporating Gaseous Globules), some of which produce baby stars. The scale of this photo is vast: each of the "fingertips" at the top of the columns, from which new stars emerge, is larger than our own solar system.

The Galactic Core

The orange and red area in the photo, less than 100 light-years from the galaxy's center, is home to the Pistol star—the brightest star seen in the galaxy. In just a few million years the Pistol, like other stars in its group, will be ripped apart by forces acting at the Milky Way's core. Within the core may lie an immensely powerful black hole, which, with a mass 2.6 million times our sun, is so dense that even light cannot escape its pull.

5

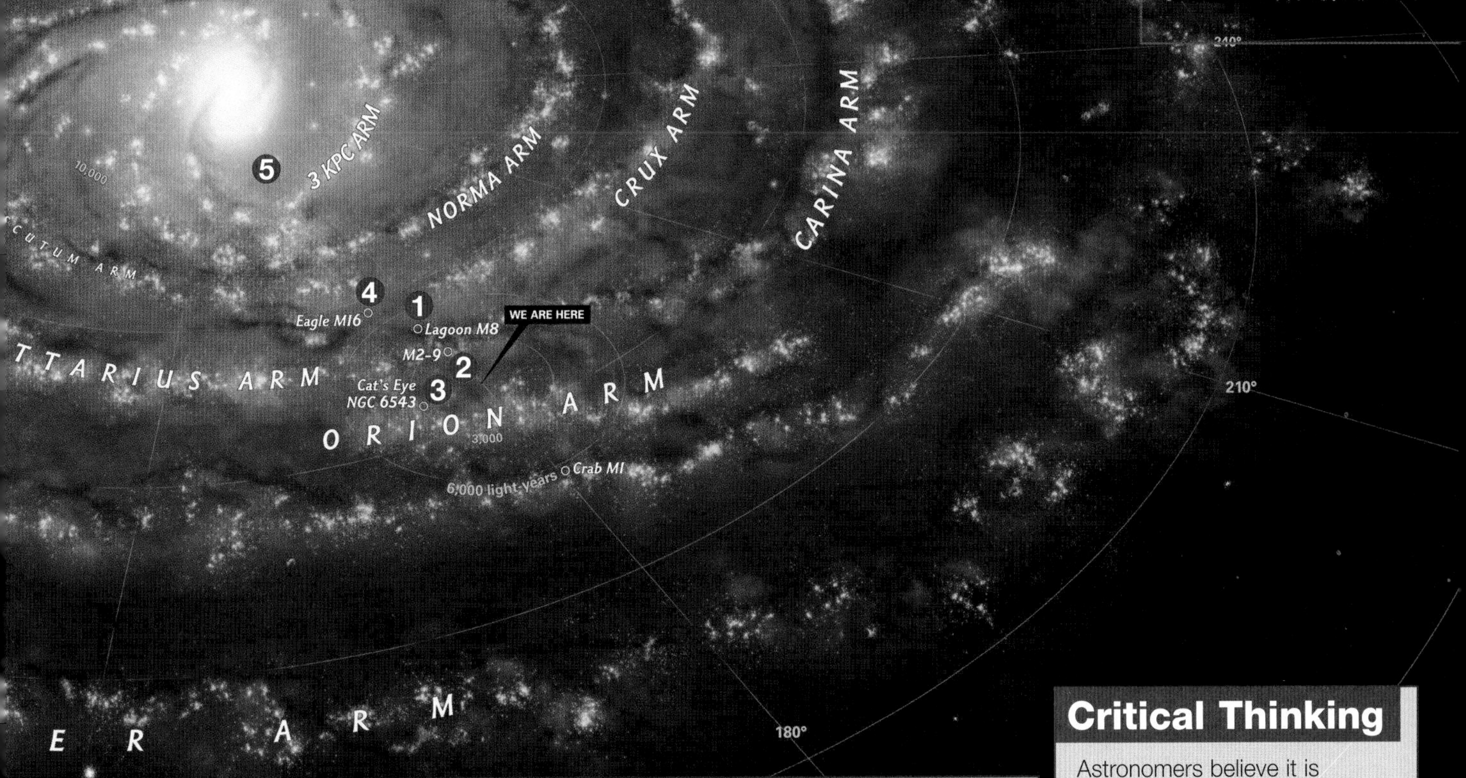

330°

270°

240°

5

10,000

3 KPC ARM

NORMA ARM

CRUX ARM

CARINA ARM

SCUTUM ARM

4 **1**

Eagle MI6

Lagoon M8

WE ARE HERE

M2-9 **2**

Cat's Eye **3**
NGC 6543

O R I O N   A R M

TTARIUS ARM

33,000

210°

6,000 light-years ○ Crab MI

E R   A R M

180°

150°

Word Link

We can replace the noun suffix **-ation** with **-ate** to form verbs, e.g., *estimation – estimate; population – populate; evaluation – evaluate; participation – participate.*

Critical Thinking

Astronomers believe it is important that we know about space. What benefits might space research bring? Do you agree it is a good use of time and money?

A. Completion. Use the correct form of words in **bold** from pages 204 to 205 to complete the passage.

A(n) **1.** _____ is a mass of stars, dust, gas, and other objects that are held together by the force of **2.** _____. According to **3.** _____, there are at least one hundred billion of them throughout the **4.** _____. Our own is called the Milky Way, and the distance from one end to the other is 100,000 **5.** _____. The Milky Way contains a few hundred billion stars, one of which is the sun. The sun, along with the planets and other objects which **6.** _____ it, make up the **7.** _____ system. The solar system and all the other stars in the Milky Way revolve around the galactic core.

B. Word Link. Many regular English verbs end in the suffix **–ate** (meaning *to do*, *to make*, or *to cause*). Complete the sentences using the correct form of words from the box. Use a dictionary to help you. One word is extra.

violate	integrate	mediate	deviate	equate
evaluate	participate	legislate	initiate	implicate

1. Because people are often unwilling to recycle their trash on their own, many cities have found it necessary to _____ it and to make recycling the law.
2. New Yorkers who _____ recycling laws face fines from $100 to $5,000.
3. Several individuals were _____ in a terrible plot to poison the city water supply.
4. Although many people _____ bottled water with purity, recent studies have found that impurities found in some bottled water are more dangerous than those in common tap water.
5. When disposing of dangerous e-waste, it is important for workers never to _____ from approved safety procedures.
6. For years the school had no recycling program, until a concerned student _____ one in 2008.
7. Several companies sell kits that allow the average person to _____ the quality of home drinking water.
8. When the city's trash collection workers went on strike and trash began to pile up, the mayor himself offered to _____ the dispute between the workers and their managers.
9. Recycling programs can only be effective if the majority of people _____.

C. Thesaurus. Write each of the six words in the box under the word they are closest to in meaning. Use your dictionary to help you. Then use the correct form of the six words to complete the sentences.

reform	deflect	dump	mutate	swerve	renounce

divert	discard	modify

1. Researchers at Albert Einstein College of Medicine have recently discovered a rare genetic _____ that may allow individuals to live 100 years and beyond.
2. Too many broken and obsolete computers are simply _____ in the trash instead of being properly recycled.
3. Meteors often seem closer than they are. Airline pilots have _____ to avoid meteors that were actually 160 kilometers (100 miles) away.
4. Bhutan's third king took action to _____ and modernize Bhutan's old-fashioned judicial system and made efforts to change the country's land ownership system.
5. In 2001, the king of Bhutan _____ absolute power and handed over the daily work of government to a council of ministers.
6. The International Space Station is protected by a large number of shields designed to _____ tiny meteorites.

D. Word Link. The suffixes **–crat** and **–arch** refer to a person who holds power or rules. Systems of government or power often include the suffixes **–cracy** or **–archy**. Look at the prefixes and their meanings. Then complete each sentence with the correct prefix.

Prefix	Meaning		Prefix	Meaning
aristo–	the best		mon–	one, alone, single
demo–	people		patri–	father
matri–	mother		theo–	god

1. _____cracy is a system of government in which religious leaders hold power.
2. In a(n) _____cracy, the general population holds the ultimate power and expresses that power in elections.
3. The _____arch of a family is its respected male leader.
4. A king or a queen who rules a nation can also be called a(n) _____arch.
5. A society or community in which respected women hold positions of power is a _____archy.
6. A(n) _____crat is someone who comes from society's upper classes and has a high social rank.

E. Word Partnership. Many phrasal verbs are of the form *verb + on* (e.g., to *continue* is to *carry on*). Complete the passage using the correct form of the words in the box.

rely	catch	live	take	draw	move	drag

THIRSTY CHINA

China's large population and booming industries have resulted in a greater need for water in the country than ever before. The Yellow River is China's second longest, and millions of people **1.** _____ on its water for their farms, animals, industries, and households. Recently, the amount of water in the river has been reduced by a long drought that has been **2.** _____ on for years. In some places, herders' animals haven't had enough grass to **3.** _____ on and have died in large numbers. Herders, with a deep love of their land and traditions, have had no choice but to **4.** _____ on, often going to live in cities. The Chinese government has **5.** _____ on the challenge of the drought by creating rain through a process called cloud seeding—the most ambitious project of its type in the world. To solve its water problems, China could **6.** _____ on the the lessons learned from one of China's driest provinces, Gansu. There, in recent decades, the practice of collecting rainwater as a source of water for toilets and for car washing has been **7.** _____ on with the general public.

F. Choosing the Right Definition. Study the numbered definitions for *lean*. Then write the number of the definition that relates to each sentence below.

lean /liːn/ (**leans, leaning, leaned, leaner, leanest**) **1** V-I When you **lean** in a particular direction, you bend your body in that direction. ❑ *He leaned out the window and shouted "Hello!"* **2** V-T/V-I If you **lean on** or **against** someone or something, you rest against them so that they partly support your weight. If you lean an object on or against something, you place the object so that it is partly supported by that thing. ❑ *The tired runner stopped and leaned on a fence.* ❑ *He leaned his shovel against the house.* **3** ADJ If you describe someone as **lean**, you mean that they are thin but look strong and healthy. ❑ *Mary looked lean after losing 10 kilos.* **4** ADJ If meat is **lean**, it does not have very much fat. **5** ADJ If you describe periods of time as **lean**, you mean that people have less of something, such as money, than they used to have, or are less successful than they used to be. ❑ *The money they saved got them through the lean years.*

_____ **a.** Various studies seem to indicate that people that are **leaner** live longer.
_____ **b.** Although Okinawan Ushi Okushima experienced the very **lean** times in Japan that followed World War II, she still succeeded in living for over 100 years.
_____ **c.** One of the world's most famous buildings is the **Leaning** Tower of Pisa—a tower that is no longer straight, and looks as though it could fall over at any time.
_____ **d.** After she reached the age of 90, Elizabeth could no longer walk without **leaning** on my arm.
_____ **e.** Although **lean** beef is better for one's health, it can be less flavorful.

Target Vocabulary

Target Vocabulary

Portrait of a Volcano

Narrator:

On the eastern frontier of Russia, there is a world unlike any other called Kamchatka. This remote and mostly untouched landscape features more than 120 volcanoes, 29 of them active.

Photographer Carsten Peter is passionate about volcanoes, a passion that motivates him to embrace new challenges.

Carsten Peter, Photographer:

"You have one of the highest density of volcanoes in the Earth. And for me it's one of the most interesting places for volcanoes."

Narrator:

Carsten and his team are on their way to several volcanoes. One of them is the highest active volcano in Asia—Klutchevskaya. He heads straight for a recently erupted volcano and lands . . . on another world. The team navigates through snow, mud, and sulfur fumes . . . to the edge of a smoking crater. They need to get closer.

Carsten wants to use a rubber raft to demonstrate how big the volcano is. But the acid in the highly acidic volcanic lake will destroy it.

Carsten Peter:

"In the sun. Paddle in the sun, but be quick."

Narrator:

Carsten is able to take just a few photos before they flee the area. But it's enough.

Their route now takes them south to Mutnovskaya Volcano. For Carsten, Mutnovskaya is worth the risk. A magnificent glacier lies in the shadow of the smoking volcano—making it the ideal subject for an adventure photographer.

Carsten has captured a powerful portrait of life beyond the lava but is obsessed with taking that one perfect picture. This is his last chance.

A new acid lake formed in the last eruption. It drains through the glacier and the hot water has melted out an unstable ice cave. Although they anticipate it's only a matter of time before the cave

gives way, Carsten and Frank hear a roar in the distance and commence into the cave.

The cave ceiling, in some places, is seven stories high. They move in, deeper and deeper, until they are blocked by an astonishing 40-foot acid waterfall. It threatens to destroy Carsten's equipment. But Carsten is no amateur and concentrates on making it work.

Carsten Peter:

"We have a hot river underneath the glacier. It's somehow unique in the world. There are only very few places where you can find that in the world, and underneath a glacier it's hard to believe."

"You never know what you expect unless you explore it. We only scratched on the surface. I will be here again, of course."

2 The Love Bird

Narrator:

This is an Australian Riflebird, which lives in the dense rainforests of northeastern Australia.

Members of the Birds of Paradise family, riflebirds may have received their name because their color resembles the uniform of early British army riflemen. A common trait of all riflebirds is that males have brighter colors than the females, which are on display during their courtship dances.

This male bounces from side to side with his wings outstretched, desperate to gain the female's attention. Unfortunately, his chances are ruined . . . by some amateur males practicing their own dances nearby. As mating season only lasts a few months, things can get rather competitive.

Another male riflebird sounds his mating call from a perch high in the canopy . . . and a nearby female, building her nest, decides she's going to check him out. He makes a brave attempt to woo the object of his affections with his passionate performance. But the female is not impressed . . . and swiftly makes her exit.

Clearly, romance does not come easily for these birds. For many species of Birds of Paradise, such elaborate rituals can last for hours.

This male has all the right moves. He pushes out his chest to make it more prominent. Some kinds of riflebirds can even clap their wings to produce a sound that can be heard up to 60 meters away. Lucky for him, the feeling is mutual. And he finishes off with a victorious pose.

Yes, it's a harsh world out there in the wild, and only the fittest survive in this mating game.

The Smelliest Fruit

Narrator:
Here in Malaysian Borneo, a battle has just begun. Hotel staff watch nervously for a food that is unwelcome in many places, yet loved by people nationwide. Meet the durian fruit. Its smell is hard to describe.

Audrey, Hotel Staff:
"It smells like . . . of rotten fish and custard."

Woman:
"A rubbish dump."

Edward, Hotel Manager:
"Blue cheese."

Elderly Man:
"Perhaps a dead dog."

Narrator:
Other cultures love foods that smell strongly. Cheese, which is actually rotted milk, is popular in the West but not so much in Asia, where many find the smell offensive.

Notwithstanding its bad smell, durian is considered precious in Southeast Asia. Some believe it's worth killing for. Durian trees sometimes take as long as 15 years to bear fruit. Known as the "King of Fruit," a single durian can cost up to 50 US dollars.

Here in Kuching, the capital of Malaysian Borneo, hotels are on the front lines of the durian war. When the fruit is in season, hotel managers maintain a constant watch to keep it out. For them, durians are bad for business. One smelly fruit can scare off a hotel full of customers.

Edward:
"So it goes into the curtains. It sticks into the carpet. It sticks into the bedspreads."

Narrator:
But since it's not feasible to check every guest, people manage to smuggle them in. And it's the hotels which have to deal with the consequences.

Every hotel has its own method of dealing with a durian alert. One is to use charcoal which absorbs odors naturally, but takes a long time. The other way is to use a machine called an ionizer, which can remove the durian's contaminating smell in less than three hours.

Audrey:
"Please no durians here. Not in the hotel. Outside . . . in the fresh air you can do it. But definitely not here."

Narrator:
In Borneo, visitors can decide for themselves if this unique fruit is delicious, or just plain disgusting . . . as long as they confine their tasting sessions to the outdoors.

4 Kinetic Sculpture

Narrator:
Welcome to the Kinetic Sculpture Race, an extraordinary event which combines crazy machines with some pretty crazy contestants.

Race Participant:
"Today is the most wonderful day."

Narrator:
Held every year in Baltimore, Maryland, U.S.A., this unusual race tests human-powered machines on an obstacle course. These are literally moving pieces of art.

It's an exhilarating display of fantasy and fantastic engineering. Teacher Jeff Bartolomeo has been helping the students of Oakland Mills High School with their entry—the Scorpion. They've been preparing for the competition for weeks.

Jen Ernst, Student:
"Some people really work on the sculpture, the scorpion sculpture, and some people have been really working on the engineering aspect."

Narrator:
The entries range from small, simple devices driven by one person to huge and complex vehicles navigated by a whole team of drivers.

Announcer:
"We now have 21 kinetic sculptures gathered here today."

Narrator:
The race commences . . .

It's the start of a 24 kilometer (15 mile) journey through water, sand, mud, and ice. Things don't go smoothly for everyone, but the race goes on nonetheless.

Jen Ernst:
"Right now we're having problems with the gears. We went down [for] the brake test this morning, and gears were fine going down and then coming back up, something happened. We're starting to clean up now and get back on the race. Try to win this thing."

Narrator:
The race originated in the late 1960s when Hobart Brown decorated his son's bicycle and raced his neighbors down Main Street, thereby starting an event that would eventually become a hugely popular phenomenon.

**Hobart Brown,
Founder of Kinetic Sculpture Race:**
"The true art work or the true art form is the participation of everybody from the kid up to the adult and the kid looks up to the adult and says I want to get older too."

Race Participant:
"We had a little accident coming through the mud pit, we broke an axle and we're trying to figure out if we're going to be able to finish the race now. We got a little bogged down."

Narrator:
The last challenge for the Scorpion—the mud pit. Gradually they make their way through.

Jeff Bartolomeo, Teacher:
"My main idea is to build a machine that can overcome all the obstacles that the race organizers set out. Now other folks could really care less, I think, about that part of the race. They just want to build something that can support their artwork. It's just a fun day of excitement."

Narrator:
The vital element of this race is not so much to win, but simply to have fun—with friends, colleagues, even complete strangers. For the students of Oakland Mills, finishing the race gives a huge sense of accomplishment. Next year, they hope to be back again—with an even better kinetic machine.

Journey of Discovery

Narrator:

Long ago, Spanish sailors were revered for their bold journeys to distant lands. Now, a modern day adventurer is setting out to outdo those brave explorers—by setting sail on a small ship . . . made entirely of reeds. From Barcelona, Spain, to Africa and across the Atlantic Ocean to Colombia.

It may seem inconceivable, but people from the Americas, Asia, and Polynesia may have crossed the oceans in such boats long before Christopher Columbus did in the 15th century.

Kitín Muñoz, Explorer:

"I have been leading these expeditions for 20 years and this has become a way of life."

Narrator:

His 20-meter boat is based on ones that were used in pre-European South America. It was built in Spain by Aymara Indians from Bolivia, without using any modern materials.

Kitín Muñoz:

"This reed that we see here for example is called 'uembe.' It comes from the jungle in the Amazon and it can last for 300 years without splitting. It is very impressive."

Narrator:

This boat is named the Mata Rangi Three. "Three" for the third journey led by Muñoz. The other two failed partly because the boats were not strong enough to endure rough weather. But Muñoz stubbornly refuses to give up.

His trip has already taken his crew from Barcelona to Morocco. It will continue along the coast of Africa to Cape Verde and then across the ocean to Cartegena, Colombia.

And so on a beautiful day off the north African coast, the crew heads for the open sea. But it is not long before the peace is disrupted by heavy winds and rough waves.

Kitín Muñoz:

"I asked Benjamin, 'Is the boat going to tip over?' Because the ship was sinking and turning. Then the masts started to bend. It was a very tense and scary moment and part of what made it scary was the noise."

Narrator:

Water starts to flood into the main cabin and Muñoz has to act quickly.

Kitín Muñoz:

"First, I yelled, 'We have to take the boat to shore.' Second, we had to be very careful, because the waves were crashing against the boat. I was worried that someone would fall into the ocean and drown. I shouted 'Hold on tight and move slowly.'"

Narrator:

Luckily, the clouds scatter and the boat makes it out of the rough seas intact. It is proof that the reeds are flexible enough to survive long periods of time in difficult conditions.

They've learned other lessons as well. Sailing on a small boat for weeks is not for everyone. Some of the hardest stretches came when there was little or no wind. The men had to fight boredom and depression.

After more than a month at sea, Cape Verde comes into view. They get back onto the mainland. And the celebration begins . . .

This is only the beginning of a much longer journey. They still have to conquer the Atlantic Ocean. But for now, they're just happy to enjoy their success, having completed an extraordinary journey of discovery.

6 Africa from the Air

Narrator:
He has flown nearly 100,000 kilometers and taken an incredible 110,000 photographs of Africa from the air, documenting a fascinating world of disappearing wildlife and growing human development.

Meet *National Geographic* Explorer In Residence, J. Michael Fay. Fay's plane has been fixed with a camera that allows him to take high quality photos as he flies back and forth low over the landscape.

J. Michael Fay, Conservationist:
"When you drive along a road or you walk on a human trail, you're in that human world. Whereas if you're flying over, you traverse those boundaries and you can go deep into landscapes where people usually don't go."

Narrator:
As Fay's innovative approach highlights, Africa's great wild animals are in danger, in part because their natural habitats are losing ground to human development.

The population of African lions has declined by 45 to 70 percent within a decade. African elephant populations have been devastated, and are now only one percent of what they were a century ago. And eastern lowland gorillas, in their main habitat in the Congo, have seen a collapse of 70 percent in just the last 10 years.

In fact, Fay discovered there are few places left where the wildlife is truly wild. These include the secluded regions of the Congo and the lonely habitat of the Sahara desert.

J. Michael Fay:
"There are a few places left on the continent where wildlife is just there because there's not enough humans to kill it off. But those places are very rare."

Narrator:
But Fay also found animals that are doing well in protected parks and game preserves. Like the successful Mala Mala game park where Fay landed briefly. Founded in 1927, Mala Mala is the largest area of privately-owned land in South Africa. In 1964, this was the first game reserve in Africa to move away from hunting safaris in order to create an authentic wildlife experience for tourists. Fay discovered humans here living in harmony with wildlife.

In contrast, he discovered a much more worrying scene in Tanzania, at the Katavi National Park. Hundreds of hippos crowd into a fast-drying river. Instinct drives them here during the dry season, but Fay believes their survival is threatened by adjacent human settlements where people use the same water for farming.

J. Michael Fay:
"You could hardly even tell they were hippos because they were just these bumps. And then you realize they're alive and you just can't believe it. If they don't get rain in another two weeks, they're dead."

Narrator:
The compilation of images Fay captured during his journeys is both devastating . . . and hopeful. Tourism has become a genuine economic incentive to protect Africa's animals. Humans, according to Fay, have the power to destroy Africa—and the power to protect it.

In the end, Fay hopes the photos will encourage people to confront the reality of Africa today, and inspire people to save what's left. This remarkable view of Africa's last wild places could help us manage the impact of our human footprint . . . and help Africa's wild animals evade the threat of extinction.

Aztec Dancer

Narrator:

Cuco Murillo lives in the house that he and his father built with their own hands. The inhabitants of the house include Cuco and his wife, Lucia, who have been married for nearly 30 years, plus their three children and two granddaughters.

Born and raised in Tecate, in northern Mexico, Cuco is a modern day descendant of the Aztecs. Four years ago, he decided to reclaim his ancient heritage. Like his ancestors, Cuco now reveres Ometoetl, the God of the Aztecs. Cuco celebrates Aztec beliefs, worshipping the Cosmos through traditional rituals and embracing Aztec folklore.

The Aztec path finds its most powerful expression through dance—a ritual that has enriched Cuco's life. After a long day's work, Cuco puts on an exotic costume in preparation to perform spiritual Aztec dances. Now fully dressed, Cuco sets out for his daily ritual.

As the sun sets over his native town, Cuco kneels in concentration to pay his respects to the Powers of the Cosmos, just as ancient practitioners did centuries before him. He prays to each of the four fundamental directions—North, South, East, and West. His dance is now ready to commence.

Cuco explains the deep significance behind each move as he gets into the rhythm of the dance.

Cuco Murillo, Aztec Indian:

"And we do these movements to represent the four elements. The movement which represents the water is this one. Make it so it would rain.

And the other is the element fire. We are jumping in the same place we are. And when we go jumping to the front and then jumping towards the rear it represents the fire element.

And the air element is when we do this movement in circles with our bodies.

And the other one, when we are walking, touching the ground—it represents the earth. It is this one. As we are touching, we love the mother earth."

Narrator:

Everything he wears has a specific meaning or theme. His breastplate symbolizes his spiritual name, Tecolate or Bull. Likewise, the object he holds in his right hand symbolizes a warrior's weapon, while painted on his shield is his Aztec name, Double Rabbit.

His ankle jewelry represents rain, a symbol of prosperity in many cultures. As Cuco says, "without rain, there is no life." He explains why Aztec dance has inspired him.

Cuco Murillo:

"Azteca dance makes me feel, you know, great! It's kind of food for my spiritual way. Aztec people, Maya people, Olmec people, they start doing this. It means traditionally something alive. That is why it is still alive. God needs that."

8 Frog Licker

Narrator:
Off the southeastern coast of Africa lies the island of Madagascar. You may know Madagascar for its exotic lemurs, but it's also home to one of the world's most colorful amphibians. The Mantella Poison Frog.

Poison frogs aren't born poisonous, but rather they are proof of the old saying, "You are what you eat." Their toxins come from something in their diet, which is mainly ants, millipedes, and mites. But which of these insects is it exactly? And will a collapse in insect diversity threaten the frogs' ability to survive?

Meet frog expert Valerie C. Clark.

Valerie Clark, Herpetologist:
"This is *Mantella Betsileo*, a very wide-spread Malagasy Poison Frog that occurs throughout the country. This appears to be a gravid female. How do I know? Because it's just very, very fat, and this is the season for love."

Narrator:
Clark and her team use GPS data to alert them to the frog's location and to relay other useful information.

Valerie Clark:
"We're right at sea level."

Narrator:
They also need to collect as many insects as possible to try and track down exactly what these frogs are eating. They have a special system to get an idea of the local insect diversity. First, they chop up and go through piles of leaves. Then they put the leaves in various bags, with the final plastic bag at the bottom filled with alcohol. As the soil dries out inside the first bag, the insects leave it to try and find wetter soil. They fall out into the plastic bag and become samples.

How do you sample the toxins in a frog's skin? Well, there are a couple of methods. On this trip, Clark uses tissue soaked in alcohol to wipe the frogs' backs, so she can compare different poison frogs at different areas. But Clark also has another way of testing for these toxins outdoors—what she calls a "quick lick" taste test.

Valerie Clark:
"Well, let's see. Oh it's definitely bitter."

Narrator:
Bitterness equals toxic. Clark assures us the poison will not affect her because Mantella are only mildly toxic to humans. They are brightly colored as a way of deterring potential predators from coming near them. The chemicals in the frogs' skin may be harmful to other animals, but could be helpful to humans. Some scientists are proponents of the idea that chemicals from frogs could hold the key to new medicines, such as pain relievers and heart-disease fighting drugs.

Valerie Clark:
"By sampling frogs for their toxic chemicals, we're effectively taking a shortcut to the many, many chemicals that exist in countless insects in the rainforest."

Narrator:
Clark is committed to raising public awareness of poison frogs, like Madagascar's famous chameleons and lemurs.

Valerie Clark:
"I believe that they're really, really important not only because they lead us to drugs and potential green pesticides, but also just because they're gorgeous!"

Narrator:
Back in the village, the results are promising.

Valerie Clark:
"Here we go!"

Narrator:
Clarke has found a little purple millipede that has several chemicals in common with Mantella poison frogs.

Valerie Clark:
"This is certainly making up the great portion of the Mantella diet and has great potential to end up being some of the sources of their chemicals."

Narrator:

In order for the frogs' toxins to work, they need a variety of insects to dine on, and the bigger the forest, the more insects to choose from. The frogs have more of these different chemicals in untouched primary rainforest. This means if the seemingly relentless destruction of the rainforest doesn't cease, there will be fewer toxic chemicals with the potential to be used in drugs.

Valerie Clark:

"So the more primary forest that we have, the better chance we have of finding new drug leads."

Narrator:

Near the end of her journey, Clark has collected a grand total of 500 tubes of insects. These are important clues that could lead her to some sources of the frogs' toxins.

Valerie Clark:

"I believe that understanding factors that affect Mantella distribution is critical for designing good conservation strategies."

Narrator:

Clearly she has a lot of work ahead of her, but already she is coming to one conclusion: More than ever, there is a compelling need to save the rainforest habitat, with its diversity of insects, if we are to save the poison frogs of Madagascar.

Queen of Egypt

Narrator:

She has a reputation for beauty, power, controversy, and ultimately, tragedy. In 69 B.C., Cleopatra was born into Egypt's Ptolemaic dynasty—a dynasty in decline and under the protection of Rome.

At the age of 18, she became queen and ruled Egypt along with her younger brother, Ptolemy the 13th, as king and husband. But the royal couple did not have a good relationship, and Cleopatra was soon forced from power.

But losing did not suit Cleopatra and she waited for a chance to prove her capabilities. That opportunity came when Julius Caesar, the winner in Rome's recent civil war, arrived in Alexandria, Egypt, in pursuit of a rival Roman general.

According to legend, Cleopatra managed to get herself into Caesar's private room rolled up inside a rug. Caesar was completely charmed and they soon fell in love. He defeated Cleopatra's rivals and helped her seize the throne. Shortly after, she gave birth to a boy, Caesarion, whom she claimed was Caesar's son.

Egypt was a very rich country and Cleopatra was fiercely determined to keep it independent of Rome. Her relationship with Caesar kept the Romans from taking direct control of Egypt. But after Caesar's murder, her position, and the future of her country, became uncertain.

Searching for people who could help her among Rome's new leaders, she was overjoyed when Marc Antony, one of Caesar's potential successors, sent for her. Like Caesar before him, Marc Antony fell in love with the elegant Egyptian queen . . . and her riches. Together they ruled Alexandria, an arrangement that made Cleopatra a fully independent ruler.

Cleopatra and Antony shared a legendary love matched by their hunger for power. They eventually married and became the power couple of the Eastern Mediterranean. Antony tried to help her acquire some Roman lands. And he declared Cleopatra's son Caesarion to be the son and true successor to Julius Caesar.

That insulted and infuriated Mark Antony's Roman rival, Octavian, who went to war against them. Antony and Cleopatra were quickly beaten at the Battle of Actium in 31 B.C.

Legend tells us that Cleopatra spread numerous false rumors of her death. His mind distorted by grief, Antony killed himself. But word came she was still alive, and Antony's followers carried him to Cleopatra where he died in her arms.

After 22 years as queen, Cleopatra was fighting a losing battle. She tried unsuccessfully to make peace with Octavian. Utterly unable to bear the pain of losing to the Romans, she took hold of a poisonous snake and let it kill her with its bite.

With her death, the Ptolemaic dynasty was finished, and Egypt fell firmly into Roman hands. Although her ambitions were never realized, Cleopatra lives on in history through her personal story of love and tragedy.

10 Solar System

Narrator:

The Milky Way galaxy. Home to our solar system.

It is believed our solar system formed at least four and a half billion years ago, when a huge cloud of dust and gas collapsed into a dense mass. That mass began to rotate and flatten into a disc. Over time, the center grew hotter and hotter until finally, a new star, our sun, was born. Leftover dust and gases continued to circle the sun and, over millions of years, cohered to form the planets and moons that make up our solar system.

The sun is the center and foundation of our solar system. Its gravity holds everything together. It is so massive it accounts for 99 percent of all the solar system's mass.

The closest planet to the sun is Mercury, a relatively small planet known for extreme temperatures—above 400 degrees Celsius in the day and minus 150 degrees at night.

Next is Venus, which is nearly identical to the Earth in terms of size, mass, and density. Its atmosphere is mostly carbon dioxide, a gas that traps the sun's heat and raises the surface temperature to nearly 480 degrees Celsius. The planet is surrounded by clouds of sulfuric acid.

The third planet is Earth, an active planet that's constantly engaged in change. More than 70 percent of its surface is covered by water. Earth is filled with life, something that so far has been found nowhere else.

Just beyond Earth lies Mars—a dry planet with distinctive geographic features including red soil, canyons four times deeper than the Grand Canyon, and polar ice.

Between Mars and the next planet is the asteroid belt. This is made up of millions of rocky fragments, most no more than a kilometer across.

The fifth planet from the sun is by far the largest—Jupiter, a gaseous giant big enough to hold over 1,300 Earths. Its great red spot alone, an awesome hurricane-like storm, is twice as wide as Earth.

Saturn, the second largest planet, is next. It is famous for its massive rings of ice and ice-covered particles.

Seventh from the sun is Uranus, an intriguing planet which rotates on its side. It too has rings, and at least 27 moons.

Neptune, the eighth planet, is perhaps the windiest place in the solar system, with winds of over 1,200 miles per hour. Neptune marks the end of the planets, but not the end of the solar system.

Farther on is the former planet Pluto, more than seven billion kilometers (four and a half billion miles) from the sun. Pluto's small size posed a dilemma to astronomers, and, in 2006, it was re-classified as a dwarf planet.

As spectacular and diverse as our solar system is, it's just one in a galaxy of billions of stars . . . in a universe comprised of billions of galaxies.

Drought

Narrator:

Its signs arrive slowly, quietly. The earth dries. Water levels fall. The rains do not come. And the land is gripped by drought.

At its most simple, a drought occurs when more water is used than is replenished. It depends on how much water there is, and how much is used up, whereby both natural and human factors come into play. Normally, low pressure systems in the atmosphere create rainclouds that support the environment. But a high pressure system forces the air upwards, preventing clouds from forming and rain from falling.

If the system lasts only a short while and the rains return, it is only considered a dry spell. But if this problem becomes a long-term trend, then drought can set in for months, years, decades, or longer. Depending on the demand for water, a drought can be a minor hazard, or a life-threatening situation.

Farms are heavily dependent on water to grow crops and maintain grazing fields for their animals. By over-cropping and over-grazing, farms may erode the soil and divert large amounts of water from natural sources. Urban areas also place huge demands on available water supplies. If these demands pile up and can't be reduced, then a drought begins to take effect.

Crops eventually dry up and die. Soil erodes away into clouds of dust. Forest fires spread rapidly. The damage to the environment can have colossal consequences for its human population. A short-term drought can cause higher prices and great distress to both people and their surroundings. Long-term droughts can lead to even worse consequences like war and famine.

Without food and water, society cannot function. In the 1930s, a severe drought in the Great Plains caused massive crop failures. So much soil blew away it became known as the Dust Bowl. Over 20 million hectares of land (50 million acres) were affected, forcing many farmers to discard their useless property. In some places, the drought lasted eight years. However, many droughts in history have surpassed the Dust Bowl's severity. Other droughts have lasted for decades, some possibly even for centuries. Famine caused by droughts killed over 40 million people in the 20th century alone.

Like other forms of weather, droughts are one of Earth's natural processes and there is little we can do to stop them. The best we can do is modify our water consumption, and help societies prepare for when droughts do come . . . before everything blows away.

12 The Science of Stress

Woman:

"Hello, good morning! How was your sleep?"

Narrator:

Six A.M. and the stress of everyday life kicks in. Family . . . home . . . work . . . over and over again. We need at least a minimal amount of stress to give us enough energy to get through the day. But a busy daily lifestyle can have a negative effect on our bodies.

In a special lab at Arizona State University, researchers are investigating exactly what stress does to a body. Kathy Matt and her research team are proving what most of us already know deep inside. That stress is not just in our mind.

Dr. Kathy Matt, Arizona State University:

"Stress, good or bad, is not just psychological. It's physiological as well."

Narrator:

So, stress from rush hour traffic actually shows up as a chemical in the blood.

Dr. Kathy Matt:

"In these samples we are measuring cortisol, which is a stress hormone."

Narrator:

When our body detects stress, it lets out two hormones: Adrenaline, to help our body react quickly and with more force. And cortisol, which gives us the energy we need for that quick physical push. That's great when you're being chased by a lion. But when the baby is crying, you don't need a physical boost. Unfortunately, the body can't tell the difference between the two types of stress.

Dr. Kathy Matt:

"But in a psychological stress, you're not utilizing fuel. You're not depleting fuel sources and yet you are increasing this cortisol."

Narrator:

Dr. Matt and her team have assembled a series of tests to show the effects of stress on the body. As the speed of the treadmill goes up, so does the heart rate and breathing. Right now the adrenaline and cortisol levels are booming. And while heart rate and oxygen levels show this woman is releasing a lot of stress hormones, she's also exploiting every bit of energy they create. So she passes the first test. Her body deals with physical stress pretty well. But what about mental stress?

Doctor:

"It's vital that you perform at your highest capable level for each of the tests."

Narrator:

With the pressure on . . .

Doctor:

"Come on Allysa, as fast as you can . . ."

Narrator:

The heart races . . . The blood pressure rises . . . Again those stress hormones are kicking in.

This time, the chemicals do not seem as compatible with the situation. Under constant psychological stress, the body releases cortisol but doesn't burn the extra fuel. And that leads to all sorts of problems. This machine checks bone density. Too much cortisol erodes the bone, potentially leading to problems that can affect our longevity.

Doctor:

"Here's your bone density. So you're really right on this norm."

Narrator:

So far so good. According to the researchers' guidelines, this woman shows no long term effects from psychological stress. But that doesn't mean she can just ignore it. Putting the body through the stress of exercise trains it to relieve psychological stress, and keeps us lean too!

And remember, not all stress is bad. Every now and then we need a good dose of those hormones to help us get to the end of the day.

Photo Credits

3 Michael S. Yamashita/NGIC, 4, 5 (clockwise from l) David McLain/NGIC, James L. Stanfield/NGIC, Michael S. Yamashita/NGIC, Robert Clark/NGIC, Peter Essick/NGIC, Pablo Corral Vega/NGIC, Richard Nowitz/NGIC, 6, 7 (clockwise from t, l) Michael Nichols/NGIC (first two), Konrad Wothe/Minden Pictures, George Steinmetz/NGIC, Tim Laman/NGIC, Luis César Tejo/Shutterstock, Randy Olson/NGIC, Heather Perry/NGIC, Tom Murphy/NGIC, David McLain/NGIC, Bob Krist/NGIC, Peter Essick/NGIC, Michael Nichols/NGIC, Jim Richardson/NGIC, 8 (t) Tino Soriano/NGIC, (b) Jason Edwards/NGIC, 9–13 (all) Michael S. Yamashita/NGIC, 15 (b) Neale Cousland/Shutterstock, 16 (t) Michael S. Yamashita/NGIC (b) Susan Welchman/NGIC, 17–20 (all) Michael S. Yamashita/NGIC, 21 elwynn/Shutterstock, 22 (t) Klaus Nigge/NGIC, (c) Stephen Alvarez/NGIC 23 Tom Murphy/NGIC 24 Justin Guariglia/NGIC 25–27 (all) Jodi Cobb/NGIC, 29 Heather Perry/NGIC, 31–33, 35, 36 (r) Tim Laman/NGIC, 37–41 (all) Jim Richardson/NGIC, 43 Elke Dennis/Shutterstock, 44–47, 49 (all) Jim Richardson/NGIC, 50 (from t to b) Jeryl Tan/iStockphoto, Augapfel/Flickr, Japanese_photo/iStockphoto, Wikimedia Commons, 51 Michael S. Yamashita/NGIC, 52, 53 (b/g and b) Michael S. Yamashita/NGIC (t) Taylor S. Kennedy/NGIC, 54, 55 (t, l to r) Jim Richardson/NGIC, Heather Perry/NGIC, Jim Richardson/NGIC, Elke Dennis/Shutterstock, Jim Richardson/NGIC (c, l to r) suravid/Shutterstock, kRie/Shutterstock (b, l to r) Jim Richardson/NGIC, Luis César Tejo/Shutterstock, 57 (l) Heather Perry/NGIC, (r) Elke Dennis/Shutterstock, 59–63 (all) Robert Clark/NGIC, 65 (t, r and b) Robert Clark/NGIC, 66 Cary Wolinsky, David Deranian and Barbara Emmel/NGIC, 67 (t) Cary Wolinsky and David Deranian/NGIC (b) Cary Wolinsky/NGIC, 68, 69 Cary Wolinsky/NGIC, 71 Ira Block/NGIC, 72 Roman Blazic/Flickr, 73 Joe McNally/NGIC 75 (l) Michael Nichols/NGIC (c) Joel Sartore/NGIC (r) David Edwards/NGIC, 77 Mark Thiessen/NGIC, 81, 82 Stephen Alvarez/NGIC, 85 Kenneth Garrett/NGIC, 86 Cesar Rangel /AP Photo, 87 Suzi Eszterhas/Minden Pictures, 89–91 Alex Webb/NGIC, 93 (r) Suzi Eszterhas/Minden, 94–97 (all) Michael Nichols/NGIC, 99 (r) Brent Stirton/NGIC, 100 (t) George Steinmetz/NGIC, 101 Stephen Alvarez/NGIC, 102, 103 (b/g) Stephen Alvarez/NGIC (t, r) Martin Gray/NGIC (b, r) Richard Nowitz/NGIC, 104, 105 (t, l to r) Cary Wolinsky/NGIC, Joel Sartore/NGIC, Michael Nicols/NGIC, David Edwards/NGIC, Raghubir Singh/NGIC, Joel Sartore /NGIC, 107 (from l to r) Joel Sartore/NGIC, David Edwards/NGIC, Raghubir Singh/NGIC, 109 Michael Melford/NGIC, 110–113 (all) William Albert Allard/NGIC, 115 Justin Guariglia/NGIC, 116–119 (all) Pablo Corral Vega/NGIC, 121 Raul Touzon/NGIC, 122 (r) Knumina/Shutterstock, 123 Todd Gipstein/NGIC, 124 (c and b), 126 Cary Wolinsky/NGIC, 127 (l) Cary Wolinsky/NGIC (r) Gordon Gahan/NGIC, 129 (t) Norbert Wu/Minden Pictures, 130 Mark Thiessen/NGIC, 131–133 (all) George Steinmetz/NGIC, 135 (t) Nina Berman/NGIC, 136 (r) Rebecca Hale/NGIC, 137 Bob Krist/NGIC, 139–141 (all) James L. Stanfield/NGIC, 144 (r), 145 Sisse Brimberg/NGIC, 146 (l) Cary Wolinsky/NGIC (r and b) Sisse Brimberg/NGIC, 147 Sisse Brimberg/NGIC, 150 (r) The Kobal Collection/20th Century Fox, 151 Dean Conger/NGIC, 152, 153 (clockwise from l) Sailorr/Shutterstock, Vladimir Wrangel/Shutterstock, shipov/iStockphoto, 154, 155 (t, from l to r) Peter Ginter/NGIC, William Albert Allard/NGIC, George Steinmetz/NGIC (last 3), 157 Peter Ginter/NGIC, George Steinmetz/NGIC, 159 James P. Blair/NGIC, 161, 162 Peter Ginter/NGIC, 163, 165 Mark Thiessen/NGIC, 168 (l) Randy Olson/NGIC (r) Leonard Kulik/NGIC (b) Stephen Alvarez/NGIC 169 (t) Dan Durda/NGIC (b) NASA/JPL/Caltech, 171 NASA/JPL/Caltech, 173 Tyrone Turner/NGIC, 175–177 (all) Peter Essick/NGIC, 179 Vincent Laforet/NGIC, 181–183 (all) Peter Essick/NGIC, 185 (t) Peter Essick/NGIC, 186 Thomas J. Abercrombie/NGIC, 187 David McLain/NGIC, 188–191, 193 (all) Lynsey Addario/NGIC, 194–197, 199 (all) David McLain/NGIC, 200 Kevin Cole/Flickr, 201 Konrad Wothe/Minden Pictures, 202, 203 (b/g) Konrad Wothe/Minden Pictures, (t and c) Joel Sartore/NGIC (b) JupiterImages, 204, 205 (t, l to r) NASA/JPL/Caltech, Randy Olson/NGIC, Mark Thiessen/NGIC, Don Dixon/Cosmographica.com, NASA/JPL/Caltech, Moonrunner Design Ltd/NGIC (b/g and inset) NASA/JPL/Caltech, 207 (l)

NASA/JPL/Caltech, (r) Randy Olson/NGIC, **211** (t) Klaus Nigge/NGIC, (b) Stephen Alvarez/NGIC, **212** Tim Laman/NGIC, **213** (clockwise from t) Jeryl Tan/ iStockphoto, Wikimedia Commons, Augapfel/Flickr, Japanese_photo/iStockphoto, **214** Roman Blazic/Flickr, **215** Cesar Rangel/AP Photo, **216** George Steinmetz/ NGIC, **217** Knumina/Shutterstock, **218** Rebecca Hale/ NGIC, **221** Thomas J. Abercrombie/NGIC, **222** Kevin Cole/Flickr

Illustration Credits

4, 5 (b/g), **10** (b), **15** (t), **22** (b), **30, 36** (l), **52** (l), **53, 54, 55, 65** (l), **74, 76, 79** (l), **85** (l), **86** (l), **88, 93** (l), **94** (b), **99** (l), **100** (b), **102** (l), **104, 105, 110** (b), **116** (b), **122** (l), **124** (t, r), **129** (b), **135** (b), **136** (l), **144** (l), **150** (l), **152** (l), **154, 155, 161** (inset), **174, 175** (l), **182** (r), **185** (b), **189** (l), **195** (inset), **197** (c), **202** National Geographic Maps, **14** Mike Reagan/NGIC, **79** Joe McNally/NGIC, **80** Herbert Kane/NGIC, **83** John T. Burgoyne/NG Maps **124** (tl) Wikimedia Commons, **125** Cary Wolinsky/NGIC, **138, 143** William H. Bond/ NGIC, **149** Wikimedia Commons, **152, 153** (b/g) Javier Zarracina, **160** Moonrunner Design Ltd/NGIC, **166** Sean McNaughton/NGIC **167** Don Dixon/ Cosmographica.com, **172, 220** NASA/JPL/Caltech, **180** Don Foley/NGIC

Text Credits

11–13 Adapted from "On the Poet's Trail," by Howard Norman: NGM February 2008, **25–27** Adapted from "True Love," by Lauren Slater: NGM February 2006, **31–33** Adapted from "Birds Gone Wild," by Jennifer S. Holland: NGM July 2007, **39–41** Adapted from "Food: How Safe?" by Jennifer Ackerman: NGM May 2002, **45–47** Adapted from "Food: How Altered?" by Jennifer Ackerman: NGM May 2002, **61–63** Adapted from "Designs from Nature: Biomimetics," by Tom Meuller: NGM April 2008, **67–69** Adapted from "Dreamweavers," by Cathy Newman: NGM January 2003, **75–77** Adapted from "Human Journey," by James Shreeve: NGM March 2006, **81–83** Adapted from "Pioneers of the Pacific," by Roff Smith: NGM March 2008, **89–91** Adapted from "Farming the Amazon," by Scott Wallace: NGM January 2007 **95–97** Adapted from "Family Ties: The Elephants of Samburu," by David Quammen: NGM September 08, **111–113** Adapted from "Lights, Camera, India,"

by Suketu Mehta: NGM February 2005, **117–119** Adapted from "Tango, Soul of Argentina," by Alma Guillermoprieto: NGM December 2003 **125–127** Adapted from "Pick Your Poison," by Cathy Newman: NGM May 2005, **131–133** Adapted from "Watching You," by David Shenk: NGM May 2005, **139–141** Adapted from "Genghis Khan," by Mike Edwards: NGM December 1996, **145–147** Adapted from "Catherine the Great," by Erla Zwingle: NGM September 1998, **161–163** Adapted from "The God Particle," by Joel Achenbach: NGM March 2008, **167–169** Adapted from "Target Earth," by Richard Stone: NGM August 2008, **175–177** Adapted from "Water Pressure," by Fen Montaigne: NGM September 2002, **181–183** Adapted from "High Tech Trash," by Chris Carroll: NGM January 2008, **189–191** Adapted from "Bhutan's Experiment," by Brook Larmer: NGM March 2008, **195–197** Adapted from "New Wrinkles on Aging," by Dan Buettner: NGM November 2005

National Geographic Image Collection = NGIC
National Geographic Magazine = NGM